Moments with Our Master
365 Daily Devotionals

Copyright © 2019 Todd Tomasella
All rights reserved.

Any part of this book may be reproduced, stored in a retrieval system, or transmitted by any means <u>without</u> the written permission of the author.

All Scripture quotations deliberately taken from the Authorized Version of the Holy Bible, the King James Version

ISBN: 9781701856523

Do you desire to learn God's Word?

To receive the *Moments with Our Master* email weekly, go to SafeGuardYourSoul.com and sign up.
Or, email info@safeguardyoursoul.com

Visit SafeGuardYourSoul.com

Mailing Address:
    SafeGuardYourSoul
    9201 Warren Pkwy. Ste. 200
    Frisco, Texas 75035

Printed in the United States of America

This book is intended to be a companion to the reader's personal study of God's Word. Nothing replaces Bible reading and the individual study of God's Word, which is the command of God.

> **"Study to shew thyself approved unto God, a workman that needeth not to be ashamed, rightly dividing the word of truth."**
> **2 Timothy 2:15**

It is the author's prayer that these daily devotionals will increase the desire in the reader to know the LORD better, to seek His holy face continually, and to daily pour prayerfully over His Word—the whole of Holy Scripture. Someone wisely stated that "It takes a whole Bible to make a whole disciple" (Psalms 119).

Moments with Our Master

This book is intended to be a companion to the reader's personal study of God's Word. Nothing replaces Bible reading and the individual study of God's Word, which is the command of God.

> **"Study to shew thyself approved unto God, a workman that needeth not to be ashamed, rightly dividing the word of truth."**
> **2 Timothy 2:15**

It is the author's prayer that these daily devotionals will increase the desire in the reader to know the LORD better, to seek His holy face continually, and to daily pour prayerfully over His Word—the whole of Holy Scripture. Someone wisely stated that "It takes a whole Bible to make a whole disciple" (Psalms 119).

Moments with Our Master

Table of Contents

January	7
February	39
March	69
April	101
May	131
June	163
July	193
August	225
September	257
October	287
November	319
December	349
Addendum	381

January 1

"And this is life eternal, that they might know thee the only true God, and Jesus Christ, whom thou hast sent." John 17:3

Jesus Christ is the Sacred Substance of the Scriptures who came and died that we may know Him in a relationship (John 17:3). If we see Him not in our Bible study nor reveal His Person in our lives and our preaching, we have missed the whole point and substance of Holy Scripture and are completely deceived, being no different than the religious hypocrites Christ condemned—who had a mere **"form of godliness"** as they denied the authority, the reign of the Lord in their personal lives (2 Timothy 3:5). It is not good enough to know the written Word of God. We must know the God of the Word—the one true God the Holy Scriptures and Holy Ghost reveal. We must cry with the Greeks who sought out Jesus and declared **"Sir, we would see Jesus"** (John 12:21).

"Search the scriptures; for in them ye think ye have eternal life: and they are they which testify of me. 40 And ye will not come to me, that ye might have life." John 5:39-40

Prayer: *Father, I want to know You and Jesus my Lord better. Please make me one with You. In Jesus' name.*

Today is your day to make certain you are truly born again. Check out page 381 to make sure.

January 2

"To every thing there is a season, and a time to every purpose under the heaven:" Ecclesiastes 3:1

Seasons are temporary—good or bad. Seasons come to pass.

It is important to obey God by remaining where He's placed us in this season. Scripture reveals that **"to obey is better than sacrifice"** (1 Samuel 15:22). Abiding, waiting upon the Lord right where He presently has us, comes with the temptation of jumping out of that place with haste, especially when it's a season of turmoil. We can and have the privilege to praise Him right where we are. His will is transpiring in our lives as we abide in/with Christ (John 15). Wondering why this season seems so long and what's next? He whispers to your heart today to **"Be still, and know that I am God"** (Psalms 46:10).

Prayer: *Precious heavenly Father, I come to You in the name of Jesus and ask You to cause my heart to be content at all times, in this very season, with You. I have everything because You have me and I have You. I love You Lord Jesus. Grant Your temperance in my heart, amen.*

January 3

"Blessed are the poor in spirit: for theirs is the kingdom of heaven." Matthew 5:3

Saints, in Psalms we see the psalmist in many dire scenarios forced into a corner and blessed to cry out to the LORD in desperation of spirit. We need and must have trials. We shall never truly understand and more deeply know the LORD until we are forced to cry out in utter desperation to Him.

"The LORD is nigh unto them that are of a broken heart; and saveth such as be of a contrite spirit." Psalms 34:18

Prayer: LORD, with deep resolve, I this moment make the obedient decision to come out of the antichrist, out of the apostate religious system where men are elevated in place of You! This moment I return to You O LORD and submit my spirit and whole being into Your holy and perfect hands! I love You LORD Jesus. Please forgive my sin of idolatry and spiritual adultery and fill me with Your Holy Spirit afresh. Please cleanse me by Your blood right now LORD. Please send me forth and make my life a fruitful field to Your glory alone. In Jesus' name, Amen.

January 4

> "The sleep of a labouring man is sweet, whether he eat little or much." Ecclesiastes 5:12a

Those who work hard rest well. This makes one wonder if more activity would cure a whole lot of sleeping problems, right?

> "The abundance of the rich will not suffer him to sleep." Ecclesiastes 5:12b

Here the rich are pictured as those who have too much time on their hands and/or that they can't sleep well due to worry about their riches. The more one has, the more he has to worry about. Liquidating your riches for God's glory will liquidate your unrest.

> "For God speaketh once, yea twice, yet man perceiveth it not. 15 In a dream, in a vision of the night, when deep sleep falleth upon men, in slumberings upon the bed; 16 Then he openeth the ears of men, and sealeth their instruction, 17 That he may withdraw man from his purpose, and hide pride from man. 18 He keepeth back his soul from the pit, and his life from perishing by the sword." Job 33:14-18

> "I will both lay me down in peace, and sleep: for thou, LORD, only makest me dwell in safety." Psalms 4:8

Prayer: *LORD, please grant my sleep to be sweet. Speak to my heart! In Jesus' name, amen.*

January 5

"My brethren, count it all joy when ye fall into divers temptations; 3 Knowing this, that the trying of your faith worketh patience. 4 But let patience have her perfect work, that ye may be perfect and entire, wanting nothing." James 1:2-4

Worshipping God in and through our times of testing, trials, temptations and struggles provides the Christlikeness, the maturity our regenerated inner man desperately desires (Romans 8:28-29; James 1:2-4; 1 Peter 5:10). God's goal is much greater than just snapping His holy finger and delivering you out of the temporary trial. He's after much more. He must break down and strip us before He can re-furnish us (Jeremiah 1:10). Remember Paul's thorn (2 Corinthians 12:7-10)? What was the divine goal? Is the LORD doing a deeper work in you, preparing you for greater fruitfulness?

Prayer: *Father, please mature me. Grant grace to my heart to see these times of testing and trials as a blessing that causes You to increase while I am crucified—decreased! In Jesus' name, amen.*

January 6

"Then Saul, (who also is called Paul,) filled with the Holy Ghost, set his eyes on him, 10 And said, O full of all subtilty and all mischief, thou child of the devil, thou enemy of all righteousness, wilt thou not cease to pervert the right ways of the Lord?" **Acts 13:9-10**

Love is at times manifested in strong rebuke (Proverbs 27:5-6; Titus 1:13). Was the message of the original Gospel always soft? Did Jesus and His holy apostles pander to the sinful sentiments and whims of sinful men? No! Read God's Word for yourself as He commanded us to do—and cease now to be misled by the soft-peddling pansies of today's apostate modern church world. Repent now. Follow Jesus! Then you won't live by your sinful emotions but will rather be an authentic disciple of Jesus who loves His truth—NO MATTER WHO IT OFFENDS. But first it must offend YOU unto repentance—to drive you to real repentance and a real (crucified) walk with Jesus (Galatians 2:20). **"Let God be true and EVERY man a liar"** (Romans 3:4).

"This witness is true. Wherefore rebuke them sharply, that they may be sound in the faith;" Titus 1:13

Prayer: *Heavenly Father, embolden my spirit to speak Your truth, only as You lead. In Jesus' name, amen.*

January 7

"He that covereth his sins shall not prosper: but whoso confesseth and forsaketh them shall have mercy." Proverbs 28:13

Victory begins at the point that we become honest with the Lord. Jesus speaks of the essential of having **"an honest and good heart"** (Luke 8:15). Like David—the man after God's own heart—we must choose perpetually, to be honest, sincere, and repentant (Psalms 51; Acts 13:22). This requires a dying to self, choosing to love the Lord, not self, with a whole heart (Matthew 22:37-39).

"I acknowledged my sin unto thee, and mine iniquity have I not hid. I said, I will confess my transgressions unto the Lord; and thou forgavest the iniquity of my sin. Selah." Psalms 32:5

Humble pie is a blessing. It flattens us to the lowest position, having only one direction to look—upward.

Prayer: *Dear Father, please bless this heart to be honest before You. In Jesus' name, amen.*

January 8

"BURIED with him in baptism *(death, burial)*, **wherein also ye are RISEN with him through the faith of the operation of God, who hath raised him from the dead." Colossians 2:12**

Kingdom Perspective: Cross Economy ... **"the operation of God."** This is how God operates in His cross economy ... we die to ourselves and Christ lives and reigns in us.

As God the Father raised Jesus from the dead by the Holy Ghost, so Christ reigns in those who follow Him by consenting to their own death to self so that He reigns supreme in their lives.

"But if the Spirit of him that raised up Jesus from the dead dwell in you, he that raised up Christ from the dead shall also quicken your mortal bodies by his Spirit that dwelleth in you." Romans 8:11

Prayer: *LORD, please let Your operation take its full course in my life—raising me up as my life is laid down. In Jesus' name, amen.*

January 9

"For the kingdom of God is not meat and drink *(non-essentials)*; but righteousness, and peace, and joy in the Holy Ghost. ... For meat *(a non-essential)* destroy not the work of God. All things indeed are pure; but it is evil for that man who eateth with offence." Romans 14:17, 20

In this important chapter, the apostle Paul is establishing that God is the only Judge of His own people. He alone will judge them at the judgment of believers for their conduct in this life, namely in non-essentials and yet, we should never judge His children on their personal use of non-essentials.

It frustrates the grace and work of God when we infringe upon the liberty that He gave each individual saint in non-essentials.

If you choose to stay away from something that is not named as a sin in God's Word, that's your God-given liberty. And, He told us not to judge others for non-essentials or how they choose to exercise their God-given liberty in non-essentials. Read Romans 14.

Prayer: *May the joy of Thy salvation fill my heart dear Lord. Cause maturity to transpire in Your body, in Jesus' name, amen.*

January 10

"Be thou in the fear of the LORD all the day long." Proverbs 23:17

The earliest followers of Jesus **"were edified; and walking in the fear of the Lord, and in the comfort of the Holy Ghost, were multiplied."**

"Then had the churches rest throughout all Judaea and Galilee and Samaria, and were edified; and walking in the fear of the Lord, and in the comfort of the Holy Ghost, were multiplied." Acts 9:31

The beginning of wisdom is truly fearing God:

"The fear of the LORD is the beginning of wisdom: and the knowledge of the holy is understanding." Proverbs 9:10

The fruit of fearing the LORD:

"The fear of the LORD is to hate evil: pride, and arrogancy, and the evil way, and the froward mouth, do I hate." Proverbs 8:13

Prayer: *Unite my heart to fear Thy holy name LORD. Teach me Your wisdom. In Jesus' name, amen LORD.*

January 11

"Work out your own salvation with fear and trembling. 13 For it is God which worketh in you both to will and to do of his good pleasure." Philippians 2:12-13

The life we have with Christ is all about His cross, the cross He commanded that we take up, His resurrection life, love and grace working in us (Colossians 1:14, 20; Romans 6-8; Luke 9:23-24; Galatians 2:20; 2 Corinthians 4:10-12, etc.). The life we have with Christ does not require that we do it all but rather that we submit ourselves to the LORD, abide in Christ, working *out* (not *for*) our own salvation with fear and trembling, as He works in us to will and to do HIS good pleasure (Philippians 2:12-13).

Shall we forget that the LORD made us and found us? We didn't make ourselves nor did we, in our sin, find Him. **"We love him, because he first loved us"** (1 John 4:19).

Jesus promises His own: **"Lo, I am with you alway, even unto the end of the world. Amen"** (Matthew 28:20).

Is He not perfecting what HE began in us?

> **"The LORD will perfect that which concerneth me: thy mercy, O LORD, endureth for ever: forsake not the works of thine own hands." (Psalms 138:8).**

Prayer: *Thank You LORD for dying for me, for finding and saving me and for continually maturing me into the image of Christ. In Jesus' name, amen.*

January 12

"The entrance of thy words giveth light; it giveth understanding unto the simple." Psalms 119:130

When you read and study the words of God, you are turning on the LORD's floodlight as His light is shining into your darkened heart, divinely lighting it up.

When you are truly full of His light, continually, daily shining His holy Word into your heart, that light will shine forth in this dark world.

"Let your light so shine before men, that they may see your good works, and glorify your Father which is in heaven." Matthew 5:16

Prayer: *Father, I here and now ask You in the name of Jesus, to grant my heart an insatiable desire to devour Thy Word—to flood this heart with the light of Your holy truth. Please let Thy holy light illuminate my heart and countenance for the glory of Jesus Christ alone.*

There's an eternity of difference between being religious and being truly saved. Find out more on page 381.

January 13

> "See, I have this day set thee over the nations and over the kingdoms, to root out, and to pull down, and to destroy, and to throw down, to build, and to plant." Jeremiah 1:10

Many times, in our humanity, we view trials as obstacles to get over as soon as possible, never realizing that God has a deeper purpose.

Are you ready today to declare, to pray: *"Jesus, please strip, purge, rebuke, and change me so I can be Your vessel! I submit now to Your will my LORD Jesus."*?

WHY did Jesus tell us that He purges us?

> "Every branch that beareth fruit, he purgeth it, that it may bring forth more fruit." John 15:2

Prayer: LORD, I am not in control, You are. In accordance to Your stated will, I ask You to please bless this life You gave to be free from any and every thing that hinders my relationship with You! Father, please, this moment, wash me clean and clear, break all the chains, purge to the core of my being. In the name of Jesus. Amen.

January 14

"For there is not a just man upon earth, that doeth good, and sinneth not." Ecclesiastes 7:20

This truth is not an excuse for sin and yet, it's a sobering reality and points us to the ever-present need for the cross and grace of Christ! (See Galatians 2:20; 5:24; Romans 6-7, etc.)

No excuse for sin:

"What shall we say then? Shall we continue in sin, that grace may abound? ² God forbid. How shall we, that are dead to sin, live any longer therein?" Romans 6:1-2

Reality of the **"old man,"** the fallen nature (Ephesians 4:22-24):

"For I know that in me (that is, in my flesh,) dwelleth no good thing: for to will is present with me; but how to perform that which is good I find not." Romans 7:18

The utter need to become and remain crucified with Christ:

"But I keep under my body, and bring it into subjection: lest that by any means, when I have preached to others, I myself should be a castaway." 1 Corinthians 9:27

Prayer: *I am crucified with Christ, dead and buried, and hid with Christ in God. In Jesus' name, amen.*

January 15

"Jesus saith to him, He that is washed needeth not save to wash his feet, but is clean every whit: and ye are clean, but not all." John 13:10

ALL who are washed in Christ's regeneration (born again) need only to have their feet washed (sins forgiven if committed). 1 John is ONLY for born again Christians:

"If we confess our sins, he is faithful and just to forgive us our sins, and to cleanse us from all unrighteousness." 1 John 1:9

Is it time to give up our lives to Christ? Will we not only then find freedom and blessings from above which richly fill our lives as we look for the soon return of our LORD from Heaven (Colossians 3:1-4)? As Jesus' disciples, we must always remember that if we are not being led to the cross, we are not being led by the Spirit and are currently outside of God's will. There is no following Christ without obeying His repeated command to die so that He alone reigns (Luke 9:23-24, etc.).

Prayer: *Right this moment, dear heavenly Father, I come to You in Jesus' name. Please wash and cleanse me afresh by the blood of Jesus. Thank You LORD for Your redeeming blood. Amen.*

January 16

> "Preach the word; be instant in season, out of season; reprove, rebuke, exhort with all longsuffering and doctrine." 2 Timothy 4:2

IF you want to preach, to communicate the Word of God, you must memorize and meditate upon it! (Proverbs 4:4; 22:17-21.)

> "Let thine heart RETAIN my words." Proverbs 4:4

As you prayerfully study God's Word, He's going to make it part of your life.

> "Bow down thine ear, and hear the words of the wise, and apply thine heart unto my knowledge. 18 For it is a pleasant thing if thou keep them within thee; they shall withal be fitted in thy lips. 19 That thy trust may be in the LORD, I have made known to thee this day, even to thee. 20 Have not I written to thee excellent things in counsels and knowledge, 21 That I might make thee know the certainty of the words of truth; that thou mightest answer the words of truth to them that send unto thee?" Proverbs 22:17-21

Prayer: *Fill my heart and mind with Your Word LORD so that Your truth is what flows from this mouth and life. In Jesus' name, amen.*

January 17

"And they that are Christ's have crucified the flesh with the affections and lusts." Galatians 5:24

The truly God-fearing man realizes his utter need for the grace of Christ. He realizes that he must continue, to abide in Christ, to **"Fight the good fight of faith, lay hold on eternal life"** (1 Timothy 6:12). He views salvation as a present reality and responsibility—to remain in an intimate, abiding relationship with Christ (John 15:1-16); Colossians 2:6-7).

Those who don't walk in the cross lifestyle, will revert to type— sinful type.

The authentic disciple builds his whole life around the Bible, the cross and the throne of God (Jeremiah 17:12; Hebrews 4:14-16).

WHEN our love for God is supreme, we will daily seek Him. When we are hungering and thirsting after His righteousness, He is filling us with His overcoming, victorious grace (Matthew 5:6).

"But I keep under my body, and bring it into subjection: lest that by any means, when I have preached to others, I myself should be a castaway." 1 Corinthians 9:27

Prayer: *I am crucified with Christ, nevertheless I live, yet not I but Christ that liveth in me.*

January 18

"WE are labourers TOGETHER with God."
1 Corinthians 3:9

Each of us are individual members in Christ's one body (1 Corinthians 12). If God's people don't support HIS work, it simply does not get supported. When God's people help His other children and His work, they partake of the eternal fruit He promised (Matthew 6:19-21).

Does the LORD not fabulously promise to replenish and refill?

> **"The liberal** *(giving, generous)* **soul shall be made fat: and he that watereth shall be watered also himself. 26 He that withholdeth corn, the people shall curse him: but blessing shall be upon the head of him that selleth it." Proverbs 11:25-26**

Are you participating in supporting those saints in need and our LORD's work?

We find these red letters, the very words of our LORD, in the books of Acts:

> **"It is more blessed to give than to receive." Acts 20:35**

Prayer: *Heavenly Father, You gave Your only begotten Son for me. Bless this heart to truly trust You (knowing You own all), and to give freely as You've freely given to me. In Jesus' name, amen.*

January 19

"But by the grace of God I am what I am: and his grace which was bestowed upon me was not in vain; but I laboured more abundantly than they all: yet not I, but the grace of God which was with me." 1 Corinthians 15:10

When through the cross-life divine grace works in our lives, not only will we not burn out, we will labour **"more abundantly"**—because God's grace is defined as His operational power, His divine influence and enablement.

Those who experience what we call "burn out," do so because they are carrying burdens God alone can carry. When we truly rest in the LORD, we will not be carrying the burden He never intended us to carry and therefore will never burn out.

Memory Verse: Psalms 46:10

Prayer: *Thank You dear LORD that Your grace is sufficient in all things You've called Your people to do. Please multiply Your grace to my heart and life today. In Jesus' name, amen.*

January 20

> "**Nevertheless I have somewhat against thee, because thou hast left thy first love.** [5] **Remember therefore from whence thou art fallen, and repent, and do the first works; or else I will come unto thee quickly, and will remove thy candlestick out of his place, except thou repent.**" Revelation 2:4-5

The believers at the town of Ephesus needed to repent due to their departure from Christ. Their love for the Savior had waxed cold.

Never, ever take our God for granted. Our LORD is our **"first love"** and highest priority (Revelation 2:4-5).

The temperature of one's relationship to Christ is directly reflected in his prayer life or lack thereof. If one has no prayer life, it is because he does not count the Son of God important enough to spend the time getting to know Him. Because of this, that person allows the **"the cares of this world, and the deceitfulness of riches, and the lusts of other things"** to displace him from Christ (Mark 4:19).

Memorize Matthew 26:41.

Prayer: *Father, I repent now of the sins of pride, self-idolatry and unbelief. I lay my life in Your hands LORD. In Jesus' name, amen.*

January 21

"**The waters compassed me about, even to the soul: the depth closed me round about, the weeds were wrapped about my head ... my prayer came in unto thee, into thine holy temple ... And the LORD spake unto the fish, and it vomited out Jonah upon the dry** *land.*" **Jonah 2:5, 7, 10**

Recently, I saw a man interviewed who'd been lost in the wilderness for five days. Put yourself in his place. Five whole days lost in the wilderness with no food or water. When asked how he did it, he said he prayed. Now, do we think his prayers were lame, lukewarm? Was he yawning? No, we know his prayers to God were fervent, were on fire. We know he was crying out from the depths of his being to the LORD, just as Jonah did from deep inside that large fish.

"**This poor man cried, and the LORD heard him, and saved him out of all his troubles.**" **Psalms 34:6**

Prayer: *Dear heavenly Father, grant my heart to be one of contrition and utter humility, broken before Your Majesty. I love You, my LORD Jesus.*

January 22

> "For the eyes of the Lord are over the righteous, and his ears are open unto their prayers: but the face of the Lord is against them that do evil."
> 1 Peter 3:12

GOD is answering the prayers of His saints today (1 Peter 3:12)! *"God speaks to those (in Christ) who take time to listen, and He listens to those who take time to pray."* Unknown

The prayers of God's people, just like salvation, are based on the perfect sacrifice of Jesus Christ!

> "And whatsoever ye shall ask in my name, that will I do, that the Father may be glorified in the Son. 14 If ye shall ask any thing in my name, I will do it."
> John 14:13-14

"Pray harder"? NO! Let go and let God by trusting Him and not your own hard work! That's what faith does—it trusts God for what we are incapable of providing.

> "Now to him that worketh is the reward not reckoned of grace, but of debt. 5 But to him that worketh not, but believeth on him that justifieth the ungodly, his faith is counted for righteousness." Romans 4:4-5

> "Are ye so foolish? having begun in the Spirit, are ye now made perfect by the flesh?" Galatians 3:3

Prayer: *Father, thank You that all our prayers, prayed in Your will and in the name of Jesus, are going to be answered by You. In Jesus' name, amen.*

January 23

"Let thine heart retain my words: keep my commandments, and live." Proverbs 4:4

You will never understand a Bible truth more than when you memorize it! Writing King James Bible verses on index cards with chapter and verse references, is a fruitful way to memorize God's Word.

You cannot possibly fully, properly and most expediently meditate upon a Bible truth you don't first memorize. God's Word cannot get into us unless we get into it.

Prayer: *Father, in Jesus' name, please grant to this vessel a photographic memory for Your blessed Word.*

January 24

"But after that the kindness and love of God our Saviour toward man appeared, 5 Not by works of righteousness which we have done, but according to his mercy he saved us, by the washing of regeneration, and renewing of the Holy Ghost; 6 Which he shed on us abundantly through Jesus Christ our Saviour; 7 That being justified by his grace, we should be made heirs according to the hope of eternal life." Titus 3:4-7

The mercy of God is poured out at the cross of Christ where He was crucified for the sins of the world (1 John 2:2).

> *My hope is built on nothing less*
> *Than Jesus' blood and righteousness;*
> *I dare not trust the sweetest frame,*
> *But wholly lean on Jesus' name.*
> *On Christ the solid rock I stand;*
> *All other ground is sinking sand;*
> *All other ground is sinking sand.*

"To wit, that God was in Christ, reconciling the world unto himself, not imputing their trespasses unto them; and hath committed unto us the word of reconciliation. ... For he hath made him to be sin for us, who knew no sin; that we might be made the righteousness of God in him." 2 Corinthians 5:19, 21

Prayer: *Thank You LORD Jesus for Your perfect sacrifice for my sin. I am all Yours dear LORD!*

January 25

"Blessed *are* the poor in spirit: for theirs is the kingdom of heaven." Matthew 5:3

Note, **"poor in spirit,"** not poor financially or religiously. The two should be mutually exclusive. The Greek word translated into English as **"poor"** is *PTOCHOS*. It means pauper, beggar, poor, desperate and spiritually impoverished. Christ looks to desperate, hungry and thirsty people who want more of Him (Isaiah 66:2). Their hearts pant for more of Him (Psalms 42:1-2). They deeply desire and long for Him.

His Word is their meat.

"To this man will I look, even to him that is poor and of a contrite spirit, and trembleth at my word." Isaiah 66:2

Prayer: *Father, please bless me to be truly poor in spirit, contrite, and to tremble at Your Word. In Jesus' name, amen.*

If you died today, are you 100% certain you'd be in Heaven and not hell? God wants you with Him! Check out page 381 to make sure.

January 26

> "For I know that in me (that is, in my flesh,) dwelleth no good thing: for to will is present with me; but how to perform that which is good I find not. ... O wretched man that I am! who shall deliver me from the body of this death?" Romans 7:18, 24

The hearts of men are evil, fallen (Genesis 6:5, 12; Jeremiah 17:9; Romans 7).

Don't trust yourself, trust God and deny self!

> "He that trusteth in his own heart is a fool: but whoso walketh wisely, he shall be delivered." Proverbs 28:26

Only Satan and his children live by the diabolical edict of "be true to yourself" or "learn to love yourself." Knowing how wretched they are of themselves, without Christ, those who are known of God live by:

> "Trust in the LORD with all thine heart; and lean not unto thine own understanding. [6] In all thy ways acknowledge him, and he shall direct thy paths." Proverbs 3:5-6

Prayer: *Father, I repent of and refuse to trust my own wicked heart. You are wonderful and outside of You, I am wicked. Please cleanse my heart Father, in Jesus' name.*

January 27

> "LORD, make me to know mine end, and the measure of my days, what it is; that I may know how frail I am. 5 Behold, thou hast made my days as an handbreadth; and mine age is as nothing before thee: verily every man at his best state is altogether vanity. Selah." Psalms 39:4-5

Without Christ's righteousness, we are left with our own righteousness, which is as **"filthy rags"** in the eyes of Him who is **"Holy, holy, holy"** (Isaiah 6:3; Revelation 4:8).

> "But we are all as an unclean thing, and all our righteousnesses are as filthy rags; and we all do fade as a leaf; and our iniquities, like the wind, have taken us away." Isaiah 64:6

We must rely fully on the righteousness of God in Christ alone.

> "For he hath made him to be sin for us, who knew no sin; that we might be made the righteousness of God in him." 2 Corinthians 5:21

Prayer: *LORD, I have nothing but unrighteousness without You. Without You Jesus, I am nothing and I have nothing. I fall afresh, right this moment, upon Your mercy, laying my life in Your hands. In Jesus' name, amen.*

January 28

"<u>Examine yourselves</u>, whether ye be in the faith; prove your own selves. Know ye not your own selves, how that Jesus Christ is in you, except ye be reprobates?" 2 Corinthians 13:5

The Bible says to **"examine yourselves"** but it never says to look within yourself for any virtue or anything good at all because the heart is deceitful **"above all things and desperately wicked"**! (See 2 Corinthians 13:5; Genesis 6:5, 12; Jeremiah 17:9; Romans 3; 7:18, etc.)

Believers are instructed to **"judge ourselves"** in order to avoid damnation with the world:

> "For if we would <u>judge ourselves</u>, we should not be judged. [32] But when we are judged, we are chastened of the Lord, that we should not be condemned with the world." 1 Corinthians 11:31-32

Prayer: *Dear heavenly Father, I come to You in the name of Jesus and ask You to do Your good work in the depths of my heart. Take over this life afresh LORD Jesus. I am all Yours!*

January 29

"**Know ye not, that so many of us as were baptized into Jesus Christ were baptized into his death? 4 Therefore we are buried with him by baptism into death: that like as Christ was raised up from the dead by the glory of the Father, even so we also should walk in newness of life." Romans 6:3-4**

This is the death and burial of Christ re-enacted in our lives, daily. Here's more biblical evidence that the cross is absolutely foundational and central to our life with Christ. Water baptism, after Jesus has saved us, contains the symbolism of our life in Christ from that point onward—we are dead to self, buried, and Christ is raising us upward. This is the only way the Christian life and the kingdom of God works.

Prayer: *Father, when You found and saved me out of the miry clay of my sin, You ordained that I live crucified with Christ. And, You promised I'd be raised up by You in my daily life and eternally. Let it be done in my life* LORD, *please, in Jesus' name, amen.*

January 30

> "This book of the law shall not depart out of thy mouth; but thou shalt meditate therein day and night, that thou mayest observe to do according to all that is written therein: for then thou shalt make thy way prosperous, and then thou shalt have good success." Joshua 1:8

As we read and meditate daily upon God's Word, He will unfold His larger kingdom picture (Joshua 1:8).

While there is a large amount of pagan meditation creeping into the apostate church world, in Scripture, meditation is always connected with God's written Word. Meditation should be directly upon Holy Scripture. Being filled daily with the treasure of God's Word is essential to the blessing of growing in the grace of Christ!

> "Blessed is the man that walketh not in the counsel of the ungodly, nor standeth in the way of sinners, nor sitteth in the seat of the scornful. 2 But his delight is in the law of the LORD; and in his law doth he meditate day and night." Psalms 1:1-2

Prayer: *Thank You LORD that Your Words will fill my heart and are the counsel in which I walk and speak. You call this success. Thank You Jesus!*

January 31

> "That this is a rebellious people, lying children, children that will not hear the law of the LORD: Which say to the seers, See not; and to the prophets, Prophesy not unto us right things, speak unto us smooth things, prophesy deceits." Isaiah 30:9-10

In Isaiah's day, the people of God called for their leaders to give them "smooth things," to **prophesy deceits.**" They were unrepentant and not willing and obedient to "endure sound doctrine." Through Paul, the Holy Spirit warned us that the same thing would be transpiring among those who profess Christ in the last hour before Christ's return.

> "Preach the word; be instant in season, out of season; reprove, rebuke, exhort with all longsuffering and doctrine. 3 For the time will come when they will not endure sound doctrine; but after their own lusts shall they heap to themselves teachers, having itching ears; 4 And they shall turn away their ears from the truth, and shall be turned unto fables." 2 Timothy 4:2-4

To "endure sound doctrine" means *to hold oneself accountable to sound doctrine, the truth of God's Word.*

Prayer: *Heavenly Father, please bring my heart and life into full honesty, repentance and authenticity. I will live by the whole counsel of Your Word. In Jesus' name, amen.*

February 1

> "He hath not dealt with us after our sins; nor rewarded us according to our iniquities. 11 For as the heaven is high above the earth, so great is his mercy toward them that fear him. 12 As far as the east is from the west, so far hath he removed our transgressions from us. 13 Like as a father pitieth his children, so the LORD pitieth them that fear him." Psalms 103:10-13

God forgives sin through Christ's perfect sacrifice. What I continue to learn is that I must reckon with all the sins I have personally committed. No matter how big or little they may seem, it's the same in the eyes of a holy God. And, I must forgive others as He has mercifully forgiven me, completely undeserved. I love these passages...which I've memorized and meditate upon daily:

> "Not by works of righteousness which we have done, but according to his mercy he saved us, by the washing of regeneration, and renewing of the Holy Ghost; 6 Which he shed on us abundantly through Jesus Christ our Saviour;" Titus 3:5-6

Returning His Mercy to others:

> "And be ye kind one to another, tenderhearted, forgiving one another, even as God for Christ's sake hath forgiven you." Ephesians 4:32

Prayer: *Dear Father, as You lovingly have forgiven me through Christ's perfect sacrifice, I choose to obey You in returning that same mercy to others, by Your grace. In Jesus' name, amen.*

February 2

**"Whosoever shall seek to save his life shall lose it; and whosoever shall lose his life shall preserve it."
Luke17:33**

You must give up your life to keep it. The divine economy is a cross economy! Jesus says you must lose your own life to see it preserved of God. You must give up your life to be blessed with His life.

You can't have HIS life unless you are willing to give up your own! Go for it! Today is your day.

ALL we need today is more of Jesus! That requires declaring that HE—not us—is MASTER and LORD of our lives (Galatians 2:20; John 3:30). Amen? God works via the reality and concept of the cross—death, burial, and resurrection! How did Jesus defeat Satan? By His cross! And how did Jesus prescribe that you defeat all enemies? The daily cross. Get some saints! WARNING: If you choose to lay it down and let Christ reign in your life—you will become addicted to the blessing of the resurrection life of Christ teeming in your life … and wonder what took you so long!

Prayer: *Precious LORD Jesus, right this moment I come to You. I am crucified with You. I am dead and my life is hidden with Christ in God. I love You Jesus and will follow You from this moment forward.*

February 3

"Always bearing about in the body the dying of the Lord Jesus, that the life also of Jesus might be made manifest in our body. 11 For we which live are alway delivered unto death for Jesus' sake, that the life also of Jesus might be made manifest in our mortal flesh. 12 So then death worketh in us, but life in you." 2 Corinthians 4:10-12

Without the cross, there is no Christianity. A real walk with Jesus begins and ends in His cross—the one Jesus died on and the one He commanded us to take up daily in our walk with Him (Luke 9:23-24).

Needing to get closer to God? Die to self and He will raise you upward! Surrender afresh—today!

You can't separate Christ and His cross. You can't say *"I am saved by the crucified Savior"* while denying that the same Savior mandates our own daily crucifixion!

"But we repeat, the Cross is not only atoning, it is also exemplary. What is more logical than a crucified Christ so that He may have crucified followers. Head and members must be one. Let us not divorce the doctrine of His Cross from the endurance of our cross. God forbid that we should be saved by crucifixion and yet saved from crucifixion." L. E. Maxwell, *The Cross and the Crown*

Prayer: *Father, in this day that You've made, let me be truly crucified with Christ, in Jesus' name, amen.*

February 4

"Know ye not that they which run in a race run all, but one receiveth the prize? So run, that ye may obtain." 1 Corinthians 9:24

Let us "leave it all on the field" for Christ if you will. Beloved of God, may God continue to help you pour out His truth in His love to others. Yes, to tirelessly communicate His Gospel just as Christ poured out His last drop of blood for us, for all, and till we are soon vanished from the earth.

"And every man that striveth for the mastery is temperate in all things. Now they do it to obtain a corruptible crown; but we an incorruptible. [26] I therefore so run, not as uncertainly; so fight I, not as one that beateth the air:" 1 Corinthians 9:25-26

Prayer: *Father, please quicken my heart to do things Your way—the right way—which is recorded in Your Word. Please use me to help others—to give them Your Word. In Jesus' name, amen.*

February 5

"And he said unto me, My grace is sufficient for thee: for my strength is made perfect in weakness. Most gladly therefore will I rather glory in my infirmities, that the power of Christ may rest upon me. 10 Therefore I take pleasure in infirmities, in reproaches, in necessities, in persecutions, in distresses for Christ's sake: for when I am weak, then am I strong." 2 Corinthians 12:9-10

In Christ's kingdom, we are only made strong by Him as we are blessed to first be made weak—death, burial, resurrection. Jesus' apostle Paul was brought low by the thorn God allowed to be given him by the messenger of Satan (2 Corinthians 12:7-8). Will God allow calamity into our lives? Yes. He has a greater plan than our temporal comfort in this fleeting life. God's desire is for us to be conformed to the image of His Son as He produces in us the character of Christ. This comes via cross occasions (Romans 8:28-29).

Prayer: *Please strip and prepare me to be fruitful for Your glory* LORD *Jesus.*

February 6

"And said, Verily I say unto you, Except ye be converted, and become as little children, ye shall not enter into the kingdom of heaven. 4 Whosoever therefore shall humble himself as this little child, the same is greatest in the kingdom of heaven." Matthew 18:3-4

If you will be with Jesus and great in His kingdom, you must lay down your life and become like a little child—fully dependent upon the LORD. Non-negotiably.

And, when we humble ourselves, we become servants to all men.

"But he that is greatest among you shall be your servant." Matthew 23:11

Kingdom Truth: Wherever you are, ABS = Always Be Serving (humbly).

Prayer: *Father, in Jesus' name, I ask You to purge me deeply from pride and self—whatever it takes—and instruct me according to Your humility and servanthood. Please teach me Your ways.*

February 7

"Verily, verily, I say unto you, Except a corn of wheat fall into the ground and die, it abideth alone: but if it die, it bringeth forth much fruit. 25 He that loveth his life shall lose it; and he that hateth his life in this world shall keep it unto life eternal." John 12:24-25

Just as nothing in hell could have held Jesus in that grave, NOTHING in hell can hold down the crucified saint! The divinely volcanic resurrection life of Christ bursting forth in the life of the crucified consenting disciple will be utterly unstoppable!

"But if the Spirit of him that raised up Jesus from the dead dwell in you, he that raised up Christ from the dead shall also quicken *(make alive, raise up)* **your mortal bodies by his Spirit that dwelleth in you." Romans 8:11**

Prayer: *LORD Jesus, I am crucified with You. I am dead and my life is hidden with Christ in God. I lay my life in Your holy hands, this moment. I love You LORD Jesus.*

There's an eternity of difference between being religious and being truly saved. Find out more on page 381.

February 8

"Blessed are they which do hunger and thirst after righteousness: for they shall be filled." Matthew 5:6

Jesus promises to fill those who hunger and thirst for His righteousness. This is a promise with condition. Only those who are seeking God, hungering and thirsting for His righteousness, are being filled by Him.

All true believers desire to share the Word of God with others in this last hour. KEY: Be so full of Christ via daily fellowship in prayer, praise, and the Word, that His love overflows from your life!

"Thou anointest my head with oil; my cup runneth over." Psalms 23:5

May our Father quicken your spirit today to cry out to Him in Jesus' name for that one saint He puts on your heart.

Prayer: Heavenly Father, LORD Jesus, I now hunger and thirst after Your righteousness - to truly know You. I seek Thy holy face. My soul follows hard after Thee, O God. In Jesus' name. Amen.

February 9

> "But this I say, He which soweth sparingly shall reap also sparingly; and he which soweth bountifully shall reap also bountifully. 7 Every man according as he purposeth in his heart, so let him give; not grudgingly, or of necessity: for God loveth a cheerful giver." 2 Corinthians 9:6-7

The verse above is the command, and next is the present and eternal incentive!

> "And God is able to make all grace abound toward you; that ye, always having all sufficiency in all things, may abound to every good work: 9 (As it is written, He hath dispersed abroad; he hath given to the poor: his righteousness remaineth for ever. 10 Now he that ministereth seed to the sower both minister bread for your food, and multiply your seed sown, and increase the fruits of your righteousness.)" 2 Corinthians 9:6-10

God has reserved the blessed privilege of supporting His work for His beloved people. Certainly, we don't expect religious organizations or the world to support the true Gospel, right?

Prayer: *Father, You gave all to save me. Please cultivate in me an obedient giving heart, to obey Your command to lay up treasure in Heaven, not on this fleeting earth. In Jesus' name, amen.*

February 10

> "And in that day ye shall ask me nothing. Verily, verily, I say unto you, Whatsoever ye shall ask the Father in my name, he will give it you. 24 Hitherto have ye asked nothing in my name: ask, and ye shall receive, that your joy may be full." John 16:23-24

God has made access to Him for salvation and answered prayer exclusive. Trust the NAME of JESUS in prayer!

> "And whatsoever ye shall ask in my name, that will I do, that the Father may be glorified in the Son. 14 If ye shall ask any thing in my name, I will do it." John 14:13-14

Many times, we hear people end their prayer with "in Your name." Where's that in the Bible? Are we ashamed of Jesus Christ? Let us be intentional, unashamed, and deliberate in stating the name of Jesus—before God and men!

Prayer: *Thank You LORD Jesus for Your perfect sacrifice for my sins and giving me full and perfect access to the Father's throne of grace. I come to You LORD—daily and often to seek Your face, to receive Your mercy and grace.*

February 11

"For we wrestle not against flesh and blood, but against principalities, against powers, against the rulers of the darkness of this world, against spiritual wickedness in high places." Ephesians 6:12

Many times, we don't recognize that sin and Satan are behind the things we see and suffer (1 Thessalonians 2:16). We also don't discern what is driving the behavior of some of those around us.

When Peter sought to prevent Christ from doing what He came to do, here's what Jesus said to him:

"Then Peter took him, and began to rebuke him, saying, Be it far from thee, Lord: this shall not be unto thee. 23 But he turned, and said unto Peter, Get thee behind me, Satan: thou art an offence unto me: for thou savourest not the things that be of God, but those that be of men." Luke 22:22-23

We must recognize that our true enemy is Satan and that he can only be overcome by Christ in us—via the crucified life Jesus prescribed, commanded. See Ephesians 6:12; 2 Corinthians 4:10-12; Galatians 2:20.

Prayer: *Heavenly Father, open the eyes of my understanding. Reveal Your truth to my heart. Teach me Thy ways, in Jesus' name.*

February 12

"And take heed to yourselves, lest at any time your hearts be overcharged with surfeiting, and drunkenness, and cares of this life, and so that day come upon you unawares. 35 For as a snare shall it come on all them that dwell on the face of the whole earth. 36 Watch ye therefore, and pray always, that ye may be accounted worthy to escape all these things that shall come to pass, and to stand before the Son of man." Luke 21:34-36

After initial salvation, each believer is personally responsible to abide in, to remain with, to continue in Christ. This requires obeying His cross command or they will **"fall away"** and be shut out of the eternal kingdom of Christ just as the five foolish virgins were (Matthew 25:1-13; Luke 8:13; 9:23-24).

Prayer: *Father, in the name of my LORD Jesus Christ, please grant full repentance to my heart. Whatever it takes, please make this vessel one of complete obedience that is prepared to honor YOU dear LORD.*

February 13

"Study to shew thyself approved unto God, a workman that needeth not to be ashamed, rightly dividing the word of truth." 2 Timothy 2:15

An authentic Christian is a disciplined follower of Jesus who is personally responsible to diligently study God's Word daily. Therefore, he feels no need to pay some institution of mere men to teach him God's Word because God gave him His Word in the King James Bible. He has a copy!

"When I was a child, I spake as a child, I understood as a child, I thought as a child: but when I became a man, I put away childish things." 1 Corinthians 13:11

Prayer: *Father in Heaven, in Jesus' holy name, please forgive my sins afresh, right now. Forgive my iniquity and rebellion against You as I've not truly surrendered and put You first, as my **"first love."** Please wash and cleanse me afresh by Your holy blood my LORD Jesus.*

February 14

"Let nothing be done through strife or vainglory; but in lowliness of mind let each esteem other better than themselves. 4 Look not every man on his own things, but every man also on the things of others. 5 Let this mind be in you, which was also in Christ Jesus:" Philippians 2:3-5

As Christ's disciple, your devotion, your love is first to Him, then to your neighbor, not self (Matthew 22:37-39). You are commanded by the Savior to set self aside and to lift others above yourself—to prefer, to put God and others first. Those who do so, experience true freedom, liberty.

Being one with Christ, who gave all to save you, means your life is over—you now live to serve the Lord and others, not self (Galatians 2:20; Colossians 3:3).

Have you poured prayerfully over Philippians 2:3-5 today?

If you will begin every day this week pouring prayerfully over this passage, asking the Lord to internalize it in your heart, God will begin to deeply instill the very **"mind of Christ"** into your innermost disposition.

Prayer: *Lord, I want to walk in the disposition You walked in on earth. I will esteem You and others above myself. In Jesus' name, amen.*

February 15

> "But I keep under my body, and bring it into subjection: lest that by any means, when I have preached to others, I myself should be a castaway." 1 Corinthians 9:27

Keeping under our bodies speaks of a continual essential. Keeping under means subduing the old man by crucifying it daily. This language speaks to the necessity of the daily cross—crucifying the iniquitous, fallen nature so that Christ alone reigns (Romans 6-8, etc.).

Paul makes it plain here that he doesn't believe he is unconditionally eternally secure and that he also could be **"a castaway"** in the end if he doesn't endure to the end with Christ— which requires obedience to His cross command:

> "And he said to them all, If any man will come after me, let him deny himself, and take up his cross daily, and follow me. 24 For whosoever will save his life shall lose it: but whosoever will lose his life for my sake, the same shall save it." Luke 9:23-24

Prayer: *Father, I here and now declare myself to be crucified with Christ. Please crucify all self, self-will, self-exaltation, and self-idolatry. In Jesus' name, amen.*

February 16

"And when ye stand praying, forgive, if ye have ought against any: that your Father also which is in heaven may forgive you your trespasses. 26 But if ye do not forgive, neither will your Father which is in heaven forgive your trespasses." Mark 11:25-26

Forgiveness: God is able to break us ... when we begin to see just how wicked we are, it seems to make it much easier to forgive others, considering how God has forgiven us on Christ's behalf. Memorizing Ephesians 4:32 has immensely helped me. We ALL deserve to be judged and God forgives those who come to Him in repentance for all their sins on the sole basis of Christ's perfect sacrifice.

"And be ye kind one to another, tenderhearted, forgiving one another, even as God for Christ's sake hath forgiven you." Ephesians 4:32

Prayer: *Father, You mercifully forgave all my sins due to the merit of Christ's sacrifice alone. I here and now choose to wholly, freely forgive all who've hurt me or who I previously judged in my attitudes. Lord, please forgive my sins which came from an evil heart. In Jesus' name I pray.*

February 17

"And when Jesus had cried with a loud voice, he said, Father, into thy hands I commend my spirit: and having said thus, he gave up the ghost." Luke 23:46

The most astounding event of human history occurred when this man, Jesus Christ, died on a Roman cross. When He died, an untimely darkness covered the land at 3:00 p.m. and an earthquake occurred as He took His final breath. This man called Jesus was crucified. Three days later He was raised from the dead! Here's why He died:

"But your iniquities *(sins)* **have separated between you and your God, and your sins have hid his face from you, that he will not hear." Isaiah 59:2**

Jesus died for you. The sin state and transgressions you've committed separate you from your Maker.

Prayer: *Heavenly Father, I come to You in the name of Jesus and ask You to save and forgive me. I've sinned against You. Take me now* Lord. *I'm all Yours and I know You're all mine. I love you Jesus and from this moment forth, I live for You alone!*

February 18

"How is it that ye sought me? wist (knew) **ye not that I must be about my Father's business?" Luke 2:49**

Is your heart sown into Christ's vision or some hireling's, some local church's vision? Is Christ's vision not revealed in His Word?

There are so many wolves who manipulate and use their prey by selling them on a vision that is not God's Word.

Are you wasting your life promoting some mere man's vision? Those not in the Word cannot discern.

Ignorance is no excuse. We shall all give full account to the Lord who bought us with the price of His holy blood.

Bidding Godspeed to, that is, condoning an enemy of Christ, will bring the same judgment on themselves as will be brought on God's enemies.

"If there come any unto you, and bring not this doctrine, receive him not into your house, neither bid him God speed: 11 For he that biddeth him God speed is partaker of his evil deeds." 2 John 10-11

Prayer: *Holy Father, please grant my heart discernment and reveal to me if in any way I am bidding God speed to any of Your enemies. In Jesus' name, amen.*

February 19

> "For, brethren, ye have been called unto liberty; only use not liberty for an occasion to the flesh, but by love serve one another." **Galatians 5:13**

God should never be taken for granted. If man chooses to wane, to wax cold toward Christ, to deny Christ instead of self, going back into sin, God will justly retribute such a man.

> "He that despised Moses' law died without mercy under two or three witnesses: ²⁹ Of how much sorer punishment, suppose ye, shall he be thought worthy, who hath trodden under foot the Son of God, and hath counted the blood of the covenant, wherewith he was sanctified, an unholy thing, and hath done despite unto the Spirit of grace?" **Hebrews 10:28-29**

Prayer: *Father, I come to You in the name of my LORD Jesus. Please evoke in my bosom Your fear. Bless this life to love, worship, obey, and please You in a fruitful, abiding walk with my LORD Jesus.*

February 20

"And he spake a parable unto them to this end, that men ought always to pray, and not to faint;" Luke 18:1

Debbie Lord writes:

"Keep on praying. See it through. We're in process. We need to diligently trust God. Remember in Genesis 32:28 when Jacob struggled with the Lord all night? Here's what Donald Stamps says regarding that portion of Scripture: 'God does not want His people to be passive but to earnestly seek Him for His blessing and grace.' We need to be earnest and persistent in prayer."

Jesus promises:

> **"I tell you that he will avenge them speedily** *(those who persevere with Him in prayer)*. **Nevertheless when the Son of man cometh, shall he find faith on the earth?"** Luke 18:8

> **"Ask, and it shall be given you; seek, and ye shall find; knock, and it shall be opened unto you:" Matthew 7:7**

Here Christ conveys to us that believers are to ask and keep asking, seek and keep seeking, and to knock and keep knocking! A.S.K. = Ask, Seek, Knock.

Prayer: *Please cultivate in me a rich fellowship, a life of prayer, with You Father. In Jesus' name, amen.*

February 21

> "But thou shalt remember the LORD thy God: for it is he that giveth thee power to get wealth, that he may establish his covenant which he sware unto thy fathers, as it is this day." Deuteronomy 8:18

Remembering the LORD from whom every blessing flows:

> "All things come of thee, and of thine own have we given thee." 1 Chronicles 29:14

> "Every good gift and every perfect gift is from above, and cometh down from the Father of lights, with whom is no variableness, neither shadow of turning." James 1:17

Asking the LORD to grant us a holy fear and a heart of gratitude toward Him is key. The great danger of forgetting God is explicitly expressed in this following verse:

> "The wicked shall be turned into hell, and all the nations that forget God." Psalms 9:17

Prayer: *Holy Father, please help my heart to be wholly grateful to You. I am crucified with Christ.*

If you were to die today, are you 100% certain you'd be in Heaven and not hell? God wants you with Him! Check out page 381 to make sure.

February 22

> "For if after they have escaped the pollutions of the world through the knowledge of the Lord and Saviour Jesus Christ, they are again entangled therein, and overcome, the latter end is worse with them than the beginning. 21 For it had been better for them not to have known the way of righteousness, than, after they have known it, to turn from the holy commandment delivered unto them." 2 Peter 2:20-21

The prospect of drifting away from the LORD should haunt us.

We are secure as we abide, remain, continue in Christ—which is a daily choice. Read John 15:1-6.

> "Work out your own salvation with fear and trembling. 13 For it is God which worketh in you both to will and to do of his good pleasure." Philippians 2:12-13

Prayer: Father, in Jesus' name, may Your holy fear fill my heart always. Please bless this life to be rooted in Christ and bearing fruit to Your eternal glory.

February 23

> **"Come unto me, all ye that labour and are heavy laden, and I will give you rest. ²⁹ Take my yoke upon you, and learn of me; for I am meek and lowly in heart: and ye shall find rest unto your souls. ³⁰ For my yoke is easy, and my burden is light." Matthew 11:28-30**

Jesus calls us to come to Him. Are you ready to pass from death to life?

God wants to pardon you—before it's too late. Jesus beckons you to **"Come unto me"**—before it's too late (Matthew 11:28-30).

If you are only 99.9% sure you are going to Heaven, you are as sure for eternal hell as if you were already there. Today is your day to give your life to Jesus right now. You may not have another opportunity. Friend don't wait another minute. God is leading you to Himself. He loves you.

Prayer: *Father I have sinned against You. This moment I ask You to save me, to forgive all my sins through Jesus Christ whom I now declare to be my* L<small>ORD</small>. *Thank You for dying and rising from the dead for me* L<small>ORD</small> *Jesus. From this moment forth I will serve You.*

See page 381 *(Making Peace with God)* at the end of this book.

February 24

"For when we were yet without strength, in due time Christ died for the ungodly *(that's you)."* **Romans 5:6**

Jesus Christ bears the scars in His holy hands and feet which prove how much He loves you (Romans 5:6-9; 2 Corinthians 5:19-21; 1 John 3:16). No one else ever died for your sins on a cruel cross— to buy you back to Himself. He **"gave himself a ransom for all, to be testified in due time"** (1 Timothy 2:6).

"Giving thanks unto the Father, which hath made us meet to be partakers of the inheritance of the saints in light: 13 Who hath delivered us from the power of darkness, and hath translated us into the kingdom of his dear Son: 14 In whom we have redemption through his blood, even the forgiveness of sins:" Colossians 1:12-14

Prayer: *LORD Jesus, I am presently and forever grateful for Your perfect sacrifice that You offered on the cross for my sins—to buy me back to You! I love You LORD Jesus.*

February 25

"I am crucified with Christ: nevertheless I live; yet not I, but Christ liveth in me: and the life which I now live in the flesh I live by the faith of the Son of God, who loved me, and gave himself for me." Galatians 2:20

Being crucified with Christ means one is emptied of self, self-will—one's own agenda, and abandoned to God's will (Philippians 2). This means that such a person searches out and embraces the biblical truth, no matter where it leads. He never bends the truth to try to fit a tradition or doctrine but rather rejects any previously believed notion when the Word says differently (Romans 3:4; 2 Timothy 2:15; 3:15-17, etc.).

"I die daily." 1 Corinthians 15:31

Prayer: *My LORD Jesus, I am crucified with You today and I know You are raising up this life for Your glory alone. Right this moment, into Your holy hands I submit my spirit.*

February 26

"Jesus said unto him, Thou shalt love the Lord thy God with all thy heart, and with all thy soul, and with all thy mind. 38 This is the first and great commandment. 39 And the second is like unto it, Thou shalt love thy neighbour as thyself. 40 On these two commandments hang all the law and the prophets." Matthew 22:37-40

Unless I am missing something, it seems that Jesus gave just two commands in Matthew 22:37-39 and not three. Did you catch that in the passage above? The **"mind of Christ"** is loving God and others above our self which requires crucifying self (Philippians 2:3-5). And, Christ's apostle Paul plainly states that we already love ourselves—it comes naturally, from the adamic, the fallen nature—**"For no man ever yet hated his own flesh"** (Ephesians 5:29). Jesus introduced to us the only solution—the daily cross (Luke 9:23-24). Loving our self is the root of our problems, our sin, and not something we should learn to do.

Not only are most leaders not teaching the cross—self-denial—they are teaching the opposite—self-exaltation! ANY leader not preaching the cross is misleading! Run!

Prayer: *Father, I will love You my Lord first, foremost, and supremely. Please fill me with Your love for others, in Jesus' name.*

February 27

"I have no greater joy than to hear that my children walk in truth." 3 John 4

What did the apostle John rejoice in? John, along with every man of God, rejoices when others walk in the truth of the LORD, which is His written Word.

"Sanctify them through thy truth: thy word is truth." John 17:17

God highly aggrandizes His truth and rewards those who love His truth and punishes those who don't (2 Thessalonians 2:10-12).

Any leader posing as a man of God but does not pray, work, rejoice in, and live to see God's people walk in His truth (the Word) is a false prophet.

Prayer: *Heavenly Father, I love Your truth. Thank You my LORD Jesus for providing Your Word in written form. I love Your precepts, Your truth. I love You Jesus. Please reveal Yourself to me.*

February 28

"And they continued stedfastly in the apostles' doctrine and fellowship, and in breaking of bread, and in prayers." Acts 2:42

If your walk with Christ is centered on the Sunday morning so-called "church service," you've allowed yourself to be misled. You may choose to ask Jesus to make you His authentic, New Testament disciple.

Be not impressed or vainly satisfied that you attended a Sunday morning "church service," even if it was a good one! Compare that to the earliest followers of Jesus, full of the Holy Ghost, who couldn't get enough of Christ and met **"daily ... house to house."** Go now to Acts 2:42-47 and see how the real body of Christ functions!

"And they, CONTINUING DAILY with one accord in the temple, and breaking bread from HOUSE TO HOUSE, did eat their meat with gladness and singleness of heart." Acts 2:46

Prayer: *Father, please probe the depths of my heart. Make me Your authentic, honest, and real disciple. Take away every trace of falsity. In Jesus' name, amen.*

February 29

"Concerning the works of men, by the word of thy lips I have kept me from the paths of the destroyer." Psalms 17:4

Walking in, obeying God's Word is the only way to scam-proof your soul!

"Every word of God is pure: he is a shield *(protection)* unto them that put their trust in him." Proverbs 30:5

To be sanctified and safeguarded, one must be set apart in and by God's Word continually.

"Sanctify them through thy truth: thy word is truth." John 17:17

Prayer: *Heavenly Father, please wash me with the water of Your Word. I here and now confess my sin of self-idolatry, spiritual adultery and declare afresh LORD Jesus that You alone are the Master, the LORD of my life. In the name of Jesus, amen.*

March 1

"It is more blessed to give than to receive." Acts 20:35

The happiest, **"more blessed,"** most joyful people we meet are the givers—those who've given their life and therefore their substance (Acts 20:35). Their hearts are full of joy because as they continue to give their life and substance, they are perpetually freed of the sins of greed and covetousness. Their hearts are filled with joy for participating in the Gospel of the One they love.

> **"Lay not up for yourselves treasures upon earth, where moth and rust doth corrupt, and where thieves break through and steal: [20] But lay up for yourselves treasures in heaven, where neither moth nor rust doth corrupt, and where thieves do not break through nor steal: [21] For where your treasure is, there will your heart be also." Matthew 6:19-21**

True disciples of Jesus live with an eternal perspective, realizing that this world we now live in is temporary (2 Corinthians 4:16-18; James 4:14).

Prayer: *Holy Father, grant my heart to understand the brevity of this life and to invest in Your eternal kingdom now. In Jesus' name.*

March 2

> "Now concerning the collection for the saints, as I have given order to the churches of Galatia, even so do ye. ² Upon the first day of the week let every one of you lay by him in store, as God hath prospered him, that there be no gatherings when I come." 1 Corinthians 16:1-2

There were collections among the saints in the New Testament (1 Corinthians 16:1-3). Our LORD, in His earthly ministry, had a treasurer in case people wanted to participate and lay up treasure in Heaven.

As His disciples, we never give to get but rather in worship-filled obedience to our new Master, our LORD, in gratitude that He gave all to save us.

KINGDOM PERSPECTIVE: Money collections to do GOD's work are not a sin but rather an opportunity for God's people to crucify, to put off the sins of greed and covetousness and to lay up treasure in Heaven as He commanded (Matthew 6:19-21; Ephesians 5:7-9).

Prayer: *Holy Father, please forgive my unbelief and hoarding. Grant this heart to be a generous heart of giving to those of Your people in need and to Your work. In Jesus' name, amen* LORD.

March 3

"But the God of all grace, who hath called us unto his eternal glory by Christ Jesus, after that ye have suffered a while, make you perfect, stablish, strengthen, settle you." 1 Peter 5:10

God perfects, establishes, settles and strengthens His people as their faith is tried in the fire via afflictions.

Meditate upon the history, the stripping work of God in the lives of every man that would be used of Him (Joseph, Moses, David, Paul, Peter, etc.). For our own learning, we can read about the breaking of Jacob (Genesis 32), the calamities of beloved Joseph (Genesis 37-50), the devastation of Job, the sin, sufferings and restoration of David (Psalms 51), the sinful denial of Christ by Peter, and the stripping of Paul (2 Corinthians 6, 11, 12, etc.). Our LORD's dealings in the lives of these men plainly demonstrates that God can and will powerfully use no one until He has first brought them to the place of crucifixion—co-death with Christ (Romans 6:3-4). God will not raise up (resurrect) anyone who is not first dead and buried (1 Corinthians 15:36; 2 Corinthians 4:10-12).

Prayer: *Dear heavenly Father, thank You for allowing various afflictions in my life and teaching me to truly trust You and worship You through them. In Jesus' name.*

March 4

> "We have also a more sure word of prophecy; whereunto ye do well that ye take heed, as unto a light that shineth in a dark place, until the day dawn, and the day star arise in your hearts: [20] Knowing this first, that no prophecy of the scripture is of any private interpretation. [21] For the prophecy came not in old time by the will of man: but holy men of God spake as they were moved by the Holy Ghost." 2 Peter 1:19-21

God's written Word is the highest divine authority and nothing else, not even the audible voice of God the Father speaking from Heaven, and certainly not prophecy of mere men.

Dear student of Christ: Until you have the revelation given us in 2 Peter 1:19-21, you are vulnerable to be deceived and ultimately **"fall away"** from the LORD—to apostatize (Luke 8:13; 1 Timothy 4:1, etc.). What is the LORD conveying to us, His people, in 2 Peter 1:12-21?

Many search for someone to give them *a word* and yet aren't seeking out, studying, meditating upon and memorizing THE WORD (2 Timothy 2:15; 3:15-17).

Prayer: *Father in Heaven, please convict my heart to deeply understand that Your written Word is the highest and final divine authority on all matters of faith. In Jesus' name.*

March 5

> "For we preach not ourselves, but Christ Jesus the Lord; and ourselves your servants for Jesus' sake."
> 2 Corinthians 4:5

The God-fearing disciple is first and foremost interested in relationship with Christ, not himself!

In fact, the true servant of Jesus humbles himself, stays away from things that would draw people to himself instead of Jesus.

> "And I, brethren, when I came to you, came not with excellency of speech or of wisdom, declaring unto you the testimony of God. 2 For I determined not to know any thing among you, save Jesus Christ, and him crucified. 3 And I was with you in weakness, and in fear, and in much trembling. 4 And my speech and my preaching was not with enticing words of man's wisdom, but in demonstration of the Spirit and of power: 5 That your faith should not stand in the wisdom of men, but in the power of God." 1 Corinthians 2:1-5

Prayer: *Father, please bless this vessel to be truly crucified with Christ so Jesus alone is shining through ... and not my flesh. In Jesus' name, amen.*

March 6

"And he said to them all, If any man will come after me, let him deny himself, and take up his cross daily, and follow me. 24 For whosoever will save his life shall lose it: but whosoever will lose his life for my sake, the same shall save it." Luke 9:23-24

Jesus tells us that our walk with Him is **"daily"** as we deny self, take up the cross and follow Him, which is Christ's prescription. If today in our life is not a cross day, we should be concerned. There can and will be no raising up of our life by God if there is not first an adherence to death and burial. Are you ready to let go and let God? Are you crying out to the LORD with John the Baptist— **"He must increase, but I must decrease"**? (See John 3:30.)

The cross message must not merely be dabbled with but rather camped out on!

Prayer: *Precious Father, in Jesus' name, may my life be crucified with Christ this day.*

Are you truly saved? Check out page 381 to make sure.

March 7

> "What? know ye not that your body is the temple of the Holy Ghost which is in you, which ye have of God, and ye are not your own? [20] For ye are bought with a price: therefore glorify God in your body, and in your spirit, which are God's." 1 Corinthians 6:19-20

You have been bought with the highest price ever—the very blood of Jesus Christ.

> "For ye are dead, and your life is hid with Christ in God." Colossians 3:3

Your life is over and the sin that brought only misery and damage to your heart and life, is in your past.

> "And such were some of you: but ye are washed, but ye are sanctified, but ye are justified in the name of the Lord Jesus, and by the Spirit of our God." 1 Corinthians 6:11

Prayer: *Father, in Jesus' name, bless this life to be truly crucified with Christ.*

March 8

> **"For to this end Christ both died, and rose, and revived, that he might be Lord both of the dead and living." Romans 14:9**

Christ died to fully pay for the sins of all of humanity that He might reign in the lives of all He saves.

> **"Who will have all men to be saved, and to come unto the knowledge of the truth." 1 Timothy 2:4**

God loves us and wants us to experience relationship with Him, now and forever (John 17:3). Friend, who else has ever died for you but Jesus, the Good Shepherd? Is He not worthy of your all?

Prayer: *Lord Jesus, thank You for being crucified for my sins. Right now, this moment, if never before, I lay my life in Your perfect, almighty hands. Use me Jesus, please.*

March 9

> **"As newborn babes, desire the sincere milk of the word, that ye may grow thereby:" 1 Peter 2:2**

The divine command here is to **"desire"** God's Word. An appetite for God's Word is found in everyone who is truly known of Him. The wise virgin believers will feed that hunger daily, voraciously.

> **"Thy words were found, and I did eat them; and thy word was unto me the joy and rejoicing of mine heart: for I am called by thy name, O Lord God of hosts." Jeremiah 15:16**

ALL who are not in the Word daily have already backslidden. Falling away from Christ begins with one moment of neglect.

"If you skip one day with God, then you'll skip tomorrow too!"
Maureen Lundie

Prayer: *Father, I come to You in Jesus' name, asking You to increase in me a hunger for You and therefore for Your Word.*

March 10

> **"And lest I should be exalted above measure through the abundance of the revelations, there was given to me a thorn in the flesh, the messenger of Satan to buffet me, lest I should be exalted above measure." 2 Corinthians 12:7**

It's not God who directly breaks us, but at times, for His purposes, as was the case with Job and Paul, the LORD allows Satan to bring in the thorn, the destruction (Romans 8:28-29). See also 1 Timothy 1:18-20; Luke 22:31-33; 1 Corinthians 5:5. If we pray for Him to break us, He will answer and do it His way.

The divine goal is always to conform His children to the image of Jesus Christ.

> **"And we know that all things work together for good to them that love God, to them who are the called according to his purpose. 29 For whom he did foreknow, he also did predestinate to be conformed to the image of his Son, that he might be the firstborn among many brethren." Romans 8:28-29**

Prayer: *Thank You LORD Jesus for using all that has, is, and will happen to me in this life to conform me to Your holy, crucified image. I love You Jesus.*

March 11

"For whosoever shall call upon the name of the Lord shall be saved." Romans 10:13

Are you truly saved? If not, please go to the Addendum (page 381) of this book to learn how to be saved.

If you are truly born again, now what?

- Tell another Christian.
- Find a group of Christ-loving, Bible-living believers.
- Be water baptized.
- Read your King James Bible daily.
- Talk with God in prayer daily.
- Follow Christ to the end of your life.

Prayer: *Father, thank You so much for finding and saving me into Your family through the blood of Jesus. I love You my LORD Jesus. Please do a deeper work in my life, continue the good work You began in me when You saved me. Thank You Jesus!*

March 12

> "For the grace of God that bringeth salvation hath appeared to all men, ¹² Teaching us that, denying ungodliness and worldly lusts, we should live soberly, righteously, and godly, in this present world;" Titus 2:11-12

If we have truly received divine grace and are presently abiding in Christ, we are being taught the following by our LORD to:

- deny ungodliness,
- deny worldly lusts,
- live soberly,
- live righteously,
- live godly,
- not expect Heaven if you aren't living a sanctified life in this present world.

Saints, beware of those who promulgate a false grace that enables, allows sin against Him who is **"Holy, holy, holy"** (Isaiah 6:3; Revelation 4:8). God's grace is being perverted by **"ungodly men"** who make it out to be a license for sin (Jude 4). The LORD will not save into Heaven ANY person who dies in sin (Ezekiel 18:4; 33:12-13; Hebrews 10:26-39; 12:14, etc.).

Prayer: *Father, please multiply Your grace to my life, Your divine influence on my heart and divine enablement—to glorify You alone in this life. In Jesus' name, amen.*

March 13

"For by grace *(undeserved favor)* **are ye saved through faith; and that not of yourselves: it is the gift of God: Not of works, lest any man should boast." Ephesians 2:8-9**

We cannot earn our own way of salvation with God. We are fully guilty of sinning against Him. He sent His only begotten Son to be our Savior—the only Savior. The Son of God died and rose again to take away all your sins. He was the only One qualified for the job and He is the only One worthy of your worship. Peace with God happens when we meet the Prince of Peace—Jesus Christ.

Prayer to make sure you have peace with God: *Father in Heaven, I come to You as a sinner, asking You to forgive my sins and to save me into Your eternal kingdom. Right now,* ***if never before****, I declare Jesus Christ—who was crucified and raised again—as the* LORD *of my life.*

March 14

"We therefore ought to receive such, that we might be fellowhelpers to the truth." 3 John 8

Saints, being that the LORD has found and saved us into His kingdom, we are blessed to be **"fellow helpers to the truth."**

Truth preaching ministries are only supported by those who agree and are fed by them. This is where our opportunity is found—in working together as members of His one body to see that His Word is going forth in this late hour—just as He commanded in His Great Commission to us (Matthew 28:18-20).

May God find us faithful stewards of the myriad blessings He's bestowed upon our lives and for which we shall give full account to Him.

"WE are labourers TOGETHER with God." 1 Corinthians 3:9

Prayer: *Holy Father, I come to You in the name of Jesus and ask that You use me to help Your bless-ed Word go forth into the hearts of men—both to feed Your saints and to reach sinners.*

March 15

> "For there is not a just man upon earth, that doeth good, and sinneth not." **Ecclesiastes 7:20**

There is always the need for conviction, self-examination, fruit-inspection, repentance, and confession of sin (Proverbs 28:13; 2 Corinthians 13:5; 1 John 1:6-2:2).

> "If we say that we have no sin, we deceive ourselves, and the truth is not in us. [9] If we confess our sins, he is faithful and just to forgive us our sins, and to cleanse us from all unrighteousness. [10] If we say that we have not sinned, we make him a liar, and his word is not in us." **1 John 1:8-10**

Prayer: *Heavenly Father, please identify and correct any and all false notions I have of You. I here and now acknowledge this moment before You that You expect and require me to be completely honest about any sin I have or may commit and to confess it to You for what it is, sin. In Jesus' name.*

March 16

> **"Who will rise up for me against the evildoers? or who will stand up for me against the workers of iniquity?" Psalms 94:16**

Do we not have enough soft-peddling pastors selling their wares? Will you be yet another spineless casualty or will you stand out and preach God's Word from a fearless crucified life/disposition? (See Psalms 94:16; 2 Corinthians 4:10-12; Galatians 1:10.)

Some foolishly suppose that Jesus and His apostles were too harsh. Who do men think they are to question God? Paul told one false prophet:

> **"And said, O full of all subtilty and all mischief, thou child of the devil, thou enemy of all righteousness, wilt thou not cease to pervert the right ways of the Lord?" Acts 13:10**

SAINTS, we should care little of what those in darkness think about us! We live to please the One who died, was buried, raised again from the dead, and is coming soon (2 Corinthians 5:15).

Prayer: *Father, I ask You to embolden my spirit with Your grace —to speak Your Word in love. In Jesus' name, amen.*

March 17

> "Who gave himself for us, that he might redeem us from ALL iniquity, and purify unto himself a peculiar people, zealous of good works." Titus 2:14

Jesus died to make His people holy, to deliver His people from **"ALL"** their iniquities and not to grant them a license to sin (Jude 4).

Yet, we have a priesthood of wolves who can be discerned in that they refuse to teach or ever mention Scriptures like this, all while they talk like Christ's saints are relegated to a life of sin! Here's another verse you'll never hear out of a deceiver who poses as Christ's servant:

> "Having therefore these promises, dearly beloved, let us cleanse ourselves from all filthiness of the flesh and spirit, perfecting holiness in the fear of God." 2 Corinthians 7:1

Prayer: *Father I come to You in the name of Jesus and ask You to purify this vessel. Cleanse my heart, mind, and life of all that defiles in Your holy eyes, in Jesus' name, amen.*

March 18

"Charity out of a pure heart." 1 Timothy 1:5

The seat of a pure heart is essential to God who is love dwelling in and mightily using a man.

"And we have known and believed the love that God hath to us. God is love; and he that dwelleth in love dwelleth in God, and God in him." 1 John 4:16

Regrettably, in this late hour, it's rare to find someone who actually cares for anyone except himself. God's people must be the example (1 Timothy 1:5). This time was all foretold (Matthew 24:10-13; 2 Timothy 3:1-7, etc.). Yet, the LORD is calling His people to shine the light of His love and truth.

God's will is that His people love Him with all their heart, mind, and strength (Matthew 22:37) whereby He fills them with His holy love. Divinely blessed powerful ministry ensues.

Prayer: *Father, You are love. I here and now ask You to purify this heart and to fill me with Your love. In Jesus' name, amen.*

March 19

"Let nothing be done through strife or vainglory; but in lowliness of mind let each esteem other better than themselves. 4 Look not every man on his own things, but every man also on the things of others. 5 Let this mind be in you, which was also in Christ Jesus:" Philippians 2:3-5

Your relationships will only be as good as your personal submission to God. The above passage is one this disciple encourages you to pour prayerfully over each morning this week. Life changer!

In Christ's kingdom economy, the mind of Christ means you choose to die and to serve Jesus and others—not self! THIS is the very **"mind of Christ"** (Philippians 2:3-5).

Your whole duty as His disciple today is to forsake self and spend your time and energy serving others as unto Him.

Prayer: *Father, please bless this life to be truly crucified with Christ today— loving You and others supremely, above myself. In Jesus' name, amen my* L*ORD*.

March 20

> "For he shall have judgment without mercy, that hath shewed no mercy; and mercy rejoiceth against judgment." James 2:13

This is a severe warning with eternal consequences and should be memorized immediately and enacted in our attitudes and actions.

True followers of Christ must show mercy in order to receive mercy from God. Memorize James 2:13 today.

What is your attitude toward a brother and sister who has sinned? If your heart is not broken over it, praying and seeking to help them to be restored, you are not yet possessed with the mind of Christ. Have you memorized Galatians 6:1-2?

> "Brethren, if a man be overtaken in a fault, ye which are spiritual, restore such an one in the spirit of meekness; considering thyself, lest thou also be tempted. 2 Bear ye one another's burdens, and so fulfil the law of Christ." Galatians 6:1-2

Prayer: *Heavenly Father, I come to You in Jesus Christ alone. Please forgive my attitude of ruthlessness and murderous hatred toward others. No one needs Your mercy more than I do, a hopeless sinner without Your saving mercy in Christ. Please teach me true humility and Your desire to restore, not condemn others.*

March 21

> "One of his disciples said unto him, Lord, teach us to pray." Luke 11:1

"**Lord, teach us to pray.**" Christ's disciples should ask the LORD to "**teach us to pray.**" The disciples called on Jesus to teach them to pray—to have a prayer life. Christ answered them and us by giving the whole Church a model prayer to be followed in spontaneous and joyful relationship. Here it is:

> "And it came to pass, that, as he was praying in a certain place, when he ceased, one of his disciples said unto him, <u>Lord, teach us to pray</u>, as John also taught his disciples. 2 And he said unto them, When ye pray, say, Our Father which art in heaven, Hallowed be thy name. Thy kingdom come. Thy will be done, as in heaven, so in earth. 3 Give us day by day our daily bread. 4 And forgive us our sins; for we also forgive every one that is indebted to us. And lead us not into temptation; but deliver us from evil." Luke 11:1-4

Jesus is coming—ready or not.

Prayer: *Father in Heaven, in the name of Jesus Christ, I ask You to teach me to pray. Here and now, I lay my life into Your holy hands afresh. You must increase, and I must decrease. In the name of Jesus, please bless this life to be dead and buried and raised up by You, LORD. Amen.*

March 22

"All things come of thee, and of thine own have we given thee." 1 Chronicles 29:14

All that we have in our temporary possession, comes from the hands of our God. What will happen when we stand before Him to give account? How will we explain to Him if we've neglected His people who were in need, when He presented us the opportunity to lay up treasure in Heaven? (See Matthew 6:19-21.)

The two biblically stated priorities for giving:

- To Christians in need (Acts 2:44-45; 4:32-35; 1 Corinthians 16:1-2)

- To the work and workers (**"labourers"**) of God (Acts 4:34-35; 1 Corinthians 9:1-14; 1 Timothy 5:17-18, etc.)

Prayer: *Father, please make me a faithful, obedient steward of Your resources, a cheerful giver to Your priorities, in Jesus' name. Amen* LORD.

March 23

> **"Christ Jesus came into the world to save** *(rescue)* **sinners." 1 Timothy 1:15**

No religion or religious figure or mere man can forgive your sins or save your soul from hell (no matter what they claim). Jesus didn't come to start a religion but rather to establish His eternal kingdom in the hearts of men, granting them a relationship with God. Jesus Christ is the only One who bears nail-scarred hands and feet for your sins. He is the only way to God and your only hope.

> **"For there is ONE God, and ONE mediator between God and men, the man Christ Jesus." 1 Timothy 2:5**

Prayer: *Father in Heaven, I've sinned against You in many ways. Right this moment, if never before, I admit my sin to You and ask You to forgive my sins and save me into Your eternal family. Right this moment, I confess that Jesus Christ is my LORD who was raised from the dead after dying for my sins. I Love You Jesus and will follow You from this moment forward.*

March 24

> "And he that reapeth receiveth wages, and gathereth fruit unto life eternal: that both he that soweth and he that reapeth may rejoice together." John 4:36

Here Jesus is speaking specifically of His work—as we do His work. There's no work so important or eternal as the work of our LORD's Gospel! And Christ promises us eternal treasure as we participate, as we obey Him.

May God bless us in this endeavor saints. **"WE are labourers TOGETHER with God"** (1 Corinthians 3:9).

The beautiful feet of Christ's Gospel workers are to be prayed for and supported by us:

> **"How then shall they call on him in whom they have not believed? and how shall they believe in him of whom they have not heard? and how shall they hear without a preacher? 15 And how shall they preach, except they be sent? as it is written, How beautiful are the feet of them that preach the gospel of peace, and bring glad tidings of good things!" Romans 10:14-15**

Prayer: *Father, grant my heart to have Your kingdom perspective. Grant me a giving heart, an obedient life. In Jesus' name, amen.*

March 25

"Strive *(agonize)* to enter in at the strait gate: for many, I say unto you, will seek to enter in, and shall not be able. 25 When once the master of the house is risen up, and hath shut to the door, and ye begin to stand without, and to knock at the door, saying, Lord, Lord, open unto us; and he shall answer and say unto you, I know you not whence ye are:" Luke 13:24-25

Read these words of Christ again and take them at face value from the Son of God. This is a warning. Many who have in the past believed and been saved are not striving to enter the eternal kingdom due to the false eternal security teaching which has made them lukewarm at best (Revelation 3:15-16).

Why would Jesus be warning His own of escaping coming judgment if there were no danger of losing out?

Many have been misled. Jesus invented the term **"FALL AWAY" and so we know it's possible** (Luke 8:13). Are you going to call the Son of God a liar? If falling away wasn't possible, why did Jesus say it is possible?

Prayer: *Heavenly Father, in Jesus' name I ask You now to cleanse me afresh of all sins. Bless my whole disposition to be that of prayer-filled worship and obedience to You as I eagerly look for the soon return of Jesus.*

March 26

"Come unto me, all *ye* that labour and are heavy laden, and I will give you rest." Matthew 11:28

When we **"come unto"** Jesus we bask in the love of **"the God of all comfort"** who undertakes our cause because He promised **"Draw nigh to God, and he will draw nigh to you"** (2 Corinthians 1:2-4; James 4:8). When we return to Him, casting off pride, unbelief, self-effort and self-reliance, we are blessed to **"learn of"** Him, whereby we **"find rest"** deep in our hearts from the Savior whose **"yoke is easy"** and whose **"burden is light"** (Matthew 11:29-30).

All are invited and all who come to Jesus will be given His **"rest."**

Prayer: *LORD, I come to You now, asking You to wash me afresh of my sins. Cleanse my heart and grant Your beautiful peace, Your perfect rest, as You alone can do. I love You LORD Jesus. In the name of Jesus.*

March 27

> "Behold, all souls are mine; as the soul of the father, so also the soul of the son is mine: the soul that sinneth, it shall die." Ezekiel 18:4

Sin separates people from God, period. **"The wages of sin is death** *(separation from God)***"** (Romans 6:23).

Here is just one of the lists of soul damning sins. This list reveals 17 sins that damn the soul. This is written to believers:

> **"Now the works of the flesh are manifest, which are these; Adultery, fornication, uncleanness, lasciviousness, 20 Idolatry, witchcraft, hatred, variance, emulations, wrath, strife, seditions, heresies, 21 Envyings, murders, drunkenness, revellings, and such like: of the which I tell you before, as I have also told you in time past, that they which do such things shall not inherit the kingdom of God" Galatians 5:19-21.**

Truly abiding assures that the true disciple is not living in sin and is therefore ready to meet Jesus.

Prayer: *Father, in Jesus' name, bless this life to be crucified with Christ and abiding in You* LORD. *Please produce the fruit of holiness in this life* LORD *Jesus.*

March 28

"But now in Christ Jesus ye who sometimes were far off are made nigh by the blood of Christ. 14 For he is our peace, who hath made both one, and hath broken down the middle wall of partition between us;" Ephesians 2:13-14

At the end of a perfect (sinless) life, Christ carried the very cross He was to be nailed to. His infinite love for you, along with the nails driven through His hands and feet, held Him to that cross as He agonized for six hours in pain—to pay for your sins. He was crucified to make peace between God and man. The Son of God bridged the gap that sin had caused. This wonderful man named Jesus, was God and chose to shed His life blood (die—in excruciating pain) for you rather than live without you. He loves you and is worthy of your life, the one He gave you and for which will hold you in full account.

Prayer: *Heavenly Father, Your gift to the world, Your only begotten Son, is what saved me. I love You Jesus. Here this moment I lay my life in Your holy hands. Have Your way in me. In Jesus' name, I'm all Yours* LORD.

March 29

> "Lay not up for yourselves treasures upon earth, where moth and rust doth corrupt, and where thieves break through and steal: 20 But lay up for yourselves treasures in heaven, where neither moth nor rust doth corrupt, and where thieves do not break through nor steal: 21 For where your treasure is, there will your heart be also." **Matthew 6:19-21**

You're going to spend (invest) your life and energy doing something. Should it not be that which holds eternal value? Isn't everything else waste? Why waste your time and energy in this brief life on temporal trinkets and pursuits?

Jesus assured us that NO **good giving** will go unrewarded! Not only will it be rewarded—that reward will be forever!!!

> "And whosoever shall give to drink unto one of these little ones a cup of cold water only in the name of a disciple, verily I say unto you, he shall in no wise lose his reward." **Matthew 10:42**

Prayer: *Dear Father, in the name of Jesus, I ask You to transform, recalibrate my focus to be Your kingdom perspective. Bless this heart to be obedient. I here and now confess my sin of self-idolatry and declare You as Master of my life.*

March 30

> "Believe on the Lord Jesus Christ, and thou shalt be saved, and thy house." Acts 16:31

Are you truly saved? Have you been born again? Friend, if you hesitate to answer, if you are not 100% certain of a yes on these questions, now's your opportunity to be secured by the LORD—to be saved, forgiven, and ready to meet Jesus.

Now, with everything within you, cry out to God. Apply His holy blood to your life so that you may be saved, forgiven, and live eternally with Him. You must completely turn your life over to Him in repentance and faith. **Pray this following prayer with all of your heart ...**

Your Prayer to God ...

Pray this out loud with everything that's in you: *"Dear Lord Jesus, thank You for shedding Your holy blood for my sins to save me from sin and eternal damnation in hell. You are my only hope and the new Lord and Master of my life. Heavenly Father, I acknowledge all my sins against You right now. I am fully guilty in Your holy eyes and ask Your forgiveness through the precious blood of Jesus, who died and rose again as full payment for my sins. Thank You Jesus for dying for me, I love You. Lord Jesus, in this very moment, please take over my life. From this moment forward You are the LORD of my life. I am all Yours and thank You that You are all mine. I love You Jesus. Amen."*

For more, see Making Peace with God on page 381.

March 31

"David encouraged himself in the LORD **his God."
1 Samuel 30:6**

This disciple has been through some very dark times, seasons in which God was purging.

While singing songs of praise, this poor man has been resurrected by Jesus out of some seasons of great testing which began the ongoing process of learning that God's grace surely is sufficient for us, no matter what we face.

Two songs that begin to effortlessly flow from my lips in times of testing are…

"God is so good" and "As the deer panteth for the water, so my soul longeth after thee."

Beloved go after God the way the thirsty deer pants for and finds water to quench his thirst.

Try it. Do it. Praise Him.

> **"By him therefore let us offer the sacrifice of praise to God continually, that is, the fruit of our lips giving thanks to his name." Hebrews 13:15**

Prayer: *Heavenly Father, bring this vessel to the place of pure, authentic worship and praise. Thank You for the unfathomable gift of Your only begotten Son, Jesus Christ. I love You Jesus!*

April 1

"For what shall it profit a man, if he shall gain the whole world, and lose his own soul?" Mark 8:36

Those not spending their lives getting to know and love Christ are wasting their lives—and will perish in hell. ANYTHING else is pure waste—a throwing of your eternal soul into the fires of eternal damnation. There will be no do-overs.

"Redeeming the time, because the days are evil." Ephesians 5:16

The psalmist prayed:

"So teach us to number our days, that we may apply our hearts unto wisdom." Psalms 90:12

When a person dies, the sum total of his net riches, when laid in the balance of perfect divine justice, will be what of Christ his heart possesses.

Prayer: *Father, in Jesus name, please shake my life down. Please deeply convict my heart to cease wasting this one life You gave me and for which I shall give full account. Right now, if never before, I ask You Jesus, to be the Master of my life, from this moment forward. I love You LORD Jesus.*

April 2

> "And forgive us our debts, as we forgive our debtors." Matthew 6:12

We must forgive as God has forgiven us.

> "And be ye kind one to another, tenderhearted, forgiving one another, even as God for Christ's sake hath forgiven you." Ephesians 4:32

Making the above verse a memory verse will change your life.

We must understand that the divine revelation of Holy Scripture is that God did not come to destroy the lives of men but to rescue them—us! **"For the Son of man is not come to destroy men's lives, but to save them"** (Luke 9:56).

He saved us on behalf of Christ's sacrifice, not our own works or any goodness of our own.

> "Not by works of righteousness which we have done, but according to his mercy he saved us, by the washing of regeneration, and renewing of the Holy Ghost; 6 Which he shed on us abundantly through Jesus Christ our Saviour;" Titus 3:5-6

Prayer: *Heavenly Father, no one who has ever lived deserves Your judgment for sin more than I do. It's not by works of righteousness which I have done but according to Your mercy that You found and saved my wretched soul. Please pour out Your beautiful mercy through my life to others, in Jesus' name, amen!*

April 3

"For ye are dead, and your life is hid with Christ in God." Colossians 3:3

Your life is hidden with Christ in God as you consent to being crucified with Christ just as He commanded all who would truly know and follow Him (Luke 9:23-24).

"Know ye not, that so many of us as were baptized into Jesus Christ were baptized into his death? [4] Therefore we are buried with him by baptism into death: that like as Christ was raised up from the dead by the glory of the Father, even so we also should walk in newness of life." Romans 6:3-4

When the LORD saved us, Jesus became the new LORD of our lives. Praise His holy name, we are no longer our own but rather bought with the price of His blood.

"What? know ye not that your body is the temple of the Holy Ghost which is in you, which ye have of God, and ye are not your own? [20] For ye are bought with a price: therefore glorify God in your body, and in your spirit, which are God's." 1 Corinthians 6:19-20

Prayer: *Heavenly Father, I thank You so very much for finding and saving me from sin and damnation. I love You Jesus. Right now, into Your holy hands I submit my spirit. I am all Yours Jesus and I know You are all mine. In Jesus' name, amen.*

April 4

"Blessed are the pure in heart: for they shall see God." Matthew 5:8

David, a man of God said to have a heart after the LORD, had fallen into gross sin and was in desperate danger and need of repentance and mercy from God. Here's a portion of that prayer of repentance:

"Have mercy upon me, O God, according to thy lovingkindness: according unto the multitude of thy tender mercies blot out my transgressions. 2 Wash me throughly from mine iniquity, and cleanse me from my sin. 3 For I acknowledge my transgressions: and my sin is ever before me. 4 Against thee, thee only, have I sinned, and done this evil in thy sight: that thou mightest be justified when thou speakest, and be clear when thou judgest. 5 Behold, I was shapen in iniquity; and in sin did my mother conceive me. 6 Behold, thou desirest truth in the inward parts: and in the hidden part thou shalt make me to know wisdom. 7 Purge me with hyssop, and I shall be clean: wash me, and I shall be whiter than snow. 8 Make me to hear joy and gladness; that the bones which thou hast broken may rejoice." Psalms 51:1-8

Prayer: *Precious holy Father, please have mercy upon me for my sin of not putting You first, not honoring You. I repent, I return now to You Jesus and denounce self-idolatry and spiritual adultery. I love You supremely LORD Jesus.*

April 5

"Blessed be God, even the Father of our Lord Jesus Christ, the Father of mercies, and the God of all comfort." 2 Corinthians 1:3

This Holy Scripture surfaced in my mind, my spirit, upon awaking this beautiful morning.

This bless-ed and Holy Scripture reveals to us that God our Father is **"the Father of our Lord Jesus Christ, the Father of mercies, and the God of all comfort;"** (2 Corinthians 1:3)

Because we were born sinners and in need of the Savior, He is **"the Father of our Lord Jesus Christ."** Because we have sinned, He is **"the Father of mercies."** Because He foreknew we'd be afraid at times, the Father of our LORD Jesus Christ is to us **"the God of all comfort."**

Prayer: *Father in Heaven, I come to You as you required—in the name of Jesus Christ. I just want to thank You today that You are so very merciful, comforting and gracious to us, Your children. I love You Jesus and thank You for dying and rising from the dead to save me. You are the Master of this life. In Jesus' name, amen.*

April 6

"Seeing then that we have a great high priest, that is passed into the heavens, Jesus the Son of God, let us hold fast our profession. [15] For we have not an high priest which cannot be touched with the feeling of our infirmities; but was in all points tempted like as we are, yet without sin. [16] Let us therefore come boldly unto the throne of grace, that we may obtain mercy, and find grace to help in time of need." Hebrews 4:14-16

Due to His perfect sacrifice and redemption provided for all of fallen mankind, we who are His are invited to "**come boldly**" to His beautiful throne of grace—where His perfect blood speaks in Heaven for us, on our behalf.

As we **"come boldly unto the throne of grace"** the Lord is going to forgive us by His mercy and fill us with His grace and love.

Prayer: *Holy Father, I celebrate and thank You so very much for sending Your only begotten Son, my Lord Jesus, to pay the perfect price to buy my otherwise lost soul back to You. I come now and ask You to forgive and wash me clear and clean of all sins and to multiply Your enabling grace so I can please You in all ways as Your overcomer. In Jesus' name, amen.*

April 7

"For the wages of sin is death; but the gift of God is eternal life through Jesus Christ our Lord." Romans 6:23

God is holy and our sins separate us from Him. We have all broken God's laws by lying, dishonoring our parents, cheating, hating, committing a sex act in our mind with someone we are not married to, stealing, coveting, taking His holy name in vain, etc. These are all sins against God, and we are all guilty. You are personally and fully guilty of sinning against Your Maker. Committing any single one of these sins makes us guilty of breaking the whole law and worthy of death.

Prayer: *Father, in the face of my iniquity and sin, You sent Your only begotten Son to die and be raised again for my salvation—while I was yet a sinner. LORD Jesus, I love You. I praise You and ask You to increase in my life today. Here this moment I surrender afresh to You, to Your will. Not my will but Thine be done in this life. In Jesus' name.*

April 8

> "Walk in the Spirit, and ye shall not fulfil the lust of the flesh. 17 For the flesh lusteth against the Spirit, and the Spirit against the flesh: and these are contrary the one to the other: so that ye cannot do the things that ye would. 18 But if ye be led of the Spirit, ye are not under the law." Galatians 5:16-18

The only way to stay out of the flesh is to stay in the Spirit. Fighting the good fight of faith consists of diligently laboring daily in seeking God (1 Timothy 6:12).

> "Let us labour therefore to enter into that rest, lest any man fall after the same example of unbelief." Hebrews 4:11

If you do nothing, you lose! You are in a fight, like it or not. So, get your dukes up and start swinging and do not stop. Only then will you be able to **"rest"** in the victory of Christ due to unrelenting fellowship with Him. You are in a relationship with the Lord and He requires your full, diligent participation.

There is no peace to be found outside of the Prince of peace!

> "Thou wilt keep him in perfect peace, whose mind is stayed on thee: because he trusteth in thee." Isaiah 26:3

Prayer: *Father, in Jesus' name, teach me to war according to Your precepts. Teach me to fight the good fight of faith and not be diverted to wrestling with flesh and blood. Please bless this life to be truly crucified with Christ, amen.*

April 9

> "For God sent not his Son into the world to condemn the world; but that the world through him might be saved." John 3:17

God has been ever so merciful to us, to me, to you. Are we reflecting that same attitude of mercy toward others—in our attitudes? We were all already condemned in our sins and yet instead of doing away with His creation, God sent His only begotten Son to purchase us back to Himself—at the highest price ever paid—the blood of the Lord Jesus.

ALL of Scripture reveals that God has an open, not closed hand to all who will come to Him. Jesus died for all, ALL men and is **"not willing that any should perish"** (2 Peter 3:9).

God didn't condemn us, and we shouldn't condemn others—nor hold such evil attitudes toward them. We are called to be moved with compassion on the lost, just as Jesus was.

> "But when he *(Jesus)* saw the multitudes, he was moved with compassion on them, because they fainted, and were scattered abroad, as sheep having no shepherd." Matthew 9:36

Prayer: *Father, please cultivate in my heart an attitude of love, of compassion and mercy toward and concerning others. May the divine revelation of restoration be multiplied in my heart and life beginning right now, in Jesus' name, amen.*

April 10

> "<u>For thou, Lord, art GOOD</u>, and ready to forgive; and plenteous in mercy unto all them that call upon thee. ... But thou, O Lord, art a God full of compassion, and gracious, longsuffering, and plenteous in mercy and truth." Psalms 86:5, 15

Jesus Christ is **"the GREAT Shepherd of the sheep"** for whom He died:

> "Now the God of peace, that brought again from the dead our Lord Jesus, <u>that great shepherd of the sheep</u>, through the blood of the everlasting covenant," Hebrews 13:20

Is God good or is He great? From Genesis to Revelation we see clear evidence that God is both GOOD and GREAT.

His goodness speaks of His kindness, His graciousness to do man well. His greatness speaks of His divinity, His might and power.

God is not only good, He's great. There's a difference and He's both!

> "**For I know the thoughts that I think toward you, saith the LORD, thoughts of peace, and not of evil, to give you an expected end.**" Jeremiah 29:11

Prayer: *Father, in Jesus' name, thank You for being so good to Your people. Thank You for loving us, and Jesus thank You for dying to save us from sin and hell. I love You my LORD Jesus.*

April 11

"For I am the LORD, I change not." Malachi 3:6

God, and therefore what He's stated are unchanging, unfailing, everlasting, ever-living and ever-relevant.

"For ever, O LORD, thy word is settled in heaven." Psalms 119:89

The LORD's Word cannot and will not change because He will never change. Divinity, eternal perfection, needs no change.

"Heaven and earth shall pass away: but my words shall not pass away." Mark 13:31

Every part of His creation is changing, yet He is forever Constant.

"The grass withereth, the flower fadeth: but the word of our God shall stand for ever." Isaiah 40:8

What God has stated in His Word will come to pass and has no expiration date.

"Seek ye out of the book of the LORD, and read: no one of these shall fail." Isaiah 34:16

Prayer: *Holy Father, I know You are unchanging, and Your Word is settled in Heaven. Thank You so very much for giving us Your unalterable Word, for preserving it for us. In Jesus' name, amen.*

April 12

"Much more then, being now justified by his blood, we shall be saved from wrath through him." Romans 5:9

All men have sinned against God who is **"Holy, holy, holy"** and yet divine justice was perfectly satisfied, fulfilled in the crucifixion of Jesus Christ (Isaiah 6:3; Revelation 4:8).

"Being justified freely by his grace through the redemption that is in Christ Jesus: 25 Whom God hath set forth to be a propitiation through faith in his blood, to declare his righteousness for the remission of sins that are past, through the forbearance of God; 26 To declare, I say, at this time his righteousness: that he might be just, and the justifier of him which believeth in Jesus." Romans 3:24-26

Those truly in Christ are **"justified freely by his grace"** and yet such is not without divinely imposed condition. He gave man free will which He never withdraws, and His blessings are conditional (Deuteronomy 30:1). Although He desires to save all, **God doesn't grant His blessings of salvation to just everyone.**

Prayer: *Father, I know and embrace that You are Holy and that You require, expect me to be holy in oneness with You. Please imbue my inner man with Your holy fear, hastening me to obey You out of true love for You. In Jesus' name, amen.*

April 13

"**The <u>backslider in heart</u> shall be filled with his own ways** *(will reap an apostate heart):* **and a good man shall be satisfied from himself.**" Proverbs 14:14

"**The backslider in heart**"—notice the words above which reveal that backsliding occurs in the hearts of men. Backsliding happens in those once saved who discontinue their life of prayer with Christ. Those who maintain, who engage in daily Bible reading and prayer, will be full of God's grace and continue to abide in Christ (John 15:1-6).

Make no mistake: Prayer is a divine command and a matter of life and death. The person who doesn't find it important to live a life of prayer is not living by faith and is denying Christ, "**Having a form of godliness, but denying the power thereof: from such turn away**" (2 Timothy 3:5).

Beware of this following pitfall: Most people believe that in order to deny Christ, one must verbally denounce Him. Not so! Any person who has gotten saved and yet now does not acknowledge and enact what Jesus instructed, is in denial of Him. According to the LORD, His people must "**watch**" and "**pray**" to "**be accounted worthy to escape all these things that shall come to pass, and to stand before the Son of man**" (Luke 21:34-36).

"Prayer is to the spiritual life what breathing is to the natural life." Unknown

Prayer: *Dear LORD, please make this vessel, my life, Your house of prayer—ever praying for Your beloved people, in the name of Jesus.*

April 14

"Watch and pray, that ye enter not into temptation: the spirit indeed is willing, but the flesh is weak." Matthew 26:41

HOW did Jesus teach us to overcome temptation to sin and be ready with unspotted garments for His soon return?

Many have been misled to believe they are unconditionally eternally secure after being truly saved. The eternal security offered by the LORD is when one is actually with Him in Heaven.

Prayer is a matter of life and death. The person who doesn't find it important to pray is not engaging in a relationship with Christ, is not living by faith and is denying Christ. Most people believe that in order to deny Christ, one must verbally denounce Him. Not so! God's Word reveals to us that backsliding—departing from Christ as **"first love"**—happens in the heart (Revelation 2:4-5; Proverbs 14:14).

Prayer: *Father, right now, in the name of Jesus Christ, I return to You as first love! Please forgive my sin of self-idolatry. I ask You to please cleanse me now in Thy holy blood LORD Jesus. Amen.*

April 15

"Jesus said unto him, Thou shalt love the Lord thy God with all thy heart, and with all thy soul, and with all thy mind. 38 This is the first and great commandment. 39 And the second is like unto it, Thou shalt love thy neighbour as thyself. 40 On these two commandments hang all the law and the prophets." Matthew 22:37-40

Jesus gives us just two commandments here—to love Him with our whole being and to love our neighbor as we already love ourselves. Many today erroneously add the third here, teaching people to learn to love themselves. All men already love themselves and that self-love is their greatest sin and the antithesis of the mind of Christ (Ephesians 5:29; Philippians 2:3-5).

"All the whole law, which was given to utter our corrupt nature, is comprehended in the ten commandments. And the ten commandments are comprehended in these two, Love God and thy neighbour. And he that loveth his neighbour, in God and Christ, filfilleth these two; and consequently the ten; and finally all the other." William Tyndale, *Prologue Upon the Gospel of Matthew.*

Prayer: *Precious Father, quicken in me that which is most important to You. Please fill me with Your love. In Jesus' name, amen.*

April 16

"Who forgiveth all thine iniquities; who healeth all thy diseases." Psalms 103:3

Are you thankful today that through the perfect sacrifice of Christ, God provided the solution, the redemption of our souls and forgiveness of our sin? (Colossians 1:12-14.)

Watch this clear example of the goodness of our God and how He forgives all the iniquities of His people as they confess their sin.

Jesus went from telling Peter ...

> **"Get thee behind me, Satan: thou art an offence unto me: for thou savourest not the things that be of God, but those that be of men."**

To forgiving and restoring him and asking him ...

> **"Lovest thou me?"**

Then instructing Peter to do His work, minister His love and truth...

> **"Feed my lambs ... Feed my sheep" Matthew 16:23; John 21:15-17**

Pour prayerfully over Philippians 3:13-14. Repent afresh. Seek God. Confess all sin. March forward.

Prayer: *Thank You dear heavenly Father for providing through Christ alone the redemption—the forgiveness of sin that has saved us! I love You Lord Jesus!*

April 17

"Neither give place to the devil." Ephesians 4:27

Casting doubt on the Word of God is the work of Satan— **"hath God said?"** (Genesis 3:1). This is why I personally choose to separate from people who insist upon questioning God's Word, denying that it was preserved for us as He promised, denying that He really meant what He plainly stated (Psalms 12:6-7; Matthew 7:6; Titus 3:10-11). God's people are instructed by Him to reject doubt-casters, heretics, to not cast their pearls before such evil persons.

> **"A man that is an heretick after the first and second admonition reject; 11 Knowing that he that is such is subverted, and sinneth, being condemned of himself." Titus 3:10-11**

> **"Give not that which is holy unto the dogs, neither cast ye your pearls before swine, lest they trample them under their feet, and turn again and rend you." Matthew 7:6**

> **"And whosoever shall not receive you, nor hear your words, when ye depart out of that house or city, shake off the dust of your feet." Matthew 10:14**

Prayer: *Father, in Jesus' holy name, please teach me Your discernment, to know Your truth of a certainty and to thereby be able to discern what is not of You.*

April 18

"Brethren, if a man be overtaken in a fault, ye which are spiritual, restore such an one in the spirit of meekness; considering thyself, lest thou also be tempted." Galatians 6:1

Following biblical protocol is important when correction is needed. Otherwise, we could miss the opportunity to help a brother or sister to be restored and bring judgment on ourselves (Galatians 6:1-2).

"Judge not, that ye be not judged. 2 For with what judgment ye judge, ye shall be judged: and with what measure ye mete, it shall be measured to you again. 3 And why beholdest thou the mote that is in thy brother's eye, but considerest not the beam that is in thine own eye? 4 Or how wilt thou say to thy brother, Let me pull out the mote out of thine eye; and, behold, a beam is in thine own eye? 5 Thou hypocrite, first cast out the beam out of thine own eye; and then shalt thou see clearly to cast out the mote out of thy brother's eye." Matthew 7:1-5

Prayer: *Dear heavenly Father, no one needs You and Your mercy more than I do. Please root out every log from my own eye—whatever it takes. When it comes to sin, may I be most concerned about my own and not that of others. Please pour out Your mercy on me (for my own sin), and through me, to help others be restored to You. I ask this in Jesus' name. Amen.*

April 19

"Be ye therefore ready also: for the Son of man cometh at an hour when ye think not." Luke 12:40

There would have been no reason for Christ and His holy apostles to firmly warn all believers to be **"ready"** to meet Heaven's King at His coming if there were no danger of losing out—due to not being **"ready."**

The notion that all who've been saved will be **"ready"** when Christ returns or when they die, is pure fiction, an utter contradiction of Jesus' teachings. Example: Remember how Jesus likened His kingdom to ten virgins and said that only five made it and the other five were shut out? (Read Matthew 25:1-13.) Those who do not remain rooted in Christ will run out of His oil and **"fall away"** (Luke 8:13). Here are the people Jesus is coming for:

> **"Husbands, love your wives, even as Christ also loved the church, and gave himself for it; 26 That he might sanctify and cleanse it with the washing of water by the word, 27 That he might present it to himself a glorious church, not having spot, or wrinkle, or any such thing; but that it should be holy and without blemish." Ephesians 5:25-27**

Prayer: LORD Jesus, I know You are coming soon, and that I must be ready at Your return or if I pass before then. Purge, cleanse, and wash my life of all iniquity, in Jesus' name.

April 20

"Give instruction to a wise man, and he will be yet wiser: teach a just man, and he will increase in learning." Proverbs 9:9

The phrase **"increase in learning"** is key. Such requires a disposition transformed by Christ—in all humility.

Remaining teachable, remaining pliable, is essential for the disciple, the student of Christ. Humility before the LORD and His people underlies this bless-ed posture of heart.

"And said, Verily I say unto you, Except ye be converted, and become as little children, ye shall not enter into the kingdom of heaven. 4 Whosoever therefore shall humble himself as this little child, the same is greatest in the kingdom of heaven." Matthew 18:3-4

Prayer: *Dear Father, please grant my whole disposition, this whole heart, to be pliable, humble and teachable before You and Your body. In Jesus' name, amen.*

Would you like to know for sure that you are truly born again? Check out page 381 to be certain.

April 21

"Thy words were found, and I did eat them; and thy word was unto me the joy and rejoicing of mine heart: for I am called by thy name, O LORD God of hosts." Jeremiah 15:16

The joy of the LORD fills the lives of those who devour His words.

The student of Christ will do well to memorize the above words penned for us by Jeremiah the prophet.

God's Word cannot get into you unless you get into it.

Don't just feed your stomach, feed your spirit by devouring God's Word! (See 1 Peter 2:2; Jeremiah 15:16.)

To be inspired and encouraged to increase your love for God's Word, read about David's passion for it in Psalm 119. It's contagious!

Feed your spirit God's Word today—or you will famish and fall away as did the five foolish virgins who were shut out of the eternal kingdom (Matthew 25:1-13).

"As newborn babes, desire the sincere *(pure)* **milk of the word, that ye may grow thereby:" 1 Peter 2:2**

Prayer: *Dear LORD Jesus, increase in me the appetite for Your Word. Make this conscience miserable, unable to sleep, unless being ever more filled with Your truth in knowing You. In Jesus' name. Amen.*

April 22

"Follow peace with all men, and holiness, without which no man shall see the Lord: 15 Looking diligently lest any man fail of the grace of God." Hebrew 12:14-15

Failing or falling short of the saving grace of God is possible. Those making excuse not to **"Be ye holy"** will be rejected.

"But as he which hath called you is holy, so be ye holy in all manner of conversation; 16 Because it is written, Be ye holy; for I am holy." 1 Peter 1:15-16

Many have bought the lie that because they were initially saved, they are guaranteed to be in Heaven when they die and that they are holy before God. Not so. Initial salvation in no way excludes the mountain of Scripture concerning remaining, continuing, abiding in Christ to the end. God is holy and He alone makes one holy, as that person submits to His stated will.

Prayer: *LORD, please purify my life. Cleanse me of every notion that contradicts the whole counsel of Your Word. In Jesus' holy name, amen.*

April 23

"Trust in the LORD with all thine heart; and lean not unto thine own understanding. **6** In all thy ways acknowledge him, and he shall direct thy paths. **7** Be not wise in thine own eyes: fear the LORD, and depart from evil." Proverbs 3:5-7

There will be no victory unless we live this life God's way. All who do things any other way than God's way vainly seek to cheat the divine system. Not going to happen in even one instance (Galatians 6:7-8). Jesus informs us that these **"are thieves and robbers"** who vainly attempt to climb **"up some other way, the same is a thief and a robber"** (John 10:1, 8).

Prayer: *Holy Father, in the name of Jesus, please stop me right now, dead in my tracks, please halt the rebellion of this wicked heart LORD. Let not this life be wasted building on a sand foundation, only to be rejected in the end. In Jesus' name.*

April 24

> "Preach the word; be instant in season, out of season; reprove, rebuke, exhort with all longsuffering and doctrine. 3 For the time will come when they will not endure sound doctrine; but after their own lusts shall they heap to themselves teachers, having itching ears; 4 And they shall turn away their ears from the truth, and shall be turned unto fables." 2 Timothy 4:2-4

"Endure sound doctrine" here means to hold oneself accountable to the truth. So many today who believe they're saved refuse to submit to Christ's lordship.

Many today have bought into an easy believes that requires nothing of them. They claim that Jesus did it all, so they have no need of obedience to Him. They claim He's their Savior and yet refuse to make Him their Lord which is required to be saved (Romans 10:9-10). They love this doctrine of lasciviousness, of an unconditional eternal security because they refuse to truly repent, make Jesus the LORD, their Master, and obey Him. These are the tares, the counterfeits who seek only to have their ears tickled by false teachings given by false teachers.

Prayer: *Heavenly Father, please root out of my life the lies Satan's false ministers have put in my mind. Let my heart cling to Your truth and to be always in Your holy fear. Quicken my life in utter love and obedience to You. In Jesus' name.*

April 25

> "Wherefore the law is holy, and the commandment holy, and just, and good." Romans 7:12

Divine justice demands that our violations be punished. Because we are guilty of breaking God's holy law, we deserve to be fairly repaid for our offenses. But God doesn't want us to be punished for our sins in hell forever. So, He sent His Son to pay the debt for us, so we would not have to pay for our own sins in eternal hell as we clearly deserve, but rather live now and forever with Him. What love!

> "In this was manifested the love of God toward us, because that God sent his only begotten Son into the world, that we might live through him. [10] Herein is love, not that we loved God, but that he loved us, and sent his Son to be the propitiation for our sins." 1 John 4:9-10

Prayer: *Thank You Holy Father for sending Your only begotten Son to die to pay for my sins so I could know You. I love You Jesus.*

April 26

"For as the sufferings of Christ abound in us, so our consolation also aboundeth by Christ."
2 Corinthians 1:5

The cross is essential to experiencing divine **"comfort"** and **"consolation."** Christ's divine resurrection life fueling and lifting upward His people during their times of suffering, brings the greatest times/seasons of His blessed fruitfulness. Our beloved brother Joseph experienced something of that closeness to the LORD, didn't he? **"For God hath caused me to be fruitful in the land of my affliction"** (Genesis 41:52).

"Fruitful in the land of my affliction" is going to be our own testimony as we, like Joseph, cling and draw ever nearer to our LORD in that hour of affliction.

The reality of the comfort of God's divine love is perhaps only a truth in our minds until we are genuinely tested. Then, that truth becomes a reality in our own personal lives that forges intimacy with Him such as we have not previously experienced and are able to speak out of personal revelation to others to help and encourage them.

The story of Joseph is itself a monumental masterpiece of the comforting love of our heavenly Father (Genesis 37-50).

Prayer: *Father, I will trust You in all things. May my life be truly crucified with Christ and may the comfort of Your love fill my heart during times of trial and testing and let it abound to Your glory in comforting others. In Jesus' name, Amen.*

April 27

"Who art thou that judgest another man's servant? to his own master he standeth or falleth. Yea, he shall be holden up: for God is able to make him stand. ⁵One man esteemeth one day above another: another esteemeth every day alike. Let every man be fully persuaded in his own mind."
Romans 14:4-5

Concerning **"meat and drink,"** which represents non-essentials to salvation, Christ's apostle warns believers never to judge other believers in those things. In doing so, we will frustrate, work against, and harm the very work of God.

We err if we impose upon other saints our own personal convictions on non-essential issues—those things that are not essential to salvation. Those who cause conflict in non-essentials adding to God's Word and imposing their own conscience and convictions concerning non-essentials on others. In Romans 14 and 1 Corinthians 10, Paul taught on Christian liberties.

Prayer: *Father, please circumcise my heart. Teach me Your wisdom and to never harm Your work in others, in Jesus' name. Please use me to feed and to nourish, to serve, and to help Your people grow in Your grace.*

April 28

"Lay not up for yourselves treasures upon earth, where moth and rust doth corrupt, and where thieves break through and steal: 20 But lay up for yourselves treasures in heaven, where neither moth nor rust doth corrupt, and where thieves do not break through nor steal: 21 For where your treasure is, there will your heart be also."
Matthew 6:19-21

When you are privileged to help a believer in need or the work of Christ, that opportunity is the very gift of God to you—to lay up treasure in Heaven as He instructed you to do (Matthew 6:19-21).

Prayer: *Father, I come to You in the name of Jesus Christ. LORD, please make my heart to be a giving heart. Fashion my heart to do as You did when You opened Your loving hand and gave Your only begotten Son for the sins of the world, for my sins. I love You LORD Jesus.*

April 29

"For I will declare mine iniquity; I will be sorry for my sin." Psalms 38:18

David was bold to declare his sin and confess it to the LORD. He didn't attempt to hide it.

"He that covereth his sins shall not prosper: but whoso confesseth and forsaketh them shall have mercy." Proverbs 28:13

When we read in God's Word that all men sin, such is the occasion to repent and confess all sin and never to justify sin (Ecclesiastes 7:20; Romans 6:1-2; 2 Corinthians 7:1, etc.).

Prayer: *Holy Father, please break me. Make this vessel honest and authentic, ready to repent and confess any sin as needed. Grant a heart of flesh dear Father I ask, in Jesus' name.*

April 30

"Thou hast loved righteousness, and hated iniquity; therefore God, even thy God, hath anointed thee with the oil of gladness above thy fellows." Hebrews 1:9

Loving righteousness and hating iniquity are integral to God anointing us with His oil of gladness, the joy of His salvation (Psalms 51:10-13).

Sin makes us sad because we were created to live in worship-filled righteousness. The righteousness of God in us ensures being full of His blessed joy.

"Create in me a clean heart, O God; and renew a right spirit within me. 11 Cast me not away from thy presence; and take not thy holy spirit from me. 12 Restore unto me the joy of thy salvation; and uphold me with thy free spirit. 13 Then will I teach transgressors thy ways; and sinners shall be converted unto thee." Psalms 51:10-13

Prayer: *Father, in Jesus' name, please purify my heart and fill this life with Your great love and joy! Use me Jesus, please.*

May 1

> "The LORD recompense thy work, and a full reward be given thee of the LORD God of Israel, under whose wings thou art come to trust." Ruth 2:12

Throughout His Word, the LORD uses winged fowl to illustrate His watch care, His protection, and His provision for His people. **"...under whose wings thou art come to trust"** (Ruth 2:12).

> "For the LORD'S portion is his people; Jacob is the lot of his inheritance. 10 He found him in a desert land, and in the waste howling wilderness; he led him about, he instructed him, he kept him as the apple of his eye. 11 As an eagle stirreth up her nest, fluttereth over her young, spreadeth abroad her wings, taketh them, beareth them on her wings: 12 So the LORD alone did lead him, and there was no strange god with him." Deuteronomy 32:9-12

As the momma bird covers its chicks under her wings for warmth, for provision and for their protection, so God covers His children—those who choose to dwell **"in the secret place of the most high,"** taking refuge under the shadow of His wings (Psalms 91:1). GOD made the **"winged fowl"** (birds) for the express purpose of showing His highest creation—mankind—how much He loves us and how He comforts, cares, provides for, and protects His own (Psalms 91:1).

Prayer: *Dear Father, I love You for who You are. Thank You for Your love toward Your people, which You purchased by the blood of Your only begotten Son. I thank You now for creating, finding, and saving me into Your eternal family. In Jesus' name, amen.*

May 2

"Create in me a clean heart, O God; and renew a right spirit within me. 11 Cast me not away from thy presence; and take not thy holy spirit from me." Psalms 51:10-11

When we wisely join in fellowship, life with fellow truth-seekers, such will assist the work of God who is quickening us to honestly admit, repent afresh and confess any sin God brings to light. Anyone else ever camped out on Psalms 51—the prayer of repentance and confession of the man after God's own heart, David?

"Restore unto me the joy of thy salvation; and uphold me with thy free spirit. 13 Then will I teach transgressors thy ways; and sinners shall be converted unto thee." Psalms 51:12-13

The New Testament believer is to ever examine himself to see whether or not he is in the faith.

"Examine yourselves, whether ye be in the faith; prove your own selves. Know ye not your own selves, how that Jesus Christ is in you, except ye be reprobates?" 2 Corinthians 13:5

Prayer: *Father, in Jesus' name, here and now if never before, I submit my life to You—to Your Lordship. From this moment forth I will serve You. Jesus You are the Master of my life from now on. I love You Jesus. Please use me for Your glory.*

May 3

"These things have I spoken unto you, that my joy might remain in you, and that your joy might be full." John 15:11

Here Jesus speaks to His abiding servants—friends—and uses the words **"your joy."** Our joy is the joy we are given by being in Him, abiding in Christ—who in His earthly days was filled with more joy than anyone, ever. Jesus was given **"the oil of gladness above thy fellows"** (Hebrews 1:9).

His joy was directly connected to the holy, pure heart of God. Catch this:

"Thou hast loved righteousness, and hated iniquity; therefore God, even thy God, hath anointed thee with the oil of gladness above thy fellows." Hebrews 1:9

David, while seeking the Lord for a pure heart, prayed:

"Restore unto me the joy of thy salvation; and uphold me with thy free spirit." Psalms 51:12

Prayer: *Father, in Jesus' name, please purify this heart. Please cleanse all that does not please You Lord Jesus. Restore unto me the joy of Your salvation dear Lord. I love You Jesus.*

May 4

"That I may know him, and the power of his resurrection, and the fellowship of his sufferings, being made conformable unto his death; 11 If by any means I might attain unto the resurrection of the dead." Philippians 3:10-11

Our Father and LORD Jesus desire to be honored in our lives. We are **"the children of the highest"** and this is made possible only through Christ alone (Luke 6:35). As our Father, the only perfect parent in existence, He desires to hear and answer all our prayers. Prayer is not just asking but first and foremost, communing with our LORD (Matthew 6:6).

Beloved of God, never lose sight of the reality, the truth that God made you to fellowship with Him. Relationship.

The LORD created us to know Him (John 17:3).

"And this is life eternal, that they might know thee the only true God, and Jesus Christ, whom thou hast sent." John 17:3

Prayer: *Holy Father, I come to You now, in the name of my LORD Jesus Christ. Please make me one with You LORD. Bless this life to abide in You truly, daily, to be fruitful in Your work for Your eternal glory. In Jesus' name, amen.*

May 5

> "For by him were all things created, that are in heaven, and that are in earth, visible and invisible, whether they be thrones, or dominions, or principalities, or powers: all things were created by him, and for him: [17] And he is before all things, and by him all things consist. [18] And he is the head of the body, the church: who is the beginning, the firstborn from the dead; that in all things he might have the preeminence. [19] For it pleased the Father that in him should all fulness dwell; [20] And, having made peace through the blood of his cross, by him to reconcile all things unto himself." Colossians 1:16-20

The supremacy of Jesus Christ is revealed in no greater fashion in God's Word than in Colossians chapters 1 and 2. May the reader be encouraged to pour prayerfully over these two chapters.

ALL cults, heretical systems, and false prophets have a common denominator: They teach that Jesus Christ is not God, Creator of all that is, the only Savior, and the supreme HEAD of His one church. Colossians 1-2 is paramount to our walk with Heaven's coming KING.

> "For in him dwelleth all the fulness of the Godhead bodily. [10] And ye are complete in him, which is the head of all principality and power:" Colossians 2:9-10

Prayer: *Father, in Jesus' name, please bless me to know You and your Son, Jesus Christ, more and more.*

May 6

"And he spake a parable unto them to this end, that men ought always to pray, and not to faint;" Luke 18:1

Those who do not pray (live a life of prayer) will **"faint,"** they will grow weak and fall.

Prayer is to the spiritual life what breathing is to the physical life.

A disciple is a student, a disciplined follower. Disciples of Jesus must routinely and without fail, yet with spontaneity of heart, seek His holy face DAILY. We must obey His truth and not our feelings. None always feel like doing what is right—seeking His holy face in prayer—and yet, such is essential and all the more reason we must. The wayfaring disciple must never **"faint"** or falter. **"Men ought always to pray, and not to faint."**

Beginning our day with moments of prayer and Bible reading, study, drawing ever nigh to our LORD, is essential to growing into full maturity in Christ and nourishing our hearts as wise virgin believers—lest the oil in our lamps expire and we do not make it to the bridal chamber with our Bridegroom (Matthew 25:1-13).

Prayer: *Heavenly Father, I come to You in the name of Jesus Christ and thank You for procuring through the blood of the cross of Christ the relationship we now enjoy. Please forgive me for not loving You with all of my being. Forgive my sins afresh dear Father. In Jesus name. Amen..*

May 7

"He that covereth his sins shall not prosper: but whoso confesseth and forsaketh them shall have mercy." **Proverbs 28:13**

Note here that those who cover or seek to hide their sin **"shall not prosper."** The life of the dishonest is halted and will go no further in God until they acknowledge (agree with God) that they are in violation.

Jesus aggrandizes, values **"an honest and good heart."**

"But that on the good ground are they, which in <u>an honest and good heart</u>, having heard the word, keep it, and bring forth fruit with patience." **Luke 8:15**

The work of God, which we must request of Him daily, is to create in His people a pure heart, to renew a right spirit within them daily (Psalms 51:10).

"Who can understand his errors? cleanse thou me from secret faults. [13] Keep back thy servant also from presumptuous sins; let them not have dominion over me: then shall I be upright, and I shall be innocent from the great transgression." **Psalms 19:12-13**

Prayer: *Father, in Jesus' name, please purify this heart and life. Set me apart for Your perfect purposes. Cleanse my heart, please* LORD *Jesus. Amen.*

May 8

"Judge not, that ye be not judged. ² For with what judgment ye judge, ye shall be judged: and with what measure ye mete, it shall be measured to you again. ³ And why beholdest thou the mote that is in thy brother's eye, but considerest not the beam that is in thine own eye?" Matthew 7:1-3

Here Jesus condemns hypocritical judgment.

He condemns those who condemn others while not condemning themselves. He wants us to deal with our own sin— which is the sin that should concern us the most! Christ is speaking of the merciless attitude we show toward others while being generous with mercy toward ourselves.

Here's what the LORD says is going to happen to the merciless:

"For he shall have judgment without mercy, that hath shewed no mercy; and mercy rejoiceth against judgment." James 2:13

Prayer: *Father, thank You for sending Your only begotten Son for my sin. Please forgive my hardness—sinful, merciless attitudes. Please break me and grant this heart to be a heart of mercy, as is Yours. In Jesus' name, amen.*

May 9

> "Let us be glad and rejoice, and give honour to him: for the marriage of the Lamb is come, and his wife hath made herself ready. 8 And to her was granted that she should be arrayed in fine linen, clean and white: for the fine linen is the righteousness of saints." Revelation 19:7-8

The person who repents and is saved, and continues rooted in Christ, continuing/abiding in Him, will confess any sin committed and be perpetually transformed by Him (Proverbs 28:13; 2 Corinthians 7:1; 1 John 1:7, 9; 3:4-10).

Many have been misled. Jesus invented the term **"FALL AWAY"** (Luke 8:13). The Son of God does not lie. If falling away isn't possible, why did Jesus say it is possible?

Jesus is returning for those who are looking for Him by the way they live.

> "So Christ was once offered to bear the sins of many; and unto THEM THAT LOOK FOR HIM shall he appear the second time without sin unto salvation." Hebrews 9:28

Prayer: *Jesus, I know You are going to return for a Bride that is without spot, wrinkle, or sin of any kind. Purify this life LORD Jesus which I now submit to You without reserve.*

May 10

> "He answered and said unto them ... This people honoureth me with *their* lips, but their heart is far from me. Howbeit in vain do they worship me, teaching *for* doctrines the commandments of men. For laying aside the commandment of God, ye hold the tradition of men, *as* the washing of pots and cups: and many other such like things ye do. And he said unto them, Full well ye reject the commandment of God, that ye may keep your own tradition." **Mark 7:6-9**

The LORD has no interest in the empty worship of men or religion which is vastly prevalent today as it was in Christ's day—where men elevate traditions above truth, the Word.

> "Beware lest any man spoil you through philosophy and vain deceit, after the tradition of men, after the rudiments of the world, and not after Christ." **Colossians 2:8**

No other sin so grieved the Savior as did un-engaged, lukewarm religious pride and worship which actually insulates men from Him. No other group received more harsh and dooming words from Jesus Christ as those who were the very leaders of the religion (Matthew 23).

Prayer: *Father, I come to You through Jesus Christ, my only hope. I repent. Here and now I lay my life, my being, in Your holy hands. Please make me a person of Your truth and purge this vessel of all idolatry and religiosity. Make me Your authentic disciple. I love You Jesus, amen.*

May 11

> "And, having made peace through the blood of his cross, by him to reconcile all things unto himself; by him, I say, whether they be things in earth, or things in heaven." Colossians 1:20

As He alone could do (when man alienated himself by sin) God **"made peace"** between Himself and fallen mankind **"through the blood of his cross"**—the crucifixion—of our Lord Jesus.

May this divinely-ordained phrase— **"the blood of His cross"**— never leave our minds. May God this moment brand it indelibly upon our hearts and minds.

> "To wit, that God was in Christ, reconciling the world unto himself, not imputing their trespasses unto them; and hath committed unto us the word of reconciliation." 2 Corinthians 5:19

Before He came, Jesus was called **"The Prince of Peace"** (Isaiah 9:6-7). He came to die to atone for mankind's sin, and the blood of Christ's cross purchased us to the Father, bringing that peace.

> "Glory to God in the highest, and on earth peace, good will toward men." Luke 2:14

Prayer: *Father in Heaven, please let my heart ever glorify the name and the holy precious blood of my Lord Jesus Christ, without which there is no Gospel (Good News) and no salvation, and no eternal glory with You! I love You Jesus. My only Salvation is Your precious blood. This moment I declare "Thank You Jesus!" times a million. In Jesus' name, amen.*

May 12

> **"Know ye not, that so many of us as were baptized into Jesus Christ were baptized into his death? 4 Therefore we are buried with him by baptism into death: that like as Christ was raised up from the dead by the glory of the Father, even so we also should walk in newness of life." Romans 6:3-4**

This is speaking of the new life every born-again believer has been brought into—a life of surrender, where Jesus reigns and no longer us.

When He saved you, He inducted you into the cross life (Romans 6:3-11). Water baptism is merely an illustration of this cross dynamic which is a **"must"** for walking with Christ.

With John the Baptist, may we come to the end of sinful self and cry **"He must increase but I must decrease"** (John 3:30).

> **"For if we have been planted together in the likeness of his death, we shall be also in the likeness of his resurrection: 6 Knowing this, that our old man is crucified with him, that the body of sin might be destroyed, that henceforth we should not serve sin. 7 For he that is dead is freed from sin." Romans 6:5-7**

Prayer: *I am crucified with Christ, nevertheless I live and yet not I but Christ. The life I now live in the flesh I live by the faith of the Son of God. Lord be glorified in this life today. In Jesus' name, amen.*

May 13

> "But whoso hearkeneth unto me shall dwell safely, and shall be quiet from fear of evil." Proverbs 1:33

This is a memory truth that will be a blessing to your life till you are with Heaven's glorious King. Does it interest you to **"dwell safely, and shall be quiet from fear of evil"**? Think upon this verse. Your life cannot remain the same, if you do.

The only way to **"hearkeneth"** to the LORD is to tend diligently and daily upon His blessed precepts—to tuck our lives under the infinite shadow of His wings. It is in the comfort of His Word that we shall not be offended by anything, being possessed with the knowledge, the living revelation that He has all things under His care.

Prayer: *LORD, please bless my life to know and to abide one with You. I love You LORD Jesus. Bring this life to the fullness of what You've ordained for Your blessed glory. I am all Yours. In Jesus' name. Amen.*

May 14

"Except a corn of wheat fall into the ground and die, it abideth alone: but if it die, it bringeth forth much fruit." John 12:24

In this late hour, we hear many messages about victory and success and yet, what's left out of the false modern gospel is the cross—death and burial. The cross is never mentioned, much less camped out on. The divine economy works by the Gospel, the cross—death, burial, and resurrection. There will be no true solutions in this life or the next outside of co-dying with Christ and being raised up by Him (Romans 6; 2 Corinthians 4:10-12). Resurrection victory is only going to come by our consenting to our own death and burial. The LORD then raises us upward in HIS glorious power to please Him and be fruitful for HIS glory.

"Today, under God's economy of the cross, miracles are only wrought through the sufferings of the cross. Resurrection comes only through death (2 Corinthians 4:10-12). Renewal through surrender (Romans 12:1-2). Power is only perfected in weakness (2 Corinthians 12). Strength is not built upon strength; only upon powerlessness." A disciple

Prayer: LORD *Jesus, bless this life to be truly crucified with You. Raise this vessel to glorify You dear LORD. In Jesus' name, amen.*

May 15

"My times are in thy hand: deliver me from the hand of mine enemies, and from them that persecute me." Psalms 31:15

The battle rages all around us and iniquities rage within us until they are silenced by Christ via the crucified life He prescribed (Luke 9:23-24). The work of Christ is to bring us to being **"still."**

Living in the now—walking, abiding one with Christ as the interpenetration of His life consumes us—instills His great peace. It's only then that we are blessed to **"Be still."**

"Be still, and know that I am God: I will be exalted among the heathen, I will be exalted in the earth." Psalms 46:10

"Stillness is found in our co-death with Christ (Romans 6)." A disciple

Prayer: *Holy Father, I come to You in the name of Jesus, asking You now to still my heart. Please teach me to truly trust You. Please forgive my unbelief and increase my faith dear LORD. Amen.*

Do you have any question about your salvation? Check out page 381.

May 16

"My covenant will I not break, nor alter the thing that is gone out of my lips." Psalms 89:34

The LORD is unchanging. Therefore, His Word, what He has spoken, is **"settled in heaven."**

"For ever, O LORD, thy word is settled in heaven." Psalms 119:89

Of Psalms 119:89, F.B. Meyer wrote:

"The famous Scotch clergyman, Thomas Erskine, said that no demolition of outward authority, even if such demolition were possible, could deprive him of the conviction of the divine origin and authority of the Bible, because it so exactly coincided with the experiences of his life, and had been verified in so many remarkable instances. We have experienced God's faithfulness to His promises too often to be afraid of any attack upon the truth of Scripture. It is settled in heaven."

Prayer: *Father, I thank You for preserving for us Your Word in print. Thank You for giving us all things that pertain unto life and godliness in Your Word, the highest and final divine authority, in Jesus' name amen LORD.*

May 17

"Thou preparest a table before me in the presence of mine enemies: thou anointest my head with oil; my cup runneth over." Psalms 23:5

Each true disciple of Christ desires to share His love with others, especially as we know the end is near. May God bless us to be so full of Christ via daily abiding fellowship, that His love overflows from our lives!

May we be able to declare with beloved David, the man after God's own heart— **"my cup runneth over."**

May our hearts be quickened this day, ignited, enlightened with the light of Jesus—as we gratefully praise, seek, worship, and glorify His holy name.

"Whom having not seen, ye love; in whom, though now ye see him not, yet believing, ye rejoice with joy unspeakable and full of glory:" 1 Peter 1:8

Prayer: Father, You gave Your only begotten Son Jesus for my sins. Now, please glorify Yourself in this life. May Christ alone be magnified in this vessel, in Jesus' name. Amen LORD, *let it be!*

May 18

> "Beware of false prophets, which come to you in sheep's clothing, but inwardly they are ravening wolves. 16 Ye shall know them by their fruits." Matthew 7:15-16

Here our LORD warns of the devouring wolves who pose as His representatives. Satan's **"ministers"** operate within and behind structures, systems they create and can be discerned thereby (Matthew 7:15-20; 2 Corinthians 11:12-15). They peddle tradition instead of truth (Matthew 23; Jeremiah 23; Ezekiel 34; 3 John 9-10, etc.). While pretending to represent Christ, they instead subvert His truth to mislead their prey.

> "For such are false apostles, deceitful workers, transforming themselves into the apostles of Christ. 14 And no marvel; for Satan himself is transformed into an angel of light. 15 Therefore it is no great thing if his ministers also be transformed as the ministers of righteousness; whose end shall be according to their works." 2 Corinthians 11:13-15

Prayer: *Dear heavenly Father, I come to You now, asking You to grant me the knowledge of Your Word and Your ability to discern Your enemies. In Jesus' name.*

May 19

"I am crucified with Christ: nevertheless I live; yet not I, but Christ liveth in me: and the life which I now live in the flesh I live by the faith of the Son of God, who loved me, and gave himself for me." Galatians 2:20

Nothing in the Christian's life works without the cross at the center of it. There is no shortcut.

Many are casting off their sinful self and the futility thereof for a new life—a cross life where Jesus reigns, not them. This cross truth is central to the original Gospel, without which the Christian life doesn't work. The cross life—death, burial, and resurrection—is the power generator of the Gospel, the raising up of Christ in those who consent to their own dying.

"Always bearing about in the body the dying of the Lord Jesus, that the life also of Jesus might be made manifest in our body. 11 For we which live are alway delivered unto death for Jesus' sake, that the life also of Jesus might be made manifest in our mortal flesh. 12 So then death worketh in us, but life in you." 2 Corinthians 4:10-12

Prayer: *Father, in Jesus' name, please help me today to follow Christ truly—by the laying down of this life, the setting aside, the denial, so that Jesus reigns supreme. Let it be dear LORD.*

May 20

"Let your light so shine before men, that they may see your good works, and glorify your Father which is in heaven." Matthew 5:16

The **"good works"** of God are witnessed by all as His people dwell in His holy light—as they **"walk in the light as he is in the light"** (1 John 1:7).

Men are blessed to see these works of God shining forth from His people—so that they too can know and magnify Christ.

"For we are his workmanship, created in Christ Jesus unto good works, which God hath before ordained that we should walk in them." Ephesians 2:10

"There is a glow and a spiritual fragrance about the life of a person who is Spirit filled that is unlike anything found in natural man. The beauty of divine holiness ought to be radiated from all Christians. It is always seen in the lives of those who are truly controlled by the Spirit." G. Christian Weiss, *Insights into Bible Times and Customs*

Prayer: *Heavenly Father, I come to You now in the name of Jesus Christ my LORD, asking You to bring my heart to full worship-filled love and faith in You and ask You to shine the light of Christ into and through this heart and life. Please use me to help others to know You LORD Jesus.*

May 21

> "The light of the body is the eye: if therefore thine eye be single, thy whole body shall be full of light. 23 But if thine eye be evil, thy whole body shall be full of darkness. If therefore the light that is in thee be darkness, how great is that darkness!" Matthew 6:22-23

What is the focal point of your life? We shall be filled with light or darkness based on where we choose to aim the focusing device of our hearts. May we be full and finished with deep remorse of the lawless idolatry of seeking anywhere but in Christ. May we set the affection of our hearts upon the **"bright and morning star"** Himself this day and to relish His pure light shining in and through our lives (Revelation 22:16).

> "If ye then be risen with Christ, seek those things which are above, where Christ sitteth on the right hand of God. 2 Set your affection on things above, not on things on the earth. 3 For ye are dead, and your life is hid with Christ in God. 4 When Christ, who is our life, shall appear, then shall ye also appear with him in glory." Colossians 3:1-4

Prayer: *Heavenly Father, I come to You in Jesus' name and ask You to forgive the iniquities of my heart. Here and now I denounce the spiritual adultery that once ruled my heart and I magnify You LORD Jesus as my all in all and the Master of my life. Amen.*

May 22

> "Wherein ye greatly rejoice, though now for a season, if need be, ye are in heaviness through manifold temptations: 7 That the trial of your faith, being much more precious than of gold that perisheth, though it be tried with fire, might be found unto praise and honour and glory at the appearing of Jesus Christ." 1 Peter 1:6-7

"Now for a season," in this earthly sojourn, this passing through, the saints of Christ suffer seasons of affliction. Yet, our faith in Christ is tested and purified as we eagerly look for **"the appearing of Jesus Christ."** Being with Him eternally helps us **"count it all joy"** as we suffer the persecution of this fallen world.

> "My brethren, count it all joy when ye fall into divers *(various)* temptations; 3 Knowing this, that the trying of your faith worketh patience. 4 But let patience have her perfect work, that ye may be perfect and entire, wanting nothing." James 1:2-4

Prayer: Holy Father, thank You for finding and saving me into Your eternal kingdom through Christ's precious blood. Please purify my faith and nourish my spirit this day with an eternal perspective and great joy, knowing Your people will soon and forever be safe in Your heavenly presence. In Jesus' name, amen.

May 23

"For ye are dead, and your life is hid with Christ in God." Colossians 3:3

The safest place in the universe is in the cross of Christ: **"your life is hid with Christ in God"** (Colossians 3:3).

Our place of protection is in the love walk with the LORD where we express our love for Him in obedience to Him. Jesus commanded that we deny self, take up the cross daily and follow Him. We are full of troubles and so it should be easy to relinquish all to Him! In Christ alone is our rest from the toil of this life.

"Concerning the works of men, by the word of thy lips I have kept me from the paths of the destroyer." Psalms 17:4

Prayer: *Father, in Jesus' name, please bring me to the end of sinful self. Rebuke and remove the foolishness of this heart! I love You LORD and thank You that I am crucified with You today and that You are raising up this life for Your glory alone.*

May 24

"O God, thou knowest my foolishness; and MY SINS are not hid from thee." Psalms 69:5

David spoke of **"my sins." This means he was taking full responsibility for them before God, from which nothing can be hidden anyway.**

The psalmist honestly acknowledged and openly declared his sins before God. He sought to hide nothing.

"For I will declare mine iniquity; I will be sorry for my sin." Psalms 38:18

God can work with honesty but will not bless or save into eternal glory the dishonest.

Isn't it just better to admit when we are wrong, to openly admit we are not sinless perfection but rather utterly, perpetually in need of God's grace?

Are you deciding to be honest in all things? Are you cultivating an honest heart before the LORD? (Proverbs 28:13; Luke 8:15)

God knew the wickedness of David's heart and the hearts of all men (Jeremiah 17:9).

Prayer: *Father, in Jesus' name, grant this heart to be honest. Remove every trace of deceit. May my heart be pure in Thy holy eyes, a purity that You alone can bring. Amen.*

May 25

"Therefore if any man be in Christ, he is a new creature: old things are passed away; behold, all things are become new. 18 And all things are of God, who hath reconciled us to himself by Jesus Christ, and hath given to us the ministry of reconciliation." 2 Corinthians 5:17-18

God demonstrated His love for fallen mankind when He sent His only begotten Son to the cross.

- You are one with Christ (John 17).

- You are abiding in Christ (John 15).

- You are a new creature in Christ (2 Corinthians 5:17-18).

- You serve Christ (not man) (1 Corinthians 7:23).

- You fear the LORD, not man (Galatians 1:10).

You are Christ's ambassador—you represent Him and not yourself or any other entity (2 Corinthians 5:20). Out of that cross life, that abiding oneness with the Father and Christ, your cup overflows on others (John 15, 17). THAT is how New Testament kingdom ministry happens.

Prayer: *Father, in Jesus' name, please bless Your people to be one with You and Jesus (John 17).*

May 26

> "Forasmuch then as the children are partakers of flesh and blood, he also himself likewise took part of the same; that through death he might destroy him that had the power of death, that is, the devil; 15 And deliver them who through fear of death were all their lifetime subject to bondage."
> **Hebrews 2:14-15**

Jesus conquered sin and death by dying! (See 1 Corinthians 15:36.) And He asks you to do the same with Him (Luke 9:23-24; Romans 6:3-5; Galatians 2:20; Colossians 3:3; Hebrews 2:14-15, etc.).

Christ's apostle Paul declares that we are foolish if we believe God is going to raise up any person who isn't dead and buried with Christ (Romans 6:1-11).

> **"Thou fool, that which thou sowest** *(plant)* **is not quickened** *(made alive, resurrected),* **except it die."**
> **1 Corinthians 15:36**

Prayer: *LORD Jesus, You conquered death by dying. You were then buried and raised from the dead. Father, please teach me the way of Your only begotten Son—the cross. May my life be conformed to Your holy image. In Jesus' name, amen.*

Are you ready to meet with God on His terms? Go to page 381 at the back of this book.

May 27

> **"Rejoice in the Lord alway: and again I say, Rejoice. 5 ... The Lord is at hand. 6 Be careful for nothing; but in every thing by prayer and supplication with thanksgiving let your requests be made known unto God." Philippians 4:4-6**

Our rejoicing is in Jesus Christ. His kingdom is at hand and we seek the LORD for all our needs and desires today.

We commune and consult, we go to our Father in the holy name of our LORD—Jesus Christ—first for salvation and thereafter for all our supplications (humble requests). **"Let your requests be made known unto God."**

Daily, millions pray and yet, God only promises to answer the prayers of those who are His—born again into Christ—and asking according to His simple prescription—ask through the name of Jesus! (See 1 John 5:13-15.) Every blessing of God comes exclusively in and through Christ. His unique and perfect sacrifice alone procured to us this relationship we now experience with God (2 Corinthians 1:20).

> **"And whatsoever ye shall ask in my name, that will I do, that the Father may be glorified in the Son. 14 If ye shall ask any thing in my name, I will do it." John 14:13-14**

Prayer: *Heavenly Father, thank You so very much for sending Your only begotten Son to die to pay the price for the sins of the whole world, for my sins. I love You LORD Jesus and thank You for redeeming me. Thank You LORD for access to the throne of grace by the blood of Jesus Christ. In Jesus' name, amen.*

May 28

"Study to shew thyself approved unto God, a workman that needeth not to be ashamed, rightly dividing the word of truth." 2 Timothy 2:15

The only way we can prevent being deceived is by astute study and belief of God's Word whereby we are able to rightly divide His Word of truth (2 Timothy 2:15).

Mark Cowan writes: *"Throughout the whole world error and truth travel the same highways, work in the same fields and factories, attend the same churches, fly in the same planes and shop in the same stores. So skilled is error at imitating truth that the two are constantly being mistaken for each other. It takes a sharp eye these days to know which brother is Cain and which is Abel!"*

Concerning doctrine, the apostle Paul told us that **"A little leaven leaveneth the whole lump"** (Galatians 5:9).

Satan's most effective wolves, dressed in sheep's clothing among us, use lots of Scripture and yet sprinkle in just a tad of deadly heresy. That's all it takes to kill. Remember, Satan only added one word to what God said and it led to the fall of mankind (Genesis 2:17; 3:4).

Prayer: *Heavenly Father, in the name of Jesus, please teach Your people the importance of doctrinal exactness. LORD Jesus Bless us to know You in the power of Your resurrection and fellowship of Your sufferings.*

May 29

"And the contention was so sharp between them, that they departed asunder one from the other: and so Barnabas took Mark, and sailed unto Cyprus." Acts 15:39

Paul and Barnabas had a rift. They strongly disagreed and parted ways and yet as mature men of God, they didn't continue any strife over the matter. Also, the Bible didn't say either of them was wrong. They simply viewed a non-essential situation differently and went their separate ways in peace.

"If it be possible, as much as lieth in you, live peaceably with all men." Romans 12:18

"Behold, how good and how pleasant it is for brethren to dwell together in unity." Psalms 133:1

"And be ye kind one to another, tenderhearted, forgiving one another, even as God for Christ's sake hath forgiven you." Ephesians 4:32

Prayer: *Holy Father, please bless this life to be truly crucified with Christ so there is no pride nor participation in unnecessary strife which could bring reproach to Your holy name. In Jesus' name, amen.*

May 30

"He must increase, but I must decrease." John 3:30

May this be our prayer today, and daily.

The life of Christ in us beckons us to the crucified life out of which comes His resurrection life (2 Corinthians 4:10-12).

"A Crucified Lord must have a Crucified Bride." W.B. Dunkum

The cross—the crucified life—is the only way the kingdom disciple's life works and the only way Christ is glorified in that laid down life.

Beloved of God, have you had enough of the sinful life, the guilt, the shame of the flesh ruling, of **"the motions of sins"**? (See Romans 7:5.)

Are you ready to **"mortify the deeds of the body"** by the enabling power of the Holy Ghost?

"For if ye live after the flesh, ye shall die: but if ye through the Spirit do mortify the deeds of the body, ye shall live." Romans 8:13

Prayer: *L*ORD*, I want to know Your Son Jesus Christ in the fellowship of His sufferings and the power of His resurrection. Please let the cross takes its fullest place in my life today. In Jesus' name, amen.*

May 31

> "But as he which hath called you is holy, so be ye holy in all manner of conversation; 16 Because it is written, Be ye holy; for I am holy." 1 Peter 1:15-16

Those making excuse not to **"Be ye holy"** will be rejected.

> "Follow peace with all men, and holiness, without which no man shall see the Lord." Hebrews 12:14

Jesus died to deliver His people from **"ALL"** their iniquities and not to grant them a license to sin.

> "Who gave himself for us, that he might redeem us from ALL iniquity, and purify unto himself a peculiar people, zealous of good works." Titus 2:14

Jesus is coming back for those who choose to love, worship, obey, and abide with Christ on HIS terms and no other terms.

> "Christ also loved the church, and gave himself for it; 26 That he might sanctify and cleanse it with the washing of water by the word, 27 That he might present it to himself a glorious church, not having spot, or wrinkle, or any such thing; but that it should be holy and without blemish." Ephesians 5:25-27

Prayer: *Father, please purify my life. Search and convict me deeply and deliver my life (spirit, soul, and body) from all evil. In Jesus' name.*

June 1

> **"Thy words were found, and I did eat them; and thy word was unto me the joy and rejoicing of mine heart." Jeremiah 15:16**

One thing we can clearly observe is that when people get out of the Word, the circumcising effect of the scriptures ceases and they resort back to self, to dishonesty, to sin-justification (2 Timothy 4:2-4). The work of God discontinues ... other than drawing them back to Him in repentance (Revelation 2:4-5). Getting out of the Word always leads to a migration to false teachers who justify sin, teaching heresies, fables like eternal security (2 Timothy 4:2-4). Those who remain diligent, daily in God's Word remain convicted, repentant, and fixed upon Christ. These are the wise virgin saints who will be openly welcomed, admitted into the eternal bridal chamber with Christ their Bridegroom (Matthew 25:1-13; Ephesians 5:25-27, etc.). The foolish virgins who began with salvation in Christ and then chose to wax cold, will be shut out of the eternal abode with Christ, the New Jerusalem, Heaven.

We must remain steadfast in the Word of God saints. Our daily bread is to be continually nourished by the Savior. To continue to grow in Christ, we must feed upon the bread of life, the food for our souls, God's Word.

> **"As newborn babes, desire the sincere milk of the word, that ye may grow thereby." 1 Peter 2:2**

Prayer: *Father, thank You for placing in my bosom the insatiable desire for Your Word. In Jesus' name, amen.*

June 2

"IF we walk in the light, as he is in the light, we have fellowship one with another, and the blood of Jesus Christ his Son cleanseth us from all sin…IF we confess our sins, he is faithful and just to forgive us our sins, and to cleanse us from all unrighteousness." 1 John 1:7, 9

Once again, we witness that bone-crushing, lie-leveling two-letter word which haunts every proponent of the unconditional eternal security myth— **"If."** Read this again— **"If, if, if we confess"** then we are forgiven and cleansed, but not until the sin is confessed. *God is (without fail) faithful to forgive if we will simply and sincerely confess our sins in true repentance.*

Contrary to so much false teaching today, when God saved us, He didn't cease requiring that we love Him and walk with Him. He never promised that all present and future sins are automatically forgiven. As you study God's Word honestly, catch this two-letter nightmare of the eternal security proponents.

There are divinely required conditions for initial salvation and to **"abide,"** to remain in Christ. Read John 15:1-6.

Prayer: *Dear Father, thank You for finding and saving me through Christ my LORD. Bless this life to truly abide in Christ as You define it. From this moment forward, I choose to walk in Your truth and to deny the lukewarm lies being peddled by the wolves You so often warned us about. In Jesus' name, amen.*

June 3

"He that is of God heareth God's words: ye therefore hear them not, because ye are not of God." **John 8:47**

The true disciple is a student of Christ. He lives by the faith of Christ breathed into His spirit by the Word and the Holy Spirit (John 4:23-24; Romans 10:17; 2 Corinthians 3:6, etc.). The follower of Christ proves his love for God by seeking out, acknowledging and being obedient to the whole will, the WORD of God (Psalms 119; John 8:47). He has truly repented and therefore lives to please the Savior by adhering to the WHOLE counsel of God's Word—letting God's Word be true and EVERY mere man a liar (Acts 20:20, 27, 32; Romans 3:4; 2 Timothy 3:16-17).

Those who don't hold God's WRITTEN WORD as the absolute final authority for all matters of the Christian faith, are deceived and the very enemies of Christ (John 8:47; Acts 17:10-11; Galatians 1:6-9). Those who are not a **"Let-God-be-true-and-EVERY-man-a-liar"** disciple are **"not of God"** (Romans 3:4; John 8:47).

Prayer: *Holy Father, make me Your authentic disciple, a person who upholds Your Word as the highest divine authority. Please reveal Yourself to me dear LORD, in Jesus' name, amen.*

June 4

> "Through thy precepts I get understanding: therefore I hate every false way." Psalms 119:104

Are Christ's disciples to hate? Yes, not people but falsehoods.

> "Therefore I esteem all thy precepts concerning all things to be right; and I hate every false way." Psalms 119:128

May our love for the LORD and therefore His truth be so consuming that deceitful lies are despised in our hearts. This is the conviction for His truth the LORD wants in each of His saints.

> "Let God be true, but every man a liar." Romans 3:4

Those who get saved and then do not continue an ever-deepening relationship with Christ are **"Ever learning, and never able to come to the knowledge of the truth"** (2 Timothy 3:7). They thereby limit God or seek Him on some basis other than His Word which can only be a **"false way."** This is one reason the psalmist stated that he HATED **"EVERY false way."** Are you walking in a **"false way"**? (See Psalms 119:104, 128.)

Prayer: *Dear Father, in Jesus' name, please purify my heart today. Cleanse and clear me to truly love, seek, and know Thee. Amen.*

June 5

"And this is life eternal, that they might know thee the only true God, and Jesus Christ, whom thou hast sent." John 17:3

The whole and stated reason that God created man, in His very own image, was relationship—the very divine purpose for **"life eternal"** through Christ.

This simple, right-under-our-nose truth is so often overlooked, never mentioned.

Dear Lord, help us!

Paul declared his earnest, deepest longing and desire when he declared:

> **"That I may know him, and the power of his resurrection, and the fellowship of his sufferings, being made conformable unto his death." Philippians 3:10**

"That I may know him" was the heart cry of this holy apostle of our Lord and may it be ours also, today.

> **"Then shall we know, if we follow on to know the Lord." Hosea 6:3**

Prayer: *Father in Heaven, I come to You in the name of Jesus Christ, asking You to make me one with You. Please bring me closer and allow me to know You deeply. I love You Lord. Amen.*

June 6

> "That in the dispensation of the fulness of times he might gather together in one all things in Christ, both which are in heaven, and which are on earth; even in him:" Ephesians 1:10

Divine, eternal purpose revealed—in Ephesians 1:10 and 2:7.

> "That in the ages to come he might shew the exceeding riches of his grace in his kindness toward us through Christ Jesus." Ephesians 2:7

In eternity, the LORD is going to bring all of His people together with Him to reveal His exceeding riches (Revelation 21).

For now, His purpose/goal for our walk with Him on Earth is that His people be one with Him and the members of His body.

> "Till we all come in the unity of the faith, and of the knowledge of the Son of God, unto a perfect man, unto the measure of the stature of the fulness of Christ:" Ephesians 4:13

Prayer: *Father, thank You for solidifying the unity of Your true body—those who remain grounded upon the foundation of Your truth. We eagerly anticipate experiencing the exceeding riches of Your unfathomable grace. In Jesus' name, amen.*

June 7

"Study to shew thyself approved unto God, a workman that needeth not to be ashamed, rightly dividing the word of truth." 2 Timothy 2:15

The personal nature of this instruction is introduced at the onset of this verse— **"Study to shew thyself approved unto God."** YOU do it.

Yet, instead of personally studying the Bible organically, some want a short cut and so what they do is hook up with some ministry that is pushing a system. Laziness is also a contributing factor when men choose to go to seminary—to supposedly study a book they've had in their possession for years. Enlisting to be indoctrinated by a man-made system would sum up the course of seminarians.

Prayer: *Heavenly Father, I come to You in Jesus' name. Please teach me Your truth, Your ways. I love You Jesus. Please fill me with the Holy Ghost afresh, right now dear LORD.*

June 8

> "As ye have therefore received Christ Jesus the Lord, so walk ye in him: 7 Rooted and built up in him, and stablished in the faith, as ye have been taught, abounding therein with thanksgiving." Colossians 2:6-7

Following initial salvation, being saved into Christ's kingdom, God's will, is to root and ground His people in the solid foundation of Christ via His Word and Holy Spirit. **"Rooted and built up in him, and stablished in the faith."**

A vital component of this involves being aware of the "many false prophets" we are so often warned about and the lies they spread. The very next words of Paul are as follow:

> "Beware lest any man spoil you through philosophy and vain deceit, after the tradition of men, after the rudiments of the world, and not after Christ. 9 For in him dwelleth all the fulness of the Godhead bodily. 10 And ye are complete in him, which is the head of all principality and power." Colossians 2:8-10

Prayer: *Heavenly Father, thank You for finding and saving me into Your eternal kingdom. I love You Jesus. Please root and ground my heart and life in Your truth. Teach me to discern between truth and lies. In Jesus' name, amen.*

June 9

> "For by grace are ye saved through faith; and that not of yourselves: it is the gift of God: ⁹ Not of works, lest any man should boast." Ephesians 2:8-9

None can save himself. Only God saves through the perfect sacrifice of Jesus Christ on the cross of Calvary.

> "For God so loved the world, that he gave his only begotten Son, that whosoever believeth in him should not perish, but have everlasting life." John 3:16

Especially with the upsurge of Judaizers and the law-keeping doctrines they perpetrate, every born-again believer should pray and study to be grounded in God's saving grace in Christ.

> "Be not carried about with divers and strange doctrines. For it is a good thing that the heart be established with grace." Hebrews 13:9

Saints, we are saved by the Lord Himself, by His grace and not our own works. People who are still self-righteous, thinking they are earning their own justification, get very uneasy when the saving grace of God is preached. They are not yet students of New Testament truth. We must have an ever-deepening biblical revelation of God's justification by grace and faith! Please begin by memorizing Romans 5:1-2. And, please read Romans chapters 3-5 repeatedly, prayerfully.

Prayer: *Lord, please establish Your people in Your grace. Thank You Father in Jesus' name.*

June 10

"Father, if thou be willing, remove this cup from me: nevertheless not my will, but thine, be done."
Luke 22:42

Here are the words of our LORD Jesus, as He anguished to the point of sweating blood, crying out to the Father at Gethsemane.

"Not my will, but thine, be done" is a perfect cross prayer for every disciple as we daily relinquish the control of our lives to the LORD.

If not, we forfeit the divine life of Christ when we choose to retain instead of release to Him the right to our lives. When we taste and see that the LORD is so very good, an addiction may begin! Let the addiction begin!

Once you choose to obey the LORD and take up the daily cross, your feeble life will be exchanged for His divine life (2 Corinthians 4:10-12). The joy of the LORD will fill your heart and life and He will resurrect you in His power; bringing you through every trial, temptation, and obstacle to His eternal glory. Let the addiction begin!

NEWS FLASH: There will be no divine raising if there is no death and burial.

Prayer: *Father, in Jesus' name, let me this moment be truly crucified with Christ that Your resurrection grace will raise up this vessel for Your glory. Thank You Jesus. I am all Yours and You are all mine!*

June 11

"For his anger *(for our sin)* **endureth but a moment; in his favour is life: weeping may endure for a night, but joy cometh in the morning." Psalms 30:5**

In Christ's kingdom, the only way up is down. Here, again, we see the cross—death, burial, resurrection.

The LORD is so gracious that He gives us His resurrection joy after a season, a time of weeping/mourning—death and burial.

"Thou hast turned for me my mourning into dancing: thou hast put off my sackcloth *(concerns a time of repentance)*, **and girded me with gladness." Psalms 30:11**

Here we see how God clothes His people with His righteousness as they come before Him in true repentance. And He fills them with His joy!

Prayer: *Holy Father, in the name of Jesus, thank You for Your ever-deepening work in my life—to crucify this vessel that You might raise it for Your glory. In Jesus' name, amen.*

Have you genuinely repented and received salvation and forgiveness from God? Go to page 381 if you are uncertain.

June 12

"Now the works of the flesh are manifest, which are these; Adultery, fornication, uncleanness, lasciviousness, [20] Idolatry, witchcraft, hatred, variance, emulations, wrath, strife, seditions, heresies, [21] Envyings, murders, drunkenness, revellings, and such like: of the which I tell you before, as I have also told you in time past, that they which do such things shall not inherit the kingdom of God. Galatians 5:19-21

Writing to the church in Galatia, Paul specifically cites by name, 17 sins, works of the flesh, which reveal the person who has fallen away from Christ. Committing these sins proves they are not abiding in Christ (John 15:1-6). Sin must be called by name, from the King James Bible.

SIN BY ANY OTHER NAME IS STILL SIN:

- It is not an affair, it is adultery
- It is not premarital sex, it is fornication
- It is not homosexuality, it is sodomy
- It is not an obsession, it is idolatry
- It is not fibbing, it is lying
- It is not abortion, it is murder

Don't white-wash sin, repent of it! Lay down your life and follow Christ to the end of your life.

Prayer: *Holy Father, I love You. Please forgive my sin, change my heart. Cleanse me dear LORD. In Jesus' name, amen.*

June 13

"And David was greatly distressed; for the people spake of stoning him, ... but David encouraged himself in the Lord his God." 1 Samuel 30:6

During seasons of great stress, this man after God's own heart sought the Lord. This time only served as a blessing, hastening David to the feet of Christ. Beloved David gave us the most amazing Scriptures concerning seeking God.

"My soul followeth hard after thee." Psalms 63:8

"As the hart panteth after the water brooks, so panteth my soul after thee, O God. 2 My soul thirsteth for God, for the living God: when shall I come and appear before God?" Psalms 42:1-2

"One thing have I desired of the Lord, that will I seek after; that I may dwell in the house of the Lord all the days of my life, to behold the beauty of the Lord, and to enquire in his temple." Psalms 27:4

"When thou saidst, Seek ye my face; my heart said unto thee, Thy face, Lord, will I seek." Psalms 27:8

Prayer: *Father in Heaven, in the name of Jesus, please grant me, Your mere servant, to be possessed with a heart after You dear Lord. I love You Jesus.*

June 14

"Remember the former things of old: for I am God, and there is none else; I am God, and there is none like me, ¹⁰ Declaring the end from the beginning, and from ancient times the things that are not yet done, saying, My counsel shall stand, and I will do all my pleasure." Isaiah 46:9-10

"Declaring the end from the beginning"—only God can do this. The Lord alone knows the future.

Fulfilled prophecy: this is how we know without question that the Bible is the only holy book on God's earth.

This is an essential component of divine truth, imperative for a sound foundation.

God's Word foretells in detail, beforehand, over 300 events that have come to pass just as they were spoken hundreds and sometimes thousands of years before they happened. For example: the exact town the Messiah was to be born in was foretold (Bethlehem)—and He was (Micah 5:2; Matthew 2:1); that he would be miraculously born of a virgin—and he was (Isaiah 7:14; Matthew 1:23); that he would be called Emmanuel (God with us)—and he was and is (Isaiah 7:14; Matthew 1:23) and that he would be betrayed for 30 pieces of silver—and he was (Zechariah 11:12-13; Matthew 27:9).

Prayer: *Heavenly Father, please establish my life on the rock foundation of Your Word. In Jesus' name, amen.*

June 15

"He that dwelleth in the secret place of the most High shall abide under the shadow of the Almighty." Psalms 91:1

Read Psalm 91. GOD creatively made his birds, and one of the reasons for this creature is the purpose of showing us how much He loves us and how He comforts, cares, provides for and protects His own (Ps 91:1). The LORD tells us that He is our divine Comforter, the One who truly cares, our Protector, our Provider.

"He shall cover thee with his feathers, and under his wings shalt thou trust: his truth shall be thy shield and buckler." Psalms 91:4

Prayer: *Father, thank You for creating me, and for sending Your only begotten Son to die for my sins, so we can have a relationship both now and forever. You are my Provider, my Protector, and my Safety. I love You my LORD. In Jesus' name, amen.*

Are you ready to enter a relationship with God as your good Father, Savior, Provider and Comforter? Go to page 381 at the back of this book.

June 16

> **"Holding forth the word of life; that I may rejoice in the day of Christ, that I have not run in vain, neither laboured in vain." Philippians 2:16**

In the abiding life Jesus calls us to, we are **"filled"** with His presence which is shining forth the light of Christ's truth and love in the midst of this dark generation, as we eagerly anticipate His return (Matthew 5:6, 16).

> **"Blessed are they which do hunger and thirst after righteousness: for they shall be filled. ... Let your light so shine before men, that they may see your good works, and glorify your Father which is in heaven." Matthew 5:6, 16**

As the light of Christ fills His saints, those beams of divine blessings are to flow through His disciples into a dark world of lost souls in need of the Savior.

> **"Ye are the light of the world. A city that is set on an hill cannot be hid." Mathew 5:14**

Prayer: *LORD please bless this heart to truly and insatiably hunger and thirst for Your righteousness. Thank You for filling Your people and letting Your love shine through them to those in need of knowing You. Thank You Father, in Jesus' name, amen.*

June 17

> "In the mouth of two or three witnesses shall every word be established." 2 Corinthians 13:1

Just because someone's book, website, or some man standing in a pulpit says something, in no way makes it true. You must **"prove *(test)* all things"** and only hold fast the truth (1 Thessalonians 5:21).

> "For every one that useth milk is unskilful in the word of righteousness: for he is a babe. 14 But strong meat belongeth to them that are of full age, even those who by reason of use have their senses exercised to discern both good and evil." Hebrews 5:13-14

This is exactly what the disciples at Berea did when they heard Paul preach—they put what he taught to the test, diligently searching Holy Scripture to see if it was God's truth:

> "And the brethren immediately sent away Paul and Silas by night unto Berea: who coming thither went into the synagogue of the Jews. 11 These were more noble than those in Thessalonica, in that they received the word with all readiness of mind, and searched the scriptures daily, whether those things were so." Acts 17:10-11

Prayer: *Heavenly Father, cause my conscience to be captive to Your Word. In Jesus' name, amen.*

June 18

> "But as touching brotherly love ye need not that I write unto you: for ye yourselves are TAUGHT OF GOD to love one another." 1 Thessalonians 4:9

Are you being **"taught of God"** or are you being taught of men?

> "It is written in the prophets, And they shall be all TAUGHT OF GOD. Every man therefore that hath heard, and hath learned of the Father, cometh unto me." John 6:45

Jesus warns us of false religious leaders who are **"teaching for doctrines the commandments of men."**

> "Howbeit in vain do they worship me, teaching for doctrines the commandments of men." Mark 7:7

Paul warns of **"doctrines of devils"**:

> "Now the Spirit speaketh expressly, that in the latter times some shall depart from the faith, giving heed to seducing spirits, and doctrines of devils;" 1 Timothy 4:1

Prayer: *Heavenly Father, in the name of Jesus I ask You to circumcise my heart and to teach me Thy truth. Please protect me from all error. Amen.*

June 19

"By this shall all men know that ye are my disciples, IF ye have LOVE one to another." John 13:35

Search out this matter in God's Word. Make it your priority. Learn it. Pray to Him for it. Ask the LORD to help you to be consumed in His love. Keep yourself in His love (Jude 21).

"Keep yourselves in the love of God, looking for the mercy of our Lord Jesus Christ unto eternal life." Jude 21

Grow, increase in God's love (1 Thessalonians 4:9-10). Find every single verse in the Bible on this essential subject that is so very close to the heart of Him who **"is love"** (1 John 4:16). Write the verses and their references on index cards so you can learn, memorize, meditate upon them, pray them and do them. **"Ask and ye shall receive"** says our LORD (Matthew 7:7). Read the love chapter, 1 Corinthians 13, and consider prayerfully reading and drinking it in at least once weekly.

Prayer: *Father, in the name of Jesus, please help us to love You with our whole hearts and to treat others as we would have others treat us (Matthew 22:37-40).*

June 20

"Seek ye out of the book of the LORD, and read: no one of these shall fail." Isaiah 34:16

As you seek the LORD in **"the book of the LORD"** which is the Bible, He is going to reveal Himself to You by His Spirit.

Not one of God's promises have ever failed, and never will— **"no one of these shall fail."**

God's Word is just like His divine nature—unchanging perfection.

"The grass withereth, the flower fadeth: but the word of our God shall stand for ever." Isaiah 40:8

Praying in the name of Jesus to the Father, asking Him to help you learn and know His truth and to never be misled, is important.

"Thy word is a lamp unto my feet, and a light unto my path." Psalms 119:105

Prayer: *Heavenly Father, teach me Your ways. I love You. Reveal Yourself to me, LORD, through Your Word. In Jesus' name, amen.*

June 21

> "For the eyes of the Lord are over the righteous, and his ears are open unto their prayers: but the face of the Lord is against them that do evil." **1 Peter 3:12**

God is answering the prayers of His saints today in Jesus Christ! (1 Peter 3:12)

> "The eyes of the Lord are over the righteous, and his ears are open unto their prayers."

God's people are **"the children of the highest"** (Luke 6:35). As our heavenly Father, the only perfect parent in existence, He desires to hear and answer all our prayers—with a yes, no, or wait. Let us readily make our needs and desires known to Him in prayer.

> **"Be careful for nothing; but in every thing by prayer and supplication with thanksgiving let your requests be made known unto God." Philippians 4:6**

Prayer: *Heavenly Father, teach me to pray, to seek Your face in abiding oneness and communion with You first and foremost. I love You Jesus and thank You for Your perfect redemption which alone grants full access to the throne of grace in Your name, amen.*

June 22

"They hate him that rebuketh in the gate, and they abhor him that speaketh uprightly." Amos 5:10

As was the case when the LORD's prophets preached His truth to backslidden Israel, so today men hate the messengers of God who give forth His rebukes. Instead of repenting at the warning, rebels attack the mere messenger and thereby forsake their own mercy (Jonah 2:8).

"They that observe lying vanities forsake their own mercy." Jonah 2:8

When God uses men to speak the light of His truth into the darkened hearts of men, many times those God seeks to reach, attack the mere messenger of His truth. In doing so, they miss the opportunity to receive the correction of the loving heavenly Father—who chastens every one of His children, and those who refuse His correction will be set outside of His kingdom (Hebrews 12:5-11).

Men who love their darkness more than God's way revealed in His Word, will not be blessed with His forgiveness **and will be outside of His kingdom** (John 3:19-21).

Prayer: *Father, in Jesus' name, please quicken my spirit right now, to be deeply humble, teachable, pliable, and obedient to You. Please pour oil on this heart, remove the stony places, and grant a heart of flesh dear LORD. I love You Jesus. Amen.*

June 23

> "I exhort therefore, that, first of all, supplications, prayers, intercessions, and giving of thanks, be made for all men; 2 For kings, and for all that are in authority; that we may lead a quiet and peaceable life in all godliness and honesty. 3 For this is good and acceptable in the sight of God our Saviour."
> **1 Timothy 2:1-3**

"**Quiet and peaceable lives**" is what the LORD has stated as His will and the reason we pray for those who lead (1 Timothy 2:1-6).

Here we have the specific instruction to pray for **"all that are in authority"** and then He gives us the reason— **"that we may lead a quiet and peaceable life in all godliness and honesty."** Then the apostle tells us that this is pleasing to our God— **"this is good and acceptable in the sight of God our Saviour."**

The prophet Jeremiah gives us further insight and incentive to pray for **"all that are in authority"**:

> "And seek the peace of the city whither I have caused you to be carried away captives, and pray unto the LORD for it: for in the peace thereof shall ye have peace." **Jeremiah 29:7**

Prayer: *Father, in Jesus' name, we lift in prayer to You all those in authority in the nation you have us in, asking You to help them do YOUR will, establishing law and order as you've ordained them to do, bringing to light the dark deeds, and to punish evil doers (Romans 13). Amen.*

June 24

> "Brethren, I count not myself to have apprehended: but this one thing I do, forgetting those things which are behind, and reaching forth unto those things which are before, [14] I press toward the mark for the prize of the high calling of God in Christ Jesus."
> Philippians 3:13-14

Did you catch the instructions in this passage?

- Forget – **"forgetting those things which are behind"**
- Reach – **"reaching forth unto those things which are before"**
- Press – **"press toward the mark for the prize of the high calling of God in Christ Jesus"**

Prayer: Father, I come to you in the Person, the blood, and name of Jesus Christ. Thank You for sending Your only begotten Son to die for me and all my sins. Right this moment, if never before, I call upon You Jesus to apprehend me afresh. I turn my life fully to You LORD Jesus and ask You to deliver me from all sin and inroads of the enemy into my life. I openly forgive all who have wronged me in any way as I submit my life to You. LORD Jesus, thank You that Your sinless blood washes away all my past sins right this moment and touches to the depth and core of my conscience, cleansing it perfectly. Thank You LORD that Your banner over me is love. Please multiply Your grace to my life and cause fruitfulness to abound to Your blessed glory. Deliver me from any influence of sin and Satan. Amen.

June 25

"Seek the LORD, and ye shall live." Amos 5:6

There are several platinum Bible verses instructing God's people to **"seek"** Him. Learning and memorizing these utterly changed the life of this disciple—as I am now able to recite them prayerfully. It's a divine super charge! Here are a few:

"Seek the LORD and his strength, seek his face continually." 1 Chronicles 16:11

"Now set your heart and your soul to seek the LORD your God." 1 Chronicles 22:19

"One thing have I desired of the LORD, that will I seek after; that I may dwell in the house of the LORD all the days of my life, to behold the beauty of the LORD, and to enquire in his temple." Psalms 27:4

"When thou saidst, Seek ye my face; my heart said unto thee, Thy face, LORD, will I seek." Psalms 27:8

"My soul followeth hard after thee: thy right hand upholdeth me." Psalms 63:8

"But seek ye first the kingdom of God, and his righteousness; and all these things shall be added unto you." Matthew 6:33

Prayer: *Heavenly Father, grant my heart to be a heart after You as was David's. I seek Your face, in Jesus' name.*

June 26

"That this is a rebellious people, lying children, children that will not hear the law of the LORD: 10 Which say to the seers, See not; and to the prophets, Prophesy not unto us right things, speak unto us smooth things, prophesy deceits." Isaiah 30:9-10

Such as was the case in the days when the LORD's prophets preached to His rebellious people, many today want preachers who are story tellers— **"speak unto us smooth things"**—instead of true ministers of Christ who preach the whole counsel of His Word.

The apostle Paul foretells of this same phenomenon occurring in the final days leading up to Christ' return.

"Preach the word; be instant in season, out of season; reprove, rebuke, exhort with all longsuffering and doctrine. 3 For the time will come when they will not endure sound doctrine; but after their own lusts shall they heap to themselves teachers, having itching ears; 4 And they shall turn away their ears from the truth, and shall be turned unto fables." 2 Timothy 4:2-4

Prayer: LORD, please make this vessel authentic, to the core of my being. Help me to endure, to hold myself accountable to Your truth. In Jesus' name.

June 27

"Feed the Flock of God." 1 Peter 5:2

First, it's God's flock, paid for with the very blood of Jesus Christ (Acts 20:28).

Jesus Christ is **"that great shepherd of the sheep"** (Hebrews 13:20). He instructed us to follow Him and, in doing so, to **"FEED my sheep"** (John 21:15-17). Tending to the sheep of Christ's pasture involves nourishing them with His Word, warning them, comforting them, and at times admonishing or rebuking.

Every single disciple of Christ should pray to be pastoral in heart and life. We are each to tend to our fellowship with Christ daily and to minister His grace to His people as we ourselves grow in His grace.

In this, we must ask Him to grant our hearts a kingdom perspective, not a local church attendance perspective. Christ and the apostles were the salt and light every day. They had no building. They went to the people as did all the disciples upon being scattered from Jerusalem during persecution. **"They that were scattered abroad went everywhere preaching the word"** (Acts 8:4).

> **"Simon, son of Jonas, lovest thou me more than these? He saith unto him, Yea, Lord; thou knowest that I love thee. He saith unto him, Feed my lambs."**
> **John 21:15**

Prayer: *Father, in Jesus' name, please nourish my heart in Your truth, fill me with Your Spirit afresh, and use me to refresh Your saints. Amen* LORD.

June 28

> "And be renewed in the spirit of your mind; 24 And that ye put on the new man, which after God is created in righteousness and true holiness." Ephesians 4:23-24

"True holiness" is brought out by GOD, as His disciple humbles himself, consenting to his own death that Christ might reign.

> "Neither yield ye your members as instruments of unrighteousness unto sin: but yield yourselves unto God, as those that are alive from the dead, and your members as instruments of righteousness unto God." Romans 6:13

"True holiness" is never a work of the flesh but rather the work of God, raising up the crucified saint (2 Corinthians 4:10-12). Any *surface* holiness that doesn't come out of the cross life, is not according to the original Gospel, but is rather a dead work of the flesh, vainly attempting to bring about a self-manufactured holiness.

Prayer: *Heavenly Father, please do Your ever-deepening work in my heart and life. Bless this vessel to be purified, cleansed of all iniquity and falsity, made authentic by You dear LORD. In Jesus' name, amen.*

June 29

"That if thou shalt confess with thy mouth the Lord Jesus, and shalt believe in thine heart that God hath raised him from the dead, thou shalt be saved. 10 For with the heart man believeth unto righteousness; and with the mouth confession is made unto salvation." Romans 10:9-10

Are you not yet saved from sin—by and for Christ? If that is the case, it is by no accident you are reading this message. This is your moment to be saved. Praying and doing good deeds and going to church will save no person from eternal punishment.

Only the perfect work of Christ shedding His sinless blood on the cross for you will save your soul as you repent before a holy and righteous God and Judge. If you are going to get right with the LORD and go to Heaven, there must be a moment of reckoning. Now is your time to be saved.

Your Prayer to God to be Saved: *Dear God, I have grossly sinned against You and yet You gave Jesus Christ on the cross to forgive and save me. Right this moment I put my trust in You my LORD Jesus, declaring You as the Master of my life, asking You to wash away all my sins. I lay my life in Your holy hands right this moment and with Your grace will follow You from this moment forward till I am with You in Heaven. Thank You for saving me LORD Jesus. Please use me to help others. In Jesus' name, amen.*

See *Making Peace with God* beginning on page 381 of this book.

June 30

"In whom are hid all the treasures of wisdom and knowledge." Colossians 2:3

Secret knowledge is a deception of the enemy of all souls. In fact, all divine knowledge available to men, is only found in Christ— granted exclusively to those truly known of Him.

God grants access to Himself and the treasures of His divinely granted salvation, wholeness, healing and wisdom exclusively through Jesus Christ.

Today some among us pretend to have special knowledge above others—and more insidious are the seminarians among us who pretend to have superior knowledge, wielding their deception over the common people. Beware. Christ is Creator and **"the Almighty"** (Colossians 1:16; Revelation 1:8). There is no thing or no one on His divine level, or superior to Heaven's KING. Paul warns:

> **"Beware lest any man spoil you through philosophy and vain deceit, after the tradition of men, after the rudiments of the world, and not after Christ. ⁹ For in him dwelleth all the fulness of the Godhead bodily. ¹⁰ And ye are complete in him, which is the head of all principality and power." Colossians 2:8-10**

Prayer: *Heavenly Father, thank You that I am complete in Christ alone. In Jesus' name I ask that you please protect Your people from the many deceptions and false prophets of Satan. Ground my heart in You LORD. I love You LORD, amen.*

July 1

> **"Watch and pray, that ye enter not into temptation: the spirit indeed is willing, but the flesh is weak." Matthew 26:41**

No, you are not capable of overcoming sin and Satan. You are no match for either and must **"Watch and pray"** in order to overcome. Only Christ has triumphed and remains triumphant over sin, Satan and death, and it's only by being truly crucified with Him that His victory will prevail in your life (Galatians 2:20). This is that cross life modern wolves hide from the people and yet is the only divine solution, the prescription for total victory. In order for Jesus to reign in your life, you must set self aside, deny self, and seek His face in prayer. It's only then, as your life is laid down and His life is reigning in you, that His victory will come to pass. Pour prayerfully over 2 Corinthians 4:10-12 today beloved.

Denying self, taking up the cross, and following Jesus means He is in control of your life and not you. This means you are given over to His will and not your own. And His stated will is that you seek Him **"daily"** in prayer and the study of His Word.

Jesus says, in this dark world we must **"Watch and pray, that ye enter not into temptation."** This means it's essential to **"Watch and pray,"** to be in close communion with Him, or temptation will prevail against us.

Prayer: *Precious LORD, quicken my spirit with Your holy fear, to hasten me to Your beautiful feet—to worship You in spirit and in truth. In Jesus' name, amen.*

July 2

"All things come of thee, and of thine own have we given thee." 1 Chronicles 29:14

All that we have or ever will have, comes from God, who made and owns all. Provision for those in need and Christ's work happens when His people obey Him by giving out of what He's given them (1 Chronicles 29:14; Proverbs 3:9-10; Luke 6:38; 2 Corinthians 9:6-11; etc.).

WE are Christ's body. As such, **"WE are labourers TOGETHER with God"**—here to display His love (1 Corinthians 3:9).

The giving of His saints, first of their lives, and then of the substance in their temporal possession, is the divine method for laying up eternal treasure for His saints.

> **"Lay not up for yourselves treasures upon earth, where moth and rust doth corrupt, and where thieves break through and steal: [20] But lay up for yourselves treasures in heaven, where neither moth nor rust doth corrupt, and where thieves do not break through nor steal: [21] For where your treasure is, there will your heart be also." Matthew 6:19-21**

Prayer: *Father, You were unfathomably generous when You sent Your only begotten Son to die for the sins of mankind. Please cause the hearts of Your people to genuinely trust You wholly, and to have hearts that are generous in cheerful giving. Thank You for storing up eternal treasure for Your people. In Jesus' name, amen.*

July 3

> "Beloved, think it not strange concerning the fiery trial which is to try you, as though some strange thing happened unto you: 13 But rejoice, inasmuch as ye are partakers of Christ's sufferings; that, when his glory shall be revealed, ye may be glad also with exceeding joy. 14 If ye be reproached for the name of Christ, happy are ye; for the spirit of glory and of God resteth upon you: on their part he is evil spoken of, but on your part he is glorified."
> **1 Peter 4:12-14**

When persecuted for our life with Christ, Scripture here exhorts us to **"Think it not strange"** or something that is out of the ordinary for Christ's people.

> **"Yea, and all that will live godly in Christ Jesus shall suffer persecution." 2 Timothy 3:12**

A kingdom perspective would be to rejoice at persecutions and to be concerned if we are not being persecuted for Christ in this fallen world.

> **"Woe unto you, when all men shall speak well of you! for so did their fathers to the false prophets."**
> **Luke 6:26**

Prayer: *Heavenly Father, in the name of Jesus Christ, I ask You to teach me Your ways and to multiply Your grace to my heart. Bless with multiplied love and the understanding that we wrestle not against flesh and blood. I love You Jesus and rejoice to be counted worthy to suffer for Your name.*

July 4

"Brethren, I count not myself to have apprehended: but this one thing I do, forgetting those things which are behind, and reaching forth unto those things which are before, 14 I press toward the mark for the prize of the high calling of God in Christ Jesus." Philippians 3:13-14

Did you catch that? With God, your past is just that—passed, behind you! Good or bad things, God says to put them in the past.

It's easy to forget the good things of the past, but not the sins we've committed, right? So, you have past sins? Join the club called humanity! AND, know that Jesus paid for this too! He desires you to have a conscience that is cleansed of your past transgressions (Hebrews 9:14; 1 John 1:9). The good news is that vanquishing your past sins means that you are not chained to the past! Jesus will deliver you now. You can let it all go, now. Let us reason: WHAT sins did Jesus NOT die to forgive?

Prayer: *Heavenly Father, through the blood of my LORD Jesus Christ, I now obey Your command for me to forget the things which are behind, reaching forth unto the things You've put before me, and pressing toward the mark of knowing You and making You known. In Jesus' name, amen dear LORD.*

July 5

> "It is <u>better</u> to go to the house of mourning, than to go to the house of feasting: for that is the end of all men; and the living will lay it to his heart. ³ Sorrow is <u>better</u> than laughter: for <u>by the sadness of the countenance the heart is made better</u>. ⁴ The heart of the wise is in the house of mourning; but the heart of fools is in the house of mirth. ⁵ It is <u>better</u> to hear the rebuke of the wise, than for a man to hear the song of fools." Ecclesiastes 7:2-5

Perhaps, when we begin to grasp this divine truth and cherish the outcome of it, we will welcome times of mourning, weeping and repentance in returning to the Lord as our **"first love"** (Revelation 2:4-5).

Most messages we hear today in the modern church world speak of success, pumping yourself up, reaching for the stars, reaching your destiny, giving it all you've got, etc. But the Lord calls us to another life—a life of seeking demotion, not promotion. The demotion is a downward dying, the death and burial, The Lord will then raise our lives upward—into His promotion.

> **"For promotion cometh neither from the east, nor from the west, nor from the south. ⁷ But God is the judge: he putteth down one, and setteth up another." Psalms 75:6-7**

Prayer: *Father, please teach me Your cross. Here and now I declare that I am crucified with Christ. Into Your hands I submit my life dear Lord, in Jesus' name, amen.*

July 6

"Though I speak with the tongues of men and of angels, and have not charity, I am become as sounding brass, or a tinkling cymbal. And though I have the gift of prophecy, and understand all mysteries, and all knowledge; and though I have all faith, so that I could remove mountains, and have not charity, I am nothing. And though I bestow all my goods to feed the poor, and though I give my body to be burned, and have not charity, it profiteth me nothing. Charity suffereth long, and is kind; charity envieth not; charity vaunteth not itself, is not puffed up, Doth not behave itself unseemly, seeketh not her own, is not easily provoked, thinketh no evil; Rejoiceth not in iniquity, but rejoiceth in the truth; Beareth all things, believeth all things, hopeth all things, endureth all things. Charity never faileth: but whether there be prophecies, they shall fail; whether there be tongues, they shall cease; whether there be knowledge, it shall vanish away. For we know in part, and we prophesy in part. But when that which is perfect is come, then that which is in part shall be done away. When I was a child, I spake as a child, I understood as a child, I thought as a child: but when I became a man, I put away childish things. For now we see through a glass, darkly; but then face to face: now I know in part; but then shall I know even as also I am known. And now abideth faith, hope, charity, these three; but the greatest of these is charity." 1 Corinthians 13

Prayer: *Father, please fill me with Your love, in Jesus' name.*

July 7

"Now set your heart and your soul to seek the Lord your God." 1 Chronicles 22:19

SET-ting up for success means doing things God's way and no other. It's a deliberate act of obedience.

Setting, programming, fixing our hearts, our lives, our minds to seek the Lord is essential, especially in this dark hour where everything around us seeks to entice and draw us away, to stray from that which is most important—seeking the Lord's holy face.

"My heart is fixed, O God, my heart is fixed: I will sing and give praise." Psalms 57:7

When you truly worship the Lord, you no longer worship the false, frail god of self. This means you are submitted to God and not self—not the dictates of sinful self.

"Submit yourselves therefore to God. Resist the devil, and he will flee from you." James 4:7

As the disciple of Jesus, you are crucified with Him—crucified to your own will and way and abandoned to His!

"For ye are dead, and your life is hid with Christ in God." Colossians 3:3

Prayer: *Dear Father, I am crucified with Christ, I am dead, and my life is hidden with Christ in God. My heart is fixed O God, my heart is fixed upon You. I love You Lord and thank You for finding and saving me. My life is given over to You this day. Not my will but Thine be done. In Jesus' name. Amen.*

July 8

> **"But thou, when thou prayest, enter into thy closet, and when thou hast shut thy door, pray to thy Father which is in secret; and thy Father which seeth in secret shall reward thee openly." Matthew 6:6**

Prayer is not just asking but first and foremost, communing with our LORD (Matthew 6:6). And as we do, He promises to openly reward us. Those who seek God in private, will have His reward upon their lives—His presence, His favor, His grace, strength and blessing.

We commune and consult, we go to our Father in Jesus' name for all our supplications (humble requests). We never ever take our God for granted. He is our first love and highest priority.

No, we are not earning our way into divine justification and yet, having been justified by the perfect sacrifice of Christ, we obey our God. We seek His face in this abiding relationship. We serve Him.

We choose to love Him supremely and therefore seek to ever more know Him—the divine purpose for which He made us and saved us.

> **"And this is life eternal, that they might know thee the only true God, and Jesus Christ, whom thou hast sent." John 17:3**

Prayer: *Father, help me to know You more, to be one with You, and to be used of You. In Jesus' name, amen.*

July 9

"For the time will come when they will not endure sound doctrine; but after their own lusts shall they heap to themselves teachers, having itching ears." 2 Timothy 4:3

The divide between the wheat and the tares is seen here. Counterfeits evade truth and truth-tellers—and run to the liars. The true remnant of Christ is known in that they **"endure sound doctrine."** To **"endure"** here is *to hold oneself accountable to.*

Our LORD Jesus told us exactly how to know who is **"of God"** and who is **"not of God."**

"He that is of God heareth God's words: ye therefore hear them not, because ye are not of God." John 8:47

Those who are truly **"of God"** are known by the fruit of their obedience to the Word of God—always putting Jesus first, as **"first love"** and not themselves—which they crucify (Luke 9:23-24; Revelation 2:4-5). In contrast, counterfeits love sin-coddling lies.

So many today, while claiming to be saved, evade divine truth that cuts, convicts and calls them to true repentance.

Prayer: *Precious Father, please forgive my sins afresh. I return to You now Jesus as the supreme love of my life. LORD please cleanse and prepare this heart and life to be used of You, in light of Your soon return. In Jesus' name, amen.*

July 10

"Remember Lot's wife." Luke 17:32

When God instructs us to **"remember"** something, He is underscoring a truth. He is warning us of danger and how to escape it.

What did Jesus want us to **"remember"** about **"Lot's wife"**? What was the sin of Lot's wife? Why was she judged? What is it about **"Lot's wife"** that the LORD wants us to beware of?

Why would Jesus warn us of an event that was thousands of years old, an account of the rebellion, the disobedience of a woman who while being delivered looked back?

WHAT'S at stake? Make no mistake: This is a real-life story about sin and judgment.

The peril of looking back should deeply concern us! This is a divine warning to each of us, make no mistake.

> **"Even as Sodom and Gomorrha, and the cities about them in like manner, giving themselves over to fornication, and going after strange flesh, are set forth for an example, suffering the vengeance of eternal fire." Jude 7**

Prayer: *Please dear LORD, help me. I hasten to You right now, asking You to cleanse my heart afresh and establish me in an abiding relationship with You. In Jesus' name.*

July 11

"Epaphras, who is one of you, a servant of Christ, saluteth you, always labouring fervently for you in prayers, that ye may stand perfect and complete in all the will of God." Colossians 4:12

This man Epaphras, a disciple among the Colossian saints whom Paul heralds here, prayed fervently for God's people to **"stand perfect and complete in all the will of God."**

The all-encompassing prayer! Simple and biblical! Life changing! We never again have to wonder how or what to pray for others or ourselves. How many times have we wondered how to pray for someone? We now know exactly how to pray for others, asking God in Jesus' name for them to **"stand perfect and complete in all the will of God."**

Prayer: *Holy Father, in Jesus' name, I ask You to fill me afresh with Your love and teach me to pray for Your perfect will to be done in the lives of Your beloved children. Amen.*

July 12

"It is more blessed to give than to receive." Acts 20:35

THE happiest, **"more blessed,"** most joyful people we meet are the givers (Acts 20:35). Their hearts are full of joy because as they give their lives to the LORD daily, they continue to be filled by Him with all the fruits of His righteousness (Matthew 5:6). These who give, in worship to the Most High, are free of greed and covetousness and their hearts are filled with joy for participating in the Gospel of the One they love (Matthew 6:21).

Debbie Lord writes: *"Speaking of Acts 20:35, blessings are best when shared with others. This is pointing to the multiplication of blessings in sharing them. 'The gift that keeps on giving!' (Feeding 5,000, etc.)"*

"Give, and it shall be given unto you; good measure, pressed down, and shaken together, and running over, shall men give into your bosom. For with the same measure that ye mete withal it shall be measured to you again." Luke 6:38

Giving our lives to Christ, who gave them to us, is always the priority. Giving is following Christ—giving love, forgiveness, mercy, treasure, comfort, etc.— **"For God so loved the world that he gave"** (John 3:16).

Prayer: *Heavenly Father, thank You for giving Your only begotten Son for my sins and for the sins of the whole world. Thank You Jesus for Your perfect sacrifice to save Your people. I ask You to grant my heart to be cheerful, joyful in giving out of that which You give. In Jesus' name, amen.*

July 11

"Epaphras, who is one of you, a servant of Christ, saluteth you, always labouring fervently for you in prayers, that ye may stand perfect and complete in all the will of God." Colossians 4:12

This man Epaphras, a disciple among the Colossian saints whom Paul heralds here, prayed fervently for God's people to **"stand perfect and complete in all the will of God."**

The all-encompassing prayer! Simple and biblical! Life changing! We never again have to wonder how or what to pray for others or ourselves. How many times have we wondered how to pray for someone? We now know exactly how to pray for others, asking God in Jesus' name for them to **"stand perfect and complete in all the will of God."**

Prayer: *Holy Father, in Jesus' name, I ask You to fill me afresh with Your love and teach me to pray for Your perfect will to be done in the lives of Your beloved children. Amen.*

July 12

"It is more blessed to give than to receive." Acts 20:35

THE happiest, **"more blessed,"** most joyful people we meet are the givers (Acts 20:35). Their hearts are full of joy because as they give their lives to the LORD daily, they continue to be filled by Him with all the fruits of His righteousness (Matthew 5:6). These who give, in worship to the Most High, are free of greed and covetousness and their hearts are filled with joy for participating in the Gospel of the One they love (Matthew 6:21).

Debbie Lord writes: *"Speaking of Acts 20:35, blessings are best when shared with others. This is pointing to the multiplication of blessings in sharing them. 'The gift that keeps on giving!' (Feeding 5,000, etc.)"*

> **"Give, and it shall be given unto you; good measure, pressed down, and shaken together, and running over, shall men give into your bosom. For with the same measure that ye mete withal it shall be measured to you again." Luke 6:38**

Giving our lives to Christ, who gave them to us, is always the priority. Giving is following Christ—giving love, forgiveness, mercy, treasure, comfort, etc.— **"For God so loved the world that he gave"** (John 3:16).

Prayer: *Heavenly Father, thank You for giving Your only begotten Son for my sins and for the sins of the whole world. Thank You Jesus for Your perfect sacrifice to save Your people. I ask You to grant my heart to be cheerful, joyful in giving out of that which You give. In Jesus' name, amen.*

July 13

"I have esteemed the words of his mouth more than my necessary food." Job 23:12

Job counted God's words to be more important than feeding his flesh. This must become the reality of Christ's disciples. You MUST eat, you must devour God's Word daily or you will fall away! Keep in mind that once you've arrived at your eternal destination there are no do-overs! Follow Jesus. Obey Christ. Living by truth and not feelings is essential.

Nourishment: What's fatter—your belly or your spirit? What's been fed more?

"As newborn babes, desire the sincere milk of the word, that ye may grow thereby:" 1 Peter 2:2

In order to grow, at any stage of maturity, the disciple of Jesus must desire and devour the words of God.

"Thy words were found, and I did eat them; and thy word was unto me the joy and rejoicing of mine heart: for I am called by thy name, O Lord God of hosts." Jeremiah 15:16

As we **"eat"** or ingest, devour the words of God, it is **"the joy and rejoicing"** of our hearts (Jeremiah 15:16).

Prayer: *Heavenly Father, please deepen the hunger in my heart for more of You, for Your precious words. In Jesus' name, amen.*

July 14

"If we say that we have no sin, we deceive ourselves, and the truth is not in us. ⁹ If we confess our sins, he is faithful and just to forgive us our sins, and to cleanse us from all unrighteousness. ¹⁰ If we say that we have not sinned, we make him a liar, and his word is not in us." 1 John 1:8-10

God can work with the honest—no matter what they've done. He cannot and will not work with a deceitful heart, a dishonest person.

"He that covereth his sins shall not prosper: but whoso confesseth and forsaketh them shall have mercy." Proverbs 28:13

There is no justifying the sin Jesus died to forgive and deliver us **"FROM"**! (See Matthew 1:21; John 1:29; Romans 6:1-2.) One of those sins is self-reliance/pride/self-righteousness, which is not admitting our utter, present, perpetual need for divine mercy and grace (Matthew 5:3; Romans 7:18). You are nothing and can do nothing to please God without Jesus, even in your **"best state"** (Psalms 39:4-5; John 15:5).

Those who aren't honest with their sin and with the whole counsel of Scripture clearly prove their hearts are not authentic and sincere before the LORD (Luke 8:15; John 7:16; 2 Corinthians 2:17; 2 Peter 3:16, etc.).

Prayer: *Father, please do Your deeper work in my life. Create in me a clean heart and establish Your truth in my life. In Jesus' name I pray.*

July 13

"I have esteemed the words of his mouth more than my necessary food." Job 23:12

Job counted God's words to be more important than feeding his flesh. This must become the reality of Christ's disciples. You MUST eat, you must devour God's Word daily or you will fall away! Keep in mind that once you've arrived at your eternal destination there are no do-overs! Follow Jesus. Obey Christ. Living by truth and not feelings is essential.

Nourishment: What's fatter—your belly or your spirit? What's been fed more?

"As newborn babes, desire the sincere milk of the word, that ye may grow thereby:" 1 Peter 2:2

In order to grow, at any stage of maturity, the disciple of Jesus must desire and devour the words of God.

"Thy words were found, and I did eat them; and thy word was unto me the joy and rejoicing of mine heart: for I am called by thy name, O Lord God of hosts." Jeremiah 15:16

As we **"eat"** or ingest, devour the words of God, it is **"the joy and rejoicing"** of our hearts (Jeremiah 15:16).

Prayer: *Heavenly Father, please deepen the hunger in my heart for more of You, for Your precious words. In Jesus' name, amen.*

July 14

"If we say that we have no sin, we deceive ourselves, and the truth is not in us. ⁹ If we confess our sins, he is faithful and just to forgive us our sins, and to cleanse us from all unrighteousness. ¹⁰ If we say that we have not sinned, we make him a liar, and his word is not in us." 1 John 1:8-10

God can work with the honest—no matter what they've done. He cannot and will not work with a deceitful heart, a dishonest person.

"He that covereth his sins shall not prosper: but whoso confesseth and forsaketh them shall have mercy." Proverbs 28:13

There is no justifying the sin Jesus died to forgive and deliver us **"FROM"**! (See Matthew 1:21; John 1:29; Romans 6:1-2.) One of those sins is self-reliance/pride/self-righteousness, which is not admitting our utter, present, perpetual need for divine mercy and grace (Matthew 5:3; Romans 7:18). You are nothing and can do nothing to please God without Jesus, even in your **"best state"** (Psalms 39:4-5; John 15:5).

Those who aren't honest with their sin and with the whole counsel of Scripture clearly prove their hearts are not authentic and sincere before the LORD (Luke 8:15; John 7:16; 2 Corinthians 2:17; 2 Peter 3:16, etc.).

Prayer: *Father, please do Your deeper work in my life. Create in me a clean heart and establish Your truth in my life. In Jesus' name I pray.*

July 15

"Now ye are clean through the word which I have spoken unto you." John 15:3

We are cleansed by the LORD initially and perpetually by hearing, applying and adhering to God's Word.

Scripture informs us that Christ died to purchase a people unto Himself, and He is presently **"sanctify***(ing)* **and cleanse***(ing)* **it** *(His Church)* **with the washing of water by the word."** Jesus will soon return for a Church, a people He has begotten **"to himself a glorious church, not having spot, or wrinkle, or any such thing; ... holy ... without blemish."**

"Christ also loved the church, and gave himself for it; 26 That he might sanctify and cleanse it with the washing of water by the word, 27 That he might present it to himself a glorious church, not having spot, or wrinkle, or any such thing; but that it should be holy and without blemish." Ephesians 5:25-27

Any person who's been born again in the past and yet is not intimately abiding holy with Christ, enduring to the end in Him, should immediately go before the LORD, the throne of grace in repentance (Hebrews 4:14-16).

Prayer: *Father, in Jesus Christ's name I come to You, asking You to forgive my sin of self-idolatry and not seeking You. Please cleanse my heart afresh with the washing of Your Word. Daily I will seek Your face in Your Word, being cleansed continually and increasingly, as I eagerly look for Your soon return LORD Jesus.*

July 16

> "Let no man beguile you of your reward in a voluntary humility and worshipping of angels, intruding into those things which he hath not seen, vainly puffed up by his fleshly mind, ¹⁹ And <u>not holding the Head</u>, from which all the body by joints and bands having nourishment ministered, and knit together, increaseth with the increase of God." Colossians 2:18-19

Those who do not uphold Christ, the only **"Head"** of each one of His people, individually and the whole of His church, are misleading people and blocking the ministry, the divine virtue of the LORD from flowing from Heaven into His body: **"And <u>not holding the Head</u>, from which all the body by joints and bands having nourishment ministered, and knit together, increaseth with the increase of God."**

We must never get in the LORD's way as He alone who has saved a person, also matures that saint. Our walk with Christ is first and foremost an individual relationship between us and the LORD. He is continuing the good work of salvation He alone began in us the day He saved us.

> "Being confident of this very thing, that he which hath begun a good work in you will perform it until the day of Jesus Christ." Philippians 1:6

Prayer: *Thank You Jesus for dying and rising from the dead to save me and for the sins of the whole world. Please teach me Your ways, use me, and please prevent me from getting in the way of Your work in the lives of others. In Jesus' name, amen.*

July 17

"But that on the good ground are they, which in an HONEST and GOOD heart, having heard the word, keep it, and bring forth fruit with patience *(perseverance—to the end)*.**" Luke 8:15**

How much does God value honesty? The only soil that produces a Heaven-bound heart is the last of the four listed in Luke 8:5-15. Only those who choose to have an **"HONEST and GOOD heart"** will be with Him. Such a man is honest with the whole counsel of Holy Scripture

Jesus, please make me Your authentic disciple. Please purify my heart dear LORD.

"Have mercy upon me, O God, according to thy lovingkindness: according unto the multitude of thy tender mercies blot out my transgressions. 2 Wash me throughly from mine iniquity, and cleanse me from my sin. 3 For I acknowledge my transgressions: and my sin is ever before me. 4 Against thee, thee only, have I sinned, and done this evil in thy sight: that thou mightest be justified when thou speakest, and be clear when thou judgest." Psalms 51:1-4

Prayer: *Dear heavenly Father, I come to You in the name of Jesus, admitting that I have fallen short of Your glory by my sin. Here and now I turn back to You. I repent and ask You to clear and cleanse my life of all that offends You. For You are holy, holy, holy. Amen.*

July 18

"Which things also we speak, not in the words which man's wisdom teacheth, but which the Holy Ghost teacheth; comparing spiritual things with spiritual." 1 Corinthians 2:13

"Rightly dividing the word of truth" is the measure for our protection given us by the Lord. This is only possible through personal daily study of God's Word—as we stack, collate each Bible verse that speaks of the topic we are studying—be it mercy, return of Christ, justice, faith, love, judgment, etc.— **"comparing spiritual things with spiritual."**

"Study to shew thyself approved unto God, a workman that needeth not to be ashamed, rightly dividing the word of truth." 2 Timothy 2:15

The importance of personal, daily, organic Bible Study cannot be over-emphasized. Understanding divine truth according as the whole of Holy Scripture reveals it is essential to the student of Christ.

Are you in God's Word daily?

Prayer: *Father, quicken my spirit to hunger and thirst for Your righteousness. Grant a photographic memory for Your Word and a heart that is humble, contrite, authentic and obedient. Please unite my heart to fear Your holy name. In Jesus' name, amen.*

July 19

> "He hath not dealt with us after our sins; nor rewarded us according to our iniquities." Psalms 103:10

Mercy, mercy, mercy. God showed it to us and requires, non-negotiably, that we show it to all others—from our hearts (Matthew 18:21-35).

This is a test—to see if we, who've received unfathomable mercy will show mercy to others...

> **"And be ye kind one to another, tenderhearted, forgiving one another, even as God for Christ's sake hath forgiven you." Ephesians 4:32**

God is **"the Father of mercies"** (2 Corinthians 1:3).

If God wasn't so merciful, WHY would He have saved our wretched souls? Why would the Father have sent His only begotten Son for our sins while we were yet sinners? (See Romans 5:6-8.) Memorize and live Titus 3:5-6. Start now!

> **"Not by works of righteousness which we have done, but according to his mercy he saved us, by the washing of regeneration, and renewing of the Holy Ghost; 6 Which he shed on us abundantly through Jesus Christ our Saviour." Titus 3:5-6**

Prayer: LORD, please rid my heart and mind of all self-righteousness. Let me be truly poor in spirit—ever so desperate and dependent upon You, my only righteousness. In Jesus' name, amen.

July 20

"<u>Blessed is he that readeth</u>, and they that hear the words of this prophecy, and keep those things which are written therein: for the time is at hand." Revelation 1:3

NOTHING REPLACES BIBLE READING. Never has, never will.

There is no greater need in the life of the true remnant disciple than to get into and remain in God's Word (KJB) especially in light of the soon return of Christ (Colossians 3:16; 2 Timothy 2:15).

The student of Christ studies God's Word to know the LORD better, to feed His own spirit, and to share it with others! See 2 Timothy 2:15; 1 Peter 3:15; Proverbs 22:17-21.

The quickest and surest way to get blessed is to simply read God's Word. This is so simple that most miss it.

Among other amazing things, God's Word is our knowledge, our healing oil, substance, wisdom, and comfort. God blesses those who read His Word.

"Blessed is he that readeth." Revelation 1:3

Prayer: *Thank You heavenly Father for the treasure of Your Word which You chose to tangibly, lovingly, preserve for Your people and for mankind. Thank You for blessing those who read Your words. In Jesus' name, amen.*

July 21

"And he said to them all, If any man will come after me, let him deny himself, and take up his cross daily, and follow me. 24 For whosoever will save his life shall lose it: but whosoever will lose his life for my sake, the same shall save it." Luke 9:23-24

These are Jesus' stated terms. Every person following Christ on His terms, is His. All other mere professors have only a **"form of godliness"** (2 Timothy 3:5).

DENY SELF: Give up your own will. Refuse to follow your own will. Deny self any pleasure which doesn't come from nor lead to God.

TAKE UP THE CROSS: Die to sin; crucify it; go against what your flesh would choose to do and instead, embrace God's will (James 4:7).

FOLLOW: Accompany Jesus in His mission as He has given in His Word, empowered by His Spirit, and leading.

The cross—the original Gospel—is central in the divine economy to the Christian faith. Those not learning the cross are not following Jesus (Luke 9:23-24).

Prayer: *Holy Father, in Jesus' name, please bless me to be truly crucified with Christ—to consent to the death and burial of self so that Jesus reigns in this life. Let it be right now Jesus.*

Do you want to know more about how to be saved so you can genuinely follow Jesus? Got to page 381 of this book.

July 22

"But of that day and hour knoweth no man, no, not the angels of heaven, but my Father only. 37 But as the days of Noe were, so shall also the coming of the Son of man be. 38 For as in the days that were before the flood they were eating and drinking, marrying and giving in marriage, until the day that Noe entered into the ark, 39 And knew not until the flood came, and took them all away; so shall also the coming of the Son of man be." **Matthew 24:36-39**

As were the days of Noah, so it is today. Exponential end time evil was foretold (2 Timothy 3:1-7, 13 etc.). The world continues to plunge deeper into evil, calling good evil and evil good, glorying in their shame. This reveals that Christ's coming is soon (Isaiah 5:20-24; Philippians 3:19). Time is **"short"**— **"Therefore rejoice, ye heavens, and ye that dwell in them. Woe to the inhabiters of the earth and of the sea! for the devil is come down unto you, having great wrath, because HE KNOWETH THAT HE HATH BUT A SHORT TIME"** (Revelation 12:12).

Jesus is coming back soon. He warns: **"Be ye therefore ready also: for the Son of man cometh at an hour when ye think not"** (Luke 12:40).

Prayer: *Heavenly Father, I confess that I've not loved and worshipped You with my whole heart. This moment I return to You O God, asking You to forgive my sins and cleanse my heart. Please quicken my spirit to fear, love and obey You. In Jesus' name. Amen.*

July 23

"He hath not dealt with us after our sins; nor rewarded us according to our iniquities. 11 For as the heaven is high above the earth, so great is his mercy toward them that fear him. 12 As far as the east is from the west, so far hath he removed our transgressions from us." Psalms 103:10-12

Wow! Is there a confessed sin from your past or anyone else's you are elevating above the cleansing blood of Christ's Cross? That is idolatry! Repent now and rejoice in His forgiveness! (See 1 John 1:9; Hebrews 8:12; 9:14; Proverbs 28:13.)

NEWS FLASH: If you're a born-again child of God and have confessed an occurrence sin, He has forgiven you and will remember it no more! You are forgiven. You are cleansed. You are free to serve Him!

"How much more shall the blood of Christ, who through the eternal Spirit offered himself without spot to God, purge your conscience from dead works to serve the living God?" Hebrews 9:14

IMPORTANT: Read about the freedom that Christ's work in you brings—Philippians 3:13-14; Hebrews 8:12; 1 John 1:9.

Prayer: *Heavenly Father, thank You for sending Your only begotten Son to singlehandedly die for our sins, providing the perfect salvation which includes initial and ongoing forgiveness of sins as needed. Thank You Jesus for Your perfect sacrifice, redemption, and the forgiveness of all my sins. In Jesus' name, amen.*

July 24

"As newborn babes, desire the sincere milk of the word, that ye may grow thereby:" 1 Peter 2:2

Just as infants need nourishment and ingest soft substances such as milk in order to grow, so new believers must nourish their hearts with God's Word to grow. As we study God's Word, being **"nourished up in the words of faith and of good doctrine,"** we will be equipped to communicate it to others.

"If thou put the brethren in remembrance of these things, thou shalt be a good minister of Jesus Christ, nourished up in the words of faith and of good doctrine, whereunto thou hast attained." 1 Timothy 4:6

Nourishing our inner man with the spiritual food of the One who made us is essential to sustain us and for growth in Christ. To grow in the knowledge of His Word is to grow in Christ—to gain an expanded, increasing revelation of Heaven's King.

"But grow in grace, and in the knowledge of our Lord and Saviour Jesus Christ. To him be glory both now and for ever. Amen." 2 Peter 3:18

Prayer: *Father, in the name of Jesus, please give me an increased hunger for Your truth and teach me Your ways as I study Your Word. Amen.*

July 25

> **"Repent ye therefore, and be converted, that your sins may be blotted out, when the times of refreshing shall come from the presence of the Lord." Acts 3:19**

When we repent (re-turn, turn again) to the LORD with our whole hearts, **"times of refreshing shall come from the presence of the Lord."** God desires to refresh His people and tells us specifically what to do as we come before Him:

> **"O Israel, return unto the LORD thy God; for thou hast fallen by thine iniquity. 2 Take with you words, and turn to the LORD: say unto him, Take away all iniquity, and receive us graciously." Hosea 14:1-2**

In Scripture the words **"return"** and **"repent"** are synonymous. The divine essential of repentance must never be left out of the Gospel message. When it is, such a message conveys a false gospel, **"another gospel"** (Galatians 1:6-9).

Who is in need of a time of refreshing? Anyone who is honest will repent, will turn again to the LORD and seek to abide, to remain ever nearer to Him. Cleansing of sin and refreshing comes from the presence of the LORD when we repent afresh, which means when we simply re-turn, turn again to the LORD.

Prayer: *Father, You are holy. Please make my conscience ever more sensitive to Your convictions. Quicken me in Your holy fear, hasten me toward repentance and being established in Your holiness. In Jesus' name.*

July 26

"And above all these things put on charity, which is the bond of perfectness." Colossians 3:14

Being all knowing, or acting as if you are, is not the measure of your relationship with God. In fact, even if we could be all knowing, if we didn't have HIS love in our hearts and manifested in our lives, we would be nothing (1 Corinthians 13).

Correct knowledge and sound doctrine are very important, and so is *living* it (James 1:22). Sound doctrine teaches that without LOVE (the way God defines it), we are nothing and are not right with Him. Memorize this please. **"He that loveth not, knoweth not God"** (1 John 4:8). Could He have said it any clearer?

May God bless us to be vessels of His great love for others. This is the proof that we know Him and how He makes Himself known to men.

"By this shall all men know that ye are my disciples, IF ye have LOVE one to another." John 13:35

Prayer: *Father, please fill my life with Your love, as only You can do. In Jesus' name, amen.*

July 27

"If thou faint in the day of adversity, thy strength is small." Proverbs 24:10

The reason believers **"faint,"** are unable to stand strong **"in the day of adversity,"** it's because they've drifted—they're not in abiding fellowship with Christ. In other words, they aren't fueled with the Word and aren't living a life of prayer and have fallen away. Jesus is not **"first love"** and therefore they are in need of repentance (Revelation 2:4-5).

Is your strength small or is it large? One disciple said it this way:

*"Lil prayer, lil power.
Lotta prayer, lotta power."*

"Watch and pray, that ye enter not into temptation: the spirit indeed is willing, but the flesh is weak." Matthew 26:41

"But ye, beloved, building up yourselves on your most holy faith, praying in the Holy Ghost." Jude 20

Prayer: *Jesus, I here and now return to You, asking You to forgive my sin of self-idolatry, for not seeking Your holy face continually.*

July 28

> "And we know that all things work together for good to them that love God, to them who are the called according to his purpose. 29 For whom he did foreknow, he also did predestinate to be conformed to the image of his Son, that he might be the firstborn among many brethren." Romans 8:28-29

All things are NOT good— things we've done, things others have done to us, and things happening all around us. Yet GOD, **"who is rich in mercy"** (Ephesians 2:4), orchestrates **"ALL things"** to His eternal glory, using them to conform us to the image of His Son Jesus—the crucified Son who was then raised from the dead. This same death, burial, and risen Gospel is re-enacted in our lives daily.

> "I am crucified with Christ: nevertheless I live; yet not I, but Christ liveth in me: and the life which I now live in the flesh I live by the faith of the Son of God, who loved me, and gave himself for me." Galatians 2:20

In our toil, we also know that God **"is able to do exceeding abundantly above all that we ask or think, according to the power that worketh in us"** (Ephesians 3:20). We know that we are **"hid with Christ in God"** (Colossians 3:3) as we are crucified with Him.

Prayer: Father, in the name of Jesus Christ, please let the work of the cross of Christ have its full effect in my life. In Jesus' holy name.

July 29

"He saith to him again the second time, Simon, son of Jonas, lovest thou me? He saith unto him, Yea, Lord; thou knowest that I love thee. He saith unto him, Feed my sheep." John 21:16

"Feed my sheep"—nurture, feed, protect as any good shepherd would do, so much more **"that great shepherd of the sheep"** whom we serve.

"Now the God of peace, that brought again from the dead our Lord Jesus, that great shepherd of the sheep, through the blood of the everlasting covenant," Hebrews 13:20

Christ's remnant is going to continue to feed Christ's beloved sheep as there is not one thing more important transpiring in the earth (John 21:15-17).

"The lips of the righteous feed many: but fools die for want of wisdom." Proverbs 10:21

Prayer: *Heavenly Father, in Jesus' name, season Your truth in my heart and open the hearts of men to receive it. Please use me to feed Your beloved sheep Jesus. Do Your work in this vessel dear* LORD *and use me for Your glory.*

July 30

"But seek ye first the kingdom of God, and his righteousness; and all these things shall be added unto you." Matthew 6:33

"**First**" refers to priority. It's also to be taken literally by Christ's disciples.

"**First**" means you deliberately put Jesus before and above self as the final authority of your daily life.

WHEN God is truly "**first**" HE is the first One we seek. Our lives are given over to and revolve around Him, around His will and no other.

"<u>**Now set your heart and your soul to seek the L**ORD **your God**</u>**; arise therefore, and build ye the sanctuary of the** L**ORD God, to bring the ark of the covenant of the** L**ORD, and the holy vessels of God, into the house that is to be built to the name of the** L**ORD." 1 Chronicles 22:19**

We now "**set**" our hearts on Him, we seek Him and in so doing, we "**set**" ourselves up to experience His victory over all our enemies!

Prayer: Holy Father, in Jesus' holy name, I here and now set You first in my life—to seek, to worship, to obey, to place You alone as the reigning KING of this life. Into Your hands I now submit my spirit.

July 31

> "Having a form of godliness, but denying the power thereof: from such turn away." 2 Timothy 3:5

Counterfeit religionists are prevalent today and nothing new. They are known in that they put their religion, religious teachings and traditions before God's Word—which is an open denial of Christ.

> "**Well hath Esaias prophesied of you hypocrites,** as it is written, This people honoureth me with their lips, but their heart is far from me. 7 Howbeit in vain do they worship me, teaching for doctrines the commandments of men. 8 For laying aside the commandment of God, ye hold the tradition of men, as the washing of pots and cups: and many other such like things ye do. 9 And he said unto them, Full well ye reject the commandment of God, that ye may keep your own tradition. ... 13 Making the word of God of none effect through your tradition, which ye have delivered: and many such like things do ye." **Mark 7:6-9, 13**

Jesus informs us that those truly **"of God"** non-negotiably uphold His written Word as final divine authority (John 8:47).

> "Beware lest any man spoil you through philosophy and vain deceit, after the tradition of men, after the rudiments of the world, and not after Christ." **Colossians 2:8**

Prayer: *Heavenly Father, please instill in my inner man a holy trust in You, in Your unchanging Word. I love You Jesus.*

August 1

> "He found him in a desert land, and in the waste howling wilderness; he led him about, he instructed him, he kept him as the apple of his eye. 11 As an eagle stirreth up her nest, fluttereth over her young, spreadeth abroad her wings, taketh them, beareth them on her wings: 12 So the LORD alone did lead him, and there was no strange god with him." Deuteronomy 32:10-12

Notice the descriptive language, the metaphors—how the LORD illustrates how He loves, protects, and provides for His people. In Scripture, the LORD uses imagery to communicate truth.

> "He that dwelleth in the secret place of the most High shall abide under the shadow of the Almighty. 2 I will say of the LORD, He is my refuge and my fortress: my God; in him will I trust. 3 Surely he shall deliver thee from the snare of the fowler, and from the noisome pestilence. 4 He shall cover thee with his feathers, and under his wings shalt thou trust: his truth shall be thy shield and buckler." Psalms 91:1-4

Read Psalm 91 often so this truth permeates you. Here the LORD uses the imagery of His **"winged fowl"** creation (Genesis 1:21). GOD made this very creature/bird for the express purpose of showing us how much He loves us and how He comforts, cares and provides for, and protects His own (Psalms 91:1).

Prayer: *Father, please grant that I know and understand You more and more. I love You LORD. In Jesus' name. Amen*

August 2

"The heart is deceitful above all things, and desperately wicked: who can know it?" Jeremiah 17:9

The L ORD knows the wickedness of my heart and of your heart. If I choose not to be truly **"crucified with Christ"** (Galatians 2:20). and therefore, dwell on wickedness of any kind, He sees all the thoughts that I allow to occupy my mind that are not holy, but sinful— **"evil concupiscence"** (Colossians 3:5). He sees where the enemy or my own un-mortified sinful nature feeds thoughts to my mind. I have at times, not guarded my heart by casting down wicked imaginations (2 Corinthians 10:5; Proverbs 4:23). Can you relate? Yet, this must not be (Romans 8:5-8; 12:1-2; Ephesians 4:22-24).

"He that trusteth in his own heart is a fool: but whoso walketh wisely, he shall be delivered." Proverbs 28:26

Prayer: *Holy Father, in Jesus' name, I trust You alone and not my own heart. Please anoint my life to be truly crucified with Christ. Please circumcise my heart dear L ORD. Amen.*

August 3

> **"But God commendeth** (displayed) **his love toward us, in that, while we were yet sinners, Christ died for us." Romans 5:8**

Everyone loves an underdog story and there's no greater underdog story as the redemption of our Creator's fallen race. When sin and Satan had ravaged the human race, bringing incalculable destruction by the alienation of His people from their Maker, we, the whole human race, were hopelessly down and out.

> **"And I sought for a man among them, that should make up the hedge, and stand in the gap before me for the land, that I should not destroy it: but I found none." Ezekiel 22:30**

Yet, as only He could have done, the Lord instituted His plan to redeem. He provided the solution to our sin via **"the Lamb slain from the foundation of the world"** (Revelation 13:8). Throughout biblically recorded history, before the advent of Christ, God prefigures this Lamb who was not only **"slain from the foundation of the world"** but also was coming to die on Calvary for the sin of the world. Knowing all things—past, present and future—He had already determined to redeem, to buy back His fallen race, us. And He did just this as He sent His only begotten Son on a cross to buy us back to Himself!

Prayer: *Father, I want to thank You this moment and forevermore for sending Jesus to die in my place, to purchase me back to Yourself for now and forever! I love You Jesus.*

August 4

"Brethren, I count not myself to have apprehended: but this one thing I do, forgetting those things which are behind, and reaching forth unto those things which are before, ¹⁴ I press toward the mark for the prize of the high calling of God in Christ Jesus." Philippians 3:13-14

Is there anything you'd like to forget—to truly put behind you so that you can move forward with a clear conscience? Perhaps God would have you take this very thing to Him today—for severance, for clearance!

Well in His infinite love, through Christ's perfect sacrifice— **"so great salvation"**—God left nothing out of His salvation package! (See Hebrews 2:3; 2 Peter 1:3-4.)

The instruction here is **"Forgetting those things which are behind"** and when we do, He will enable us to be in His forward motion, **"reaching forth unto those things which are before,"** as we **"press toward the mark for the prize of the high calling of God in Christ Jesus."**

Prayer: *Heavenly Father, through the precious blood of Jesus I bring _____ before You now, asking You to forgive and cleanse me of this sin. I now obey You to forget it. It's now behind me. I love You Jesus and now press toward the mark for the high calling of God in Christ Jesus!*

August 5

> "My brethren, count it all joy when ye fall into divers temptations; 3 Knowing this, that the trying of your faith worketh patience. 4 But let patience have her perfect work, that ye may be perfect and entire, wanting nothing." **James 1:2-4**

To **"count it all joy"** becomes easier as we endure various trials in this life, seeing the hand of our God working in us through them—purging us of things that were a hindrance to our relationship with Him and others.

God has a much grander plan than to just comfort us by lifting us out of situations He's allowing!

While our goal may be immediate deliverance, His aim is the character of Christ being formed in us!

When maturity begins to set in, we welcome those seasons of testing, thanking our LORD for the work He's doing in our lives! (See Romans 8:28-29; Psalms 138:8; Philippians 2:12-13; Romans 5:3.)

> "Blessed is the man that endureth temptation: for when he is tried, he shall receive the crown of life, which the Lord hath promised to them that love him." **James 1:12**

Prayer: *Holy Father, You know best and I here and now thank You for the trials, and for forming Christ in me. In Jesus' name.*

August 6

"O Israel, return unto the LORD thy God; for thou hast fallen by thine iniquity. ² Take with you words, and turn to the LORD: say unto him, Take away all iniquity, and receive us graciously: so will we render the calves of our lips." Hosea 14:1-2

What a call for God's people to cry out to Him! Here the LORD calls us to **"return"** to Him—to re-turn simply means to "turn again" to Him. In His great kindness He gives specific instructions on how this is done. What love!

1. **"Take with you words, and turn to the LORD"**

2. **"say unto him, Take away all iniquity, and receive us graciously"**

The result of the LORD restoring His people is that they **"render the calves of our lips"** which refers to the fruit of their lives reflecting the forgiveness and restoration He provides.

SO, you sinned? Return to God (repentance), confess your sin, and rejoice that He forgave you (1 John 1:9). REMEMBER, God never forgave you on your own merit in the first place. Selah. No, He forgave you on the sole basis of Christ's shed blood for you! He delights to forgive His children when they simply come to Him in faith—faith in Jesus' perfect sacrifice for your sins.

Prayer: *I love You Jesus! Thank You Father for providing the way for Your people to approach You for all their needs. In Jesus' name, amen.*

August 7

> "Take heed, brethren, lest there be in any of you an evil heart of unbelief, in departing from the living God. 13 But exhort one another daily, while it is called To day; lest any of you be hardened through the deceitfulness of sin. 14 For we are made partakers of Christ, if we hold the beginning of our confidence stedfast unto the end; 15 While it is said, To day if ye will hear his voice, harden not your hearts, as in the provocation." Hebrews 3:12-15

This is a severe warning. We must take God's Word at face value and allow no man to soften the blow of this severe divine warning, this declaration. Allowing sin and refusing to repent and turn from sin is a deadly undertaking. Make no mistake: The eternal soul is in the balance. Satan is making a play to remove a child of God.

> "Therefore I will judge you, O house of Israel, every one according to his ways, saith the Lord GOD. Repent, and turn yourselves from all your transgressions; so iniquity shall not be your ruin. 31 Cast away from you all your transgressions, whereby ye have transgressed; and make you a new heart and a new spirit: for why will ye die, O house of Israel?" Ezekiel 18:30-31

Read Mark 9:43-49.

Prayer: *Dear Father, I come to You now in the name of Jesus. Please forgive all my sins, wash and cleanse me. Cause deep conviction and repentance to ever be in my bosom. You are holy!*

August 8

"To wit, that God was in Christ, reconciling the world unto himself, not imputing their trespasses unto them; and hath committed unto us the word of reconciliation." 2 Corinthians 5:19

The ultimate display of mercy is the cross of Jesus Christ.

God gave His only begotten Son for the sin of the world—to buy back a people from the grip of sin and Satan. There is no greater act of love.

"Greater love hath no man than this, that a man lay down his life for his friends." John 15:13

Will you be His? Would you like to bow your heart and head right now before Your God, receiving the blessings of His forgiveness, His salvation, by receiving Christ? Pray this from your heart—with everything that's in you:

Prayer: *Heavenly Father, I've sinned against You. I'm fully guilty and openly admit it before You now. Yet I know You gave Jesus in my place on that cross and that He singlehandedly paid the full price for my sin. Jesus, I ask You now to save, to forgive, to wash me from all my sins. Please be the LORD, the Master of my life, from this moment forward. I'm all Yours now dear LORD. Thank You for saving my soul!*

See *Making Peace with God* beginning on page 381 of this book.

August 9

"In the fear of the Lord is strong confidence: and his children shall have a place of refuge." Proverbs 14:26

"Strong confidence" is only found in fearing God. **"Confidence"** that glorifies God and not man, comes from truly fearing the Lord which means obeying Him.

"Let us hear the conclusion of the whole matter: Fear God, and keep his commandments: for this is the whole duty of man." Ecclesiastes 12:13

"In the fear of the Lord," the born-again believer is **"hid with Christ in God"** and fully assured, full of divine confidence!

"For ye are dead, and your life is hid with Christ in God." Colossians 3:3

Beware of the often-peddled cheap counterfeit, where people are instructed to learn to love themselves. The Bible commands us to love God and others, not self. In fact, loving self is the root sin that brought the original fall of mankind and remains as that sin which keeps men from God—pride in self instead of fearing God!

Prayer: *Father, in Jesus' name, please forgive me for the sin of self-idolatry and not fearing You. I now repent. Please forgive and cleanse me of this sin. I here and now declare and choose to trust You with my life. I love You Jesus!*

August 10

"And they shall teach my people the difference between the holy and profane, and cause them to discern between the unclean and the clean." Ezekiel 44:23

Leaders true to the Lord are known in that they teach discernment. The Lord says His true under-shepherds **"teach my people the difference between the holy and profane."** In doing so, they **"cause them to discern between the unclean and the clean."**

Those who teach discernment inoculate God's people from heresies, from false doctrines that would derail, deceive and damn them. Studying, knowing and understanding the Word of God is essential for the protection of God's people.

"By the word of thy lips I have kept me from the paths of the destroyer." Psalms 17:4

Prayer: *Heavenly Father, please teach me discernment, Your ways, to know You and rightly divide the Word of Your truth. In Jesus' name, amen.*

August 11

> "Beware of false prophets, which come to you in sheep's clothing, but inwardly they are ravening wolves." Matthew 7:15

We see our LORD's warning here. We see all around us those who have allowed themselves to be devoured by the wolves Jesus warns us to **"beware of"** (Matthew 7:15). So many have landed themselves on the spiritual trash heap by allowing themselves to get derailed along the way—many times by false teachers who insist on preaching things that do not align with the WHOLE counsel of God's Word (2 Thessalonians 2:10-12). Many of their prey are willing participants and pigeon-hole themselves into some doctrinal slant or religious framework, thereby living the remainder of their days deceived and ditched. They are then **"Ever learning, and never able to come to the knowledge of the truth"** (2 Timothy 3:7). They thereby limit God or seek Him on some basis other than His Word. This is one reason the psalmist stated that he HATED **"EVERY false way."** Are you walking in a **"false way"**? (See Psalms 119:104, 128.)

Being in Christ is our only safety, following His Word.

> **"Every word of God is pure: he is a shield unto them that put their trust in him. ⁶ Add thou not unto his words, lest he reprove thee, and thou be found a liar." Proverbs 30:5-6**

Prayer: *Father, please quicken my spirit to ever more diligently search and study Your Word. Please protect Thy servant dear LORD. In Jesus' name, amen.*

August 12

"That he might sanctify and cleanse it with the washing of water by the word." Ephesians 5:26

God's Word cannot get into me unless I get into it. When the Word of God is flowing into my system daily, it's like a cleansing flood that washes away the sin, refreshes, and establishes the truth of God in my life.

"Now ye are clean through the word which I have spoken unto you." John 15:3

When the Word is flowing into my heart and mind daily, it washes out the unrest, the anxiety, the fear, the stain of sin, the guilt, the unbelief, the hatred, the strivings, etc. Think: We all know the refreshing blessing of taking a shower after a sweaty day or work out and yet what about the purifying refreshment of a cleansing for the inner man? The washing of water of God's Word is something known only to those who are in His Word! Amen Jesus!

Prayer: *Holy Father, please cleanse me of all that does not belong to You. Imbue my innermost man with the deep hunger to know You, to be established in Thy truth, and to be fruitful for Your eternal glory. In Jesus' name, amen LORD.*

Have you been saved by the cleansing blood of Jesus Christ? If you would like to know more, go to page 381 of this book.

August 13

"But after that the kindness and love of God our Saviour toward man appeared." Titus 3:4

"The kindness and love of God" was never more manifested than on the cross of Christ.

> "This is a faithful saying, and worthy of all acceptation, that Christ Jesus came into the world to save sinners; of whom I am chief." 1 Timothy 1:15

God gave His only begotten Son who was crucified on a cruel wooden cross, when you and I were **"aliens ... having no hope, and without God in the world."**

> "That at that time ye were without Christ, being aliens from the commonwealth of Israel, and strangers from the covenants of promise, having no hope, and without God in the world:" Ephesians 2:12

We are fully indebted to our Savior, to our God—to live unto Him and no other!

> "And that he died for all, that they which live should not henceforth live unto themselves, but unto him which died for them, and rose again." 2 Corinthians 5:15

Prayer: *Father, in Jesus' name I thank You for the sacrifice of Your only begotten Son. I love You Jesus. Here and now I lay my life into Your holy hands. Amen.*

August 14

> "And as it is appointed unto men once to die, but after this the judgment:" Hebrews 9:27

Judgment Day is on the way. No man escapes.

> "For we must all appear before the judgment seat of Christ; that every one may receive the things done in his body, according to that he hath done, whether it be good or bad." 2 Corinthians 5:10

One writer notes: *"So it will be for the despisers of the Blood of the Covenant. One can become self-delusional about the judgment of God, believing that he or she is immune, but it will come anyway at the appointed time."*

> "Because sentence against an evil work is not executed speedily, therefore the heart of the sons of men is fully set in them to do evil." Ecclesiastes 8:11

The prayer of the psalmist:

> "So teach us to number our days, that we may apply our hearts unto wisdom." Psalms 90:12

Prayer: *Father, please quicken my spirit concerning Your judgment—that I will stand before You to give full account of my life in this world. In Jesus' name, amen.*

August 15

> **"Now unto him that is able to do exceeding abundantly above all that we ask or think, according to the power that worketh in us," Ephesians 3:20**

At times, do we not cry out in our toil, *"But I just can't do it!"* It's true that we cannot walk with the LORD in our own will power, our flesh. Yet, HE most surely can bring to pass His perfect will, with no exception, each and every day in the life of the crucified saint. Ephesians 3:20 anyone? Jesus is always able to bring to pass what He stated in His Word, what He commands, expects, what He began in us when He saved us, and what He ordains in our lives.

> **"Work out your own salvation with fear and trembling. 13 For it is God which worketh in you both to will and to do of his good pleasure." Philippians 2:12-13**

> **"The LORD will perfect that which concerneth me: thy mercy, O LORD, endureth for ever: forsake not the works of thine own hands." Psalms 138:8**

Prayer: *Holy Father, I do not want to waste another moment striving in the flesh, doing things outside of oneness, outside of an abiding intimacy with You. Do Your work in me dear LORD, I ask. I am Your clay and You are the Potter. In Jesus' name, amen.*

August 16

"And when he was demanded of the Pharisees, when the kingdom of God should come, he answered them and said, The kingdom of God cometh not with observation *(hostile watching)*: [21] **Neither shall they say, Lo here! or, lo there! for, behold, the kingdom of God is within you."　Luke 17:20-21**

We need not run around frantically looking for the coming of the KING and His kingdom because **"the kingdom of God is within you."** The domain of the KING is in us—KING-dom! That's what it means.

Some people are so busy trying to figure out exactly when Jesus is coming back and how the end time events are going to unfold that they aren't preparing themselves to meet Him! They aren't ready to meet Jesus nor helping others to be prepared for the soon return of Christ. Fruitfulness comes from an abiding relationship with Christ.

Living in fear destroys present fruitfulness. Many today jump from one end times ministry to another, fueling their anxiety with speculations. They are perpetually incapacitated from the daily abiding and fruitfulness Jesus ordains (John 15:1-16).

Prayer: *Father, please ground me in You, establish Your kingdom and its fruitfulness in my life. In Jesus' name, amen.*

August 17

> "But IF we walk in the light, as he is in the light, we have fellowship one with another, and the blood of Jesus Christ his Son cleanseth us from all sin." 1 John 1:7

After being saved initially, ongoing washing/cleansing is essential in order to remain in relationship with the LORD who is holy (1 Peter 1:15-16). Many falsely teach that salvation is a one-time event with no further personal responsibility for the recipient of the gift of God in Christ. Nonsense. Initial salvation requires repentance and faith and so does our entire abiding walk with Christ in this world—till we are with Him (John 15:1-6).

> "If we say that we have no sin, we deceive ourselves, and the truth is not in us. ⁹ If we confess our sins, he is faithful and just to forgive us our sins, and to cleanse us from all unrighteousness." 1 John 1:8-9

Our walk with God is a relationship between two parties which requires engaging with Him and remaining holy as He is holy. Any leader in the church world not teaching this is a wolf.

> "Having therefore these promises, dearly beloved, let us cleanse ourselves from all filthiness of the flesh and spirit, perfecting holiness in the fear of God." 2 Corinthians 7:1

Prayer: *Father, in Jesus' name, please teach me Your ways. Quicken my spirit in repentance, confession of all sin, and to be established soundly in Thy truth. Amen.*

August 18

> "Teach me, O Lᴏʀᴅ, the way of thy statutes; and I shall keep it unto the end." Psalms 119:33

Here is God's stated way, to be learned by each of His disciples:

Three Essentials for Christ's Saints

1. The Word

> "Study to shew thyself approved unto God, a workman that needeth not to be ashamed, rightly dividing the word of truth." 2 Timothy 2:15

2. Prayer

> "But thou, when thou prayest, enter into thy closet, and when thou hast shut thy door, pray to thy Father which in secret; and thy Father which seeth in secret shall reward thee openly." Matthew 6:6

3. Real fellowship

> "Not forsaking the assembling of ourselves together, as the manner of some is; but exhorting one another: and so much the more, as ye see the day approaching." Hebrews 10:25

Prayer: *Father, in Jesus' name, please teach me Your ways, teach me what's most important to You and bless my life with Your grace to accomplish such. Thank You* Lᴏʀᴅ *Jesus.*

August 19

> "For in my wrath I smote thee, but in my favour have I had mercy on thee." Isaiah 60:10

In their rebellion against Him, God allowed evil to come upon His children. Though He is holy and just, the LORD desires to forgive, to redeem and to restore. He requires that His conditions be met.

> "The Lord is ... longsuffering to us-ward, not willing that any should perish, but that all should come to repentance." 2 Peter 3:9

Scripture features the sin of man and the restoration of God. The sins of Abraham, Moses, and David are captured and their restoration. God requires repentance and confession of sins. They had to reap what they sowed. God didn't shut them out, turn against them or disown them. He restored them (Psalms 51; Luke 15).

Some wonder *"Has God forsaken me?" "Why do I feel He's done with me?" "Why do I not sense His presence in my life anymore?"* Also, some wonder *"Have I gone too far?! Has God rejected me?"*

The LORD gave us these patriarchal examples for our own learning and comfort.

> "For whatsoever things were written aforetime *(the Holy Scriptures)* were written for our learning, that we through patience and comfort of the scriptures might have hope." Romans 15:4

Prayer: *Father, thank You for desiring to restore. Grant my heart true and holy conviction and repentance. In Jesus' name.*

August 20

> "**For if ye live after the flesh, ye shall die: but if ye through the Spirit do mortify the deeds of the body, ye shall live. 14 For as many as are led by the Spirit of God, they are the sons of God.**" Romans 8:13-14

If you wish to be powerfully led of the Spirit of God, you must embrace the crucified life. "**If ye through the Spirit do mortify the deeds of the body, ye shall live**" (Romans 8:13). Note that as we submit our lives to the LORD, His Holy Spirit works to enable our flesh to be crucified— "**through the Spirit.**"

The primary way we are blessed to be used of God, to be dominated and led by the Holy Ghost instead of the flesh, is to be given over to the LORD in the crucified life! In the above passage, verse 13 precedes verse 14 by divine design. As we are practically "**crucified with Christ**" (Galatians 2:20), His divine life is going to teem in us and flow through us in ministry to others!

> "**So then death worketh in us, but life in you.**"
> **2 Corinthians 4:12**

Prayer: *Jesus, I am crucified with You. Thank You for anointing my life to be dead and buried and raised up in Your grace and power! In Jesus' name. Amen!*

August 21

> "Or despisest thou the riches of his goodness and forbearance and longsuffering; not knowing that the goodness of God leadeth thee to repentance? 5 But after thy hardness and impenitent heart treasurest up unto thyself wrath against the day of wrath and revelation of the righteous judgment of God; 6 Who will render to every man according to his deeds." Romans 2:4-6

It's only in Christ, presently, practically, that sin is overcome. Those living in sin are not **"in him** *(Christ)"* and under divine condemnation.

> **"Whosoever committeth sin transgresseth also the law: for sin is the transgression of the law.** 5 **And ye know that he was manifested to take away our sins; and <u>in him is no sin</u>.** 6 **Whosoever abideth** *(dwells, remains)* **IN HIM sinneth not: whosoever sinneth hath not seen him, neither known him."** 1 John 3:4-6

Prayer: *Jesus, I want to truly be in You, both positionally and practically, in reality, walking separated unto You, holy. Please do this work in me dear* LORD. *In Jesus' name, amen.*

August 22

"Study to shew thyself approved unto God, a workman that needeth not to be ashamed, rightly dividing the word of truth." 2 Timothy 2:15

To **"study"** and know, understand and rightly divide God's Word doesn't take man's seminary. We already have God's Book, the Bible. In its simplest definition to **"study"** means to read and while you read, to pay close, prayer-filled attention, asking the Author of Holy Scripture to grant you His understanding.

"Blessed is he that readeth." Revelation 1:3

- Bible reading/study is key to learning the things of God (Proverbs 22:17-21).

- Bible study is paramount to spiritual growth (1 Peter 2:2; Psalms 119).

- Reading God's Word etches the image of Christ upon the canvass of the heart (Lk 24:27; Jn 5:39, 46).

God blesses those who read His Word.

"Let the word of Christ dwell in you richly *(abundantly)* in all wisdom; teaching and admonishing one another in psalms and hymns and spiritual songs, singing with grace in your hearts to the Lord." Colossians 3:16

Prayer: *Dear Father, make me a man/woman of Your Word, Your truth. Bless this heart to be contrite, sincere and authentic. In Jesus' name, amen.*

August 23

"For ye are dead, and your life is hid with Christ in God." Colossians 3:3

Every person not **"hid with Christ in God"** is going away in judgment (Colossians 3:3; Romans 8:13; Galatians 5:19-21, 24). When we are **"hid with Christ in God,"** we are safe, secure, and under the blessings of His divine grace instead of His condemnation.

What some don't realize is that just because they were saved in the past in no way means they are still in Christ. This is why we read things like this throughout Scripture:

> **"Examine yourselves, whether ye be in the faith; prove your own selves. Know ye not your own selves, how that Jesus Christ is in you, except ye be reprobates? 2 Corinthians 13:5**

We must judge ourselves against God's Word.

> **"For if we would judge ourselves, we should not be judged. 32 But when we are judged, we are chastened of the Lord, that we should not be condemned with the world." 1 Corinthians 11:31-32**

Prayer: Father please penetrate my heart with Your holy conviction, granting true repentance and obedience. In Jesus' name, amen.

August 24

"Who is among you that feareth the LORD, that obeyeth the voice of his servant, that walketh in darkness, and hath no light? let him trust in the name of the LORD, and stay upon his God." Isaiah 50:10

God is speaking to His own people here, encouraging them to **"trust in the name of the LORD, and stay upon his God."** When difficult seasons come upon our lives, we must cling to the LORD. God seeks to purify our faith during these times.

> **"Wherein ye greatly rejoice, though now for a season, if need be, ye are in heaviness through manifold temptations** *(tests, trials)***: 7 That the trial of your faith, being much more precious than of gold that perisheth, though it be tried with fire, might be found unto praise and honour and glory at the appearing of Jesus Christ: 8 Whom having not seen, ye love; in whom, though now ye see him not, yet believing, ye rejoice with joy unspeakable and full of glory." 1 Peter 1:6-8**

Jesus suffered and promised we'd suffer for His name's sake also (Matthew 10:22; Luke 6:22-26; John 15:20, etc.).

> **"But the God of all grace, who hath called us unto his eternal glory by Christ Jesus, after that ye have suffered a while, make you perfect, stablish, strengthen, settle you." 1 Peter 5:10**

Prayer: *LORD, please purify my love, faith and life in You. In Jesus' name, amen.*

August 25

"Now when John had heard in the prison the works of Christ, he sent two of his disciples, 3 And said unto him, Art thou he that should come, or do we look for another? 4 Jesus answered and said unto them, Go and shew John again those things which ye do hear and see: 5 The blind receive their sight, and the lame walk, the lepers are cleansed, and the deaf hear, the dead are raised up, and the poor have the gospel preached to them. 6 And blessed is he, whosoever shall not be offended in me." Matthew 11:2-6

At this time John the Baptist had been taken into custody by the civil authorities for exposing the adultery of king Herod (Luke 7:18-29; Mark 6:14-29). Apparently, understandably, in his incarceration he'd grown weak in faith and so asked his disciples to go ask Jesus to confirm if He was the Messiah. To confirm to him that He's the Messiah, Jesus did not send John the Baptist a rebuke but rather a testimony of the miracles He was doing. What a Savior!

When we are weak, our Savior invites us to **"Come unto me ... ye shall find rest"** (Matthew 11:28-30). Jesus desires to build the faith of His true followers, never to injure or destroy it or them.

Prayer: *Father, in the name of Jesus, I ask You to increase my faith, to fortify and build it. Thank You my LORD.*

August 26

"And in that day ye shall ask me nothing. Verily, verily, I say unto you, Whatsoever ye shall ask the Father in my name, he will give it you. [24] Hitherto have ye asked nothing in my name: ask, and ye shall receive, that your joy may be full." John 16:23-24

Biblical protocol is praying to the Father in the name (authority) of Jesus Christ.

Successful praying is not about over-thinking and straining but rather trusting and simply praying God's Word in Jesus' mighty name for others (and yourself). God is going to answer prayer based on these things:

1. **"Ye must be born again"** (John 3:3, 7)—God only answers the prayers of those who are in His family and that only happens through Jesus Christ (John 14:6; 16:23-24; 1 Timothy 2:5; Hebrews 7:24-26, etc.).

2. We must pray to our Heavenly Father in Jesus' holy name (John 14:13; 16:23-24, etc.).

3. We must pray according to God's will which is God's Word (Psalms 119:105; James 4:3, etc.).

Prayer: *Precious Father, I come to You now in the name of Jesus, asking You to sanctify my life. Let me be truly crucified with Jesus and teach me to pray. Amen.*

August 27

"My little children, let us not love in word, neither in tongue; but in deed and in truth. 19 And hereby we know that we are of the truth, and shall assure our hearts before him." 1 John 3:18-19

Assurance in our hearts comes with our worshipful obedience to our LORD. God requires more than just lip service. Words are cheap when they are not accompanied with corresponding obedient action.

"But be ye doers of the word, and not hearers only, deceiving your own selves." James 1:22

By obeying God's Word practically, you demonstrate that you truly know and are loving Christ above self. He is the Master of your life, not yourself. We obey God out of love. Obedience to God is an expression of our love for God.

Prayer: *Father, may this life be crucified with Christ, truly. Let me be genuinely sincere and humble. Purify my heart to be authentic to the core. In Jesus' name, amen.*

There's an eternity of difference between being religious and being truly saved. If you have any doubt whatsoever, check out page 381 to make sure of your salvation.

August 28

> "The fear of the L`ORD` is a fountain of life, to depart from the snares of death." **Proverbs 14:27**

Departing from sin, which is **"the snare of death,"** is essential to enduring to the end with our L`ORD`. Read Mark 9:43-49 in the King James Bible.

Fearing God, not just reverencing but also fearing Him, is important.

> "Sanctify the L`ORD` of hosts himself; and let him be your fear, and let him be your dread." **Isaiah 8:13**

We must never soften the blow of the divine command to fear God.

> "Serve the L`ORD` with fear, and rejoice with trembling. [12] Kiss the Son, lest he be angry, and ye perish from the way, when his wrath is kindled but a little. Blessed are all they that put their trust in him." **Psalms 2:11-12**

Fearing God is a command and the beginning of wisdom (Proverbs 9:10), keeping the believer from being snared by sin and Satan. The fear of the L`ORD` is a daily choice.

> "For that they hated knowledge, and did not choose the fear of the L`ORD`." **Proverbs 1:29**

Prayer: *Father, I choose to fear You. I love You and know You are holy. I acknowledge and confess my sins to You now, asking You to forgive me, cleanse and establish Your kingdom in my life. In Jesus' name.*

August 29

"Whom we **preach**, **warning** every man, and **teaching** every man in all wisdom; that we may present every man perfect in Christ Jesus." Colossians 1:28

Here we see that the apostle Paul did three things to prepare God's people to meet Christ at His soon return. PWT = Preach, Warn, Teach. This gives us specific insight into the doctrine and ministry of Christ's apostles. Balanced ministry includes all three of these elements.

To preach is to speak the Word of God with the invitation to repent and obey it. To warn is to quicken God's people to beware of the many false prophets and to take cover in the truth lest we fall away with them. And to teach is to communicate biblical truth in order to establish, to soundly ground God's people in His Word.

In order to become a balanced, fully equipped mature disciple (1 Corinthians 4:15), we must tend to feeding, nourishing and also warning Gods' people (Colossians 1:28).

Prayer: *Father, please ground Your people in Your truth and quicken us with Your warnings. In Jesus' name, amen.*

August 30

"For as many as are led by the Spirit of God, they are the sons of God." Romans 8:14

The true disciple of Jesus desires to be led of Him and to know that such is the case. Right?

We can be assured that it is His will that we **"know"** we are saved and that we are His and being led by Him (1 John 5:13).

"The steps of a good man are ordered by the LORD: and he delighteth in his way." Psalms 37:23

As we seek God daily in His Word, asking Him to lead us by His Spirit, we can be sure that He will.

"Order my steps in thy word: and let not any iniquity have dominion over me." Psalms 119:133

Many today claim to be led of the Spirit while saying and doing things that contradict God's Word. Be sure that God will never contradict His written Word. The primary way He leads His body, His individual saints, is by His Word.

"Thy word is a lamp unto my feet, and a light unto my path." Psalms 119:105

Prayer: *Dear Father, please bless me to be led of You in all things. In Jesus' name, amen.*

August 31

"The discretion of a man deferreth his anger; and it is his glory to pass over a transgression." Proverbs 19:11

It is very important to walk in the Spirit with the LORD—to walk in the wisdom of His Word, powered by the Holy Spirit. Memorizing the following verse of Holy Scripture has immensely helped my life and will certainly bless yours if you will retain it in memory and meditation.

> "He that is slow to wrath is of great understanding: but he that is hasty of spirit exalteth folly." Proverbs 14:29

Anger destroys. The history of humanity is littered with death and destruction due to anger not dealt with in wisdom but rather acted out in wickedness.

> "Be not hasty in thy spirit to be angry: for anger resteth in the bosom of fools." Ecclesiastes 7:9

Being crucified with Christ is essential to overcoming the flesh (Galatians 2:20).

> "Be ye angry, and sin not: let not the sun go down upon your wrath: 27 Neither give place to the devil." Ephesians 4:26-27

Prayer: *Father, please fill my heart with Your love and all the fruits thereof. Get to the root of all anger in my life. Diffuse it with repentance and the establishment of Your truth. In Jesus' name, amen.*

September 1

> "But I keep under my body, and bring it into subjection: lest that by any means, when I have preached to others, I myself should be a castaway." 1 Corinthians 9:27

Keeping under our bodies speaks of a continual essential. Keeping under means subduing the old man by crucifying it daily. This language speaks to the necessity of the daily cross—crucifying the iniquitous, fallen nature so that Christ alone reigns (Romans 6-8, etc.).

Paul makes it plain that he doesn't believe he is unconditionally eternally secure and that he also could be **"a castaway"** if he doesn't endure to the end with Christ—which requires obedience to His cross command:

> "And he said to *them* all, If any *man* will come after me, let him deny himself, and take up his cross daily, and follow me. ²⁴ For whosoever will save his life shall lose it: but whosoever will lose his life for my sake, the same shall save it." Luke 9:23-24

Prayer: LORD, *in the name of Jesus I seek You! I love You Jesus and thank You so very much for dying for my sins—to bring me into relationship with You and the Father. My soul follows hard after You dear* LORD.

September 2

> **"For we are not as MANY, which corrupt** *(twist, pervert)* **the word of God: but as of sincerity, but as of God, in the sight of God speak we in Christ."**
> **2 Corinthians 2:17**

In this late hour, dishonesty with the Scriptures is at an all-time high.

All personal agendas must be crucified!

> **"Therefore seeing we have this ministry, as we have received mercy, we faint not; 2 But have renounced the hidden things of dishonesty, not walking in craftiness, nor handling the word of God deceitfully; but by manifestation of the truth commending ourselves to every man's conscience in the sight of God." 2 Corinthians 4:1-2**

Of the self-serving wolves who hold ministry positions, Paul writes:

> **"(For many walk, of whom I have told you often, and now tell you even weeping, that they are the enemies of the cross of Christ: 19 Whose end is destruction, whose God is their belly** *[carnal appetites]*, **and whose glory is in their shame, who mind earthly things.)" Philippians 3:18-19**

Prayer: *Holy Father, please purify my heart of all evil. I am crucified with Christ! In Jesus' name, amen.*

September 3

"But thou, when thou prayest, enter into thy closet, and when thou hast shut thy door, pray to thy Father which is in secret; and thy Father which seeth in secret shall reward thee openly." Matthew 6:6

Praying to the Father in *private* yields the *public* blessing of God upon our lives.

Beginning our day drawing nigh unto our LORD is the best way to begin!

"Unless in the first waking moment of the day you learn to fling the door wide back and let God in, you will work on a wrong level all day; but swing the door wide open and pray to your Father in secret, and every public thing will be stamped with the presence of God." Oswald Chambers, My Utmost for His Highest

Is your heart truly fixed upon the LORD? Are you seeking His face?

"My heart is fixed, O God, my heart is fixed: I will sing and give praise." Psalms 57:7

Prayer: *Dear LORD, I set my heart and my eyes upon You. My heart is fixed O God, my heart is fixed. I will praise, thank, worship and seek Your holy face. I love You LORD. In Jesus' name, amen.*

September 4

"Epaphras, who is one of you, a servant of Christ, saluteth you, always labouring fervently for you in prayers, that ye may stand perfect and complete in all the will of God." Colossians 4:12

Emulating Epaphras is a great endeavor—to lift God's people in prayer, which is among the most noble duties of every disciple!

Gospel Key: At the knowledge of one powerful truth, you and I never again need to wonder about how to pray for others. Here God tells us exactly how to pray! Here it is: Request of Him that God's people **"may stand perfect and complete in all the will of God."**

What an example of Christlikeness! Epaphras interceded for the saints just like Jesus did in redemption and does now in intercession for those He died to save (Hebrews 7:24-25).

Prayer: *Dear Father, please teach me to pray like Your disciple Epaphras—to seek Your face in prayer, asking You to bless Your saints to stand perfect and complete in all Your will. In Jesus' name, amen.*

September 5

> "For by grace are ye saved through faith; and that not of yourselves: it is the gift of God: [9] Not of works, lest any man should boast. [10] For we are his workmanship, created in Christ Jesus unto good works, which God hath before ordained that we should walk in them." Ephesians 2:8-10

We are saved by God **"by grace"** and not our own works. Yet, there is so much in God's Word about good fruit and good works. Good works and good fruit do not save and yet they are the proof that we possess saving faith via true repentance ... whereby the work of Christ in us manifests in the fruit of good works. Remember, those truly saved by grace **"are his workmanship"** (Ephesians 2:8-10).

The biblical correlation of true repentance and good fruit are essential in discernment. Remember how our LORD told us how we will know ourselves and others? **"By their fruits ye shall know them"** (Matthew 7:16, 20). John the Baptist commanded: **"Repent ye: for the kingdom of heaven is at hand. ... Bring forth therefore fruits meet** *(fitting)* **for repentance"** (Matthew 3:4, 8).

When a person truly repents, the good fruit will always follow.

Prayer: *Dear Father, bless me to truly abide and bear good fruit for Your glory. In Jesus' name.*

September 6

> "See, I have this day set thee over the nations and over the kingdoms, to root out, and to pull down, and to destroy, and to throw down, to build, and to plant." Jeremiah 1:10

God has a plan to remove that which does not belong in you and to establish what does.

WHEN the Word is flowing in and through your life like a river, it will cleanse like a river! A full-scale embarking on studying God's Word will cleanse you and establish you in divine truth! Dabbling in the Word is like a mere trickle.

God is working in the hearts and lives of each of His people and He requires and expects our personal participation. He has to root things out of us, every one of us, before He begins building and planting in us. Get to know Jeremiah 1:10 closely. *"LORD change me"* is a great daily prayer.

We didn't make up the terms. GOD did. We repent and obey or perish. Be engaged in His plan to cleanse you.

Prayer: *Holy Father, I ask You to change me. Do Your deeper work in my life. Here this moment I lay my life in Your hands. Have Your way dear LORD. In Jesus' name, amen.*

If you died today, are you 100% certain you'd be in Heaven and not hell? God wants you with Him! Check out page 381 to make sure.

September 7

> "And I gave her space to repent of her fornication; and she repented not." Revelation 2:21

Even Jezebel was given **"space to repent."** Repentance is a must for eternal glory. Of this, Frank Telford writes:

"Our gracious and loving heavenly Father has so much patience for His children that He gives us time to repent. Now what happens when He gives some time to repent and they choose not too? Their hearts become hard, their conscience gets seared with a hot iron and their minds become reprobate. Their sins also become more grotesque and perverted in the process."

> **"Take heed, brethren, lest there be in any of you an evil heart of unbelief, in departing from the living God. 13 But exhort one another daily, while it is called To day; lest any of you be hardened through the deceitfulness of sin. 14 For we are made partakers of Christ, if we hold the beginning of our confidence stedfast unto the end; 15 While it is said, To day if ye will hear his voice, harden not your hearts, as in the provocation." Hebrews 3:12-15**

Prayer: *Father, in Jesus' name, please grant me a heart of flesh. Take away the stony places in my heart that came through sin. Please purify this vessel of every trace of iniquity.*

September 8

"He must increase, but I must decrease." John 3:30

Have you declared this today as John the Baptist did? Is your own crucifixion with Christ a settled issue? If not, iniquity can never be overcome and will plague your life—until you consent to be truly **"crucified with Christ"** (Galatians 2:20).

Those who don't camp on this message of the cross, will not experience the victory Christ died to procure for His beloved saints. It's only in bowing down low that God will lift His people high. This is the death, burial, and resurrection in our daily lives.

Though nearly never heard in the modern church, the message of the cross is an irreplaceable mainstay of the original Gospel. The cross is central to the original Gospel.

> **"I am crucified with Christ: nevertheless I live; yet not I, but Christ liveth in me: and the life which I now live in the flesh I live by the faith of the Son of God, who loved me, and gave himself for me." Galatians 2:20**

> **"For ye are dead, and your life is hid with Christ in God." Colossians 3:3**

Prayer: Holy Father, You gave us Your only begotten Son to rescue us and You gave us Your written Word for all things that pertain unto life and godliness in this life. Please bless me to be given over to You. I declare myself to be crucified with Christ, this moment. In Jesus' name, amen.

September 9

> "And it came to pass, as he had made an end of speaking all these words, that the ground clave asunder that was under them: 32 And the earth opened her mouth, and swallowed them up, and their houses, and all the men that appertained unto Korah, and all their goods. 33 They, and all that appertained to them, went down alive into the pit, and the earth closed upon them: and they perished from among the congregation." Numbers 16:31-33

IF God doesn't send backsliders to hell, what's this? Why did God open the earth and send His own people to hell, irrevocably, if falling away from Him were not possible? Note: No person could possibly slide back from something they never possessed. 1 Corinthians 10:1-12 records the five sins that kept the very children of God out of their promised land. God is holy and the wages of sin is still death (Isaiah 6:3; Romans 6:23; Revelation 4:8).

Jesus says that someone who believes and is saved can then afterward **"fall away"** (Luke 8:13). Jesus also says, speaking of those **"in me"** that they will be cast into the fire if they do not **"abide"** in Him, which means to remain in Him (John 15:6). Paul said that if believers don't continue in the goodness of God, they will receive the **"severity"** of His judgment and be **"cut off"** (Romans 11:20-22).

Prayer: *LORD please keep me ever close to You in the abiding life You've ordained for each of Your disciples. Cleanse me afresh and protect me from following false doctrines, false teachers. In Jesus' name, amen!*

September 10

> "Till I come, give attendance to READING, to EXHORTATION, to DOCTRINE. ... Take heed unto thyself, and unto the doctrine; continue in them: for in doing this thou shalt both save thyself, and them that hear thee." 1 Timothy 4:13, 16

R.E.D. Alert – "to Reading, to Exhortation, to Doctrine"

- "Reading"—we need more Bible reading.

- "Exhortation"—we need more exhorting and daily encouraging among the body of Christ.

- "Doctrine"—our whole belief system, eternity, and lifestyle is based and contingent upon embracing sound biblical truth/doctrine. To underscore the importance placed upon correct doctrine, it is interesting to observe that the word "**doctrine**" appears 51 times in God's Word.

Saint of Christ, are you in God's Word richly and daily, being nourished with His blessed truths? (See Colossians 3:16; Acts 2:42.) If so, you are to be putting His children in remembrance of these truths as we look together for His soon return. When we do this, we are considered "**a good minister of Jesus Christ.**"

> "If thou put the brethren in remembrance of these things, thou shalt be a good minister of Jesus Christ, nourished up in the words of faith and of good doctrine, whereunto thou hast attained." 1 Timothy 4:6

Prayer: *LORD, please ground me in Thy Word, in Jesus' name.*

September 11

"Hell and destruction are before the Lord: how much more then the hearts of the children of men?" Proverbs 15:11

God looks down from Heaven with every man in mind as each is at risk of going to the place originally made for **"the devil and his angels"** when they rebelled (Matthew 25:41).

God gave His only begotten Son to save **"all men"** and yet He gave men free will—to receive or to reject Him and His plan (Joshua 24:15). Before going to the cross, Jesus declared that He was going to seek out every man, giving them the choice to be saved:

> **"Who will have all men to be saved, and to come unto the knowledge of the truth." 1 Timothy 2:4**

> **"And he is the propitiation for our sins: and not for ours only, but also for the sins of the whole world." 1 John 2:2**

> **"The Lord is ... not willing that any should perish, but that all should come to repentance." 2 Peter 3:9**

Hell is a prison which now and forever will house all who die in sin instead of in Christ. It will be cast into the lake of fire (Revelation 20:14). It's a one-way trip. There is no release date, nor will consciousness ever cease or be diminished (Mark 9:43-49).

Prayer: *Father, please use me to help inform others of Your great love for them—and how You gave Your only begotten Son to save, to forgive them. In Jesus' name, amen.*

September 12

> **"The law of thy mouth is better unto me than thousands of gold and silver." Psalms 119:72**

You can't find gold unless you dig for it! Searching, digging and unearthing the golden nuggets of truth, God's Word, is the adventure embarked upon by every true follower of Christ.

Any man or woman who ever walked closely with the LORD, esteemed His Word as the **"gold and silver"** of their lives—the highest priority. Job counted the words of God more important than physical food.

> **"Neither have I gone back from the commandment of his lips; I have esteemed the words of his mouth more than my necessary food." Job 23:13**

To study God's Word is to seek Him and to learn of Him and have Christ revealed. There is no short cut nor undertaking so rewarding. No activity on earth will yield more good fruit than the searching and studying of the very words of God.

> **"Study to shew thyself approved unto God, a workman that needeth not to be ashamed, rightly dividing the word of truth." 2 Timothy 2:15**

> **"Seek ye out of the book of the LORD, and read: no one of these shall fail." Isaiah 34:16**

Prayer: *Father, please quicken, lead and bless the study of Your Word by Your people. In Jesus' name, amen.*

September 13

> "My sheep hear my voice, and I know them, and they follow me: ²⁸ And I give unto them eternal life; and they shall never perish, neither shall any man pluck them out of my hand. ²⁹ My Father, which gave them me, is greater than all; and no man is able to pluck them out of my Father's hand." John 10:27-29

Take a closer look. Anchor the promise in verses 28-29 on verse 27 where Jesus identifies who His sheep are—those who hear and continue to hear His voice and continue to follow Him (present tense). The promise to be kept is a conditional promise requiring the individual recipient of the gift of God to continue to hear His voice and follow Him (John 10:27-29). Many today detach our Lord's words in verse 27 from verses 28-29 of John 10. In doing so, they perpetrate their "eternal security" mythology. Beware as this was the first lie Satan told mankind, which led to the fall (Genesis 2:17; 3:4).

> "Who are kept by the power of God <u>through faith unto salvation</u> ready to be revealed in the last time." 1 Peter 1:5

The recipient of salvation must **"through faith"** be **"kept."** God never removes man's free will and requires not only initial but also continued faith. Jesus foretold that some would be saved and then not continue with Him and **"fall away"** (Luke 8:12-13).

> "Receiving the end of your faith, even the salvation of your souls." 1 Peter 1:9

Prayer: *Father, You are holy and require my faith to the end of this life. Make sensitive my conscience, quicken my spirit to repentance and to be holy as You are holy. In Jesus' name.*

September 14

> **"My soul followeth hard after thee: thy right hand upholdeth me." Psalms 63:8**

The soul of the disciple must follow hard after the Lord in diligence, not slothfulness. Those who are daily diligent in seeking Jesus will be full of the Holy Spirit and prosper in Christ. Those who don't will grow weak and fall away.

> **"Slothfulness casteth into a deep sleep; and an idle soul shall suffer hunger." Proverbs 19:15**

Being filled with our Lord's presence is His gift to those who **"do hunger and thirst after righteousness."**

> **"Blessed are they which do hunger and thirst after righteousness: for they shall be filled." Matthew 5:6**

Seeking the Savior upon waking in the mornings is earnest obedience of truly putting Him first and not self. Jesus means for us to take Him seriously and literally when He says:

> **"But seek ye first the kingdom of God, and his righteousness; and all these things shall be added unto you." Matthew 6:33**

Prayer: *Lord, my soul follows hard after You. I love You Jesus and thank You for dying for my sins and reigning in my life today. This moment Lord into Your hands I submit my spirit, soul and body. In Jesus' name, amen.*

September 15

> "But by the grace of God I am what I am: and his grace which was bestowed upon me was not in vain; but I laboured more abundantly than they all: yet not I, but the grace of God which was with me." 1 Corinthians 15:10

Paul was able to boast in the LORD, not in himself. Here Christ's apostle grants us a powerful key to true New Testament ministry and how it's accomplished—by God and not us! The grace, the divine influence, the divine enablement labors in and through those yielded, crucified vessels. Christ is **"the resurrection and the life"** and He reciprocally raises up those who are humbly bowed down in death and burial (John 11:25).

> "Always bearing about in the body the dying of the Lord Jesus, that the life also of Jesus might be made manifest in our body. 11 For we which live are alway delivered unto death for Jesus' sake, that the life also of Jesus might be made manifest in our mortal flesh. 12 So then death worketh in us, but life in you." 2 Corinthians 4:10-12

Who does the LORD raise up?

> "The LORD upholdeth all that fall, and raiseth up all those that be bowed down." Psalms 145:14

Prayer: *Teach me dear LORD to consent to my own death and burial so that this life is all You! In Jesus' name, amen.*

September 16

> "And he that reapeth receiveth wages, and gathereth fruit unto life eternal: that both he that soweth and he that reapeth may rejoice together." John 4:36

There are eternal rewards, **"wages"** to be laid up. Many lay up treasure, savings for the end of their lives in this fleeting world while few lay it up in Heaven where the dividends will never cease yielding the highest rewards (Matthew 6:19-21).

Jesus commanded us to **"lay up treasure in Heaven"** and He daily lays those opportunities in front of us—to serve Him by serving others (Matthew 6:19-21; Acts 4:34-37; 1 Corinthians 16:1-2; 2 Corinthians 9:6-11; Galatians 6:6. etc.). What incentive!

> **"Lay not up for yourselves treasures upon earth, where moth and rust doth corrupt, and where thieves break through and steal: 20 But lay up for yourselves treasures in heaven, where neither moth nor rust doth corrupt, and where thieves do not break through nor steal: 21 For where your treasure is, there will your heart be also." Matthew 6:19-21**

> **"But this I say, He which soweth sparingly shall reap also sparingly; and he which soweth bountifully shall reap also bountifully. 7 Every man according as he purposeth in his heart, so let him give; not grudgingly, or of necessity: for God loveth a cheerful giver." 2 Corinthians 9:7**

Prayer: *Father, in Jesus' name, please teach my heart Your wisdom, and grant an eternal kingdom perspective.*

September 17

> "But we had the sentence of death in ourselves, that we should not trust in ourselves, but in God which raiseth the dead:" 2 Corinthians 1:9

Have you sentenced yourself to death? Declare the following words aloud, from your heart, in agreement with the Lord:

> "And they that are Christ's have crucified the flesh with the affections and lusts." Galatians 5:24

Your life is over—Christ's has begun!

> "I am crucified with Christ: nevertheless I live; yet not I, but Christ liveth in me: and the life which I now live in the flesh I live by the faith of the Son of God, who loved me, and gave himself for me." Galatians 2:20

Declare this today concerning your life:

> "For ye are dead, and your life is hid with Christ in God." Colossians 3:3

Prayer: *Heavenly Father, please anoint my life to be truly dead and buried with Christ this moment. Thank You for raising me up to please You alone. In Jesus' name, amen.*

September 18

"The lord of that servant shall come in a day when he looketh not for him." Matthew 24:50

Jesus foretells here that many will be caught off guard when He returns. As pertaining to the return of Jesus, believers are repeatedly warned, throughout Holy Scripture to **"be ye therefore ready."** If there were no danger of losing out, of being shut out of His kingdom, these divine warnings would not exist. Read Jesus' parable of the Ten Virgins in Matthew 25:1-13.

"Be ye therefore ready also: for the Son of man cometh at an hour when ye think not." Luke 12:40

JESUS IS COMING - Ready or not.

Any minister who is not constantly preaching Christ, the cross, the blood, repentance, judgment to come and being ready for the return of Jesus, is a wolf.

Prayer: *Father, deliver me from all sin and false doctrine and every false teacher. I want to know You and be with You eternally. In Jesus' name.*

Are you sure you are ready to meet Jesus when He comes? Find out for certain by turning to page 381 of this book and read about *Making Peace with God.*

September 19

"I will not drive them out from before thee in one year; lest the land become desolate, and the beast of the field multiply against thee. ³⁰ By little and little I will drive them out from before thee, until thou be increased, and inherit the land." Exodus 23:29-30

"This is a pre-figurement of progressive sanctification through the cross!" A disciple

Sanctification begins immediately when He saves us and yet doesn't happen all at once, by divine design. Have you ever felt like your walk with Christ wasn't moving forward as you had hoped? Justification is where He begins, then sanctification ensues and by divine design, it's **"little and little."**

God here promises to drive out Israel's enemies and yet, not all at once. For the good of His people, the LORD was going to drive out their enemies **"by little and little"** which means little by little. It was for their own good. Removing all our enemies suddenly could cause problems due to the abruptness of the removal of the blessed tension of warfare.

"It is important, not only to see, but to love, the gradual processes of God. ... The special subject to which the text spiritually and allegorically refers is the conquest of sin. For such as the old inhabitants of the land of Canaan were to Israel, such the old inhabitants of our hearts are to us." Unknown

Prayer: *Father, thank You for finding and saving me from sin and into Your eternal family. Thank You for continuing to work in me both to will and to do of Your good pleasure, perfecting that which concerns my life in You. In Jesus' name.*

September 20

> **"Deep calleth unto deep at the noise of thy waterspouts: all thy waves and thy billows are gone over me." Psalms 42:7**

Raising up requires dying downward. The cross life is central to the Christian life.

> **"That I may know him, and the power of his resurrection, and the fellowship of his sufferings** *(death and burial),* **being made conformable unto his death." Philippians 3:10**

One disciple penned these words:

"There is a place deep inside of me that thirsts for His living water that I might thirst no more. There is a place deep inside of me that yearns to know the breadth, the length, the depth, the height of His love. There is a place inside of me that cries out to know the power of His resurrection and what is the exceeding greatness of His power toward me. There is a place inside of me that hungers to know His Joy because it is my only strength. There is a place deep inside of me that longs for Him because I am complete only in Him. Without Him, I am nothing. There is a place inside of me that is desperate for Him. There is a place inside of me that cries out to that place deep inside of Him that I may know Him and one day see Him face to face. Did not my heart burn within me as He talked to me and while He opened to me the Scriptures? As the deer panteth for the water, so my soul longeth after thee and 'Deep cries out to Deep! O how the Spirit and the Bride say, 'Come, Lord Jesus!'"

Prayer: LORD I want to know You. Let it be, please dear LORD. I love You. In Jesus' name, amen.

September 21

> "For unto you it is given in the behalf of Christ, not only to believe on him, but also to suffer for his sake;" **Philippians 1:29**

His saints **"suffer for his sake."** Suffering in this fallen world is a reality and suffering for Christ is as much a reality. Those who are known by Him who is **"the light of the world"** shine in the darkness (John 8:12; Matthew 5:13-16). As our LORD suffered persecution, so shall His servants.

> "If the world hate you, ye know that it hated me before it hated you. [19] If ye were of the world, the world would love his own: but because ye are not of the world, but I have chosen you out of the world, therefore the world hateth you. [20] Remember the word that I said unto you, The servant is not greater than his lord. If they have persecuted me, they will also persecute you; if they have kept my saying, they will keep yours also." **John 15:18-20**

Prayer: Thank You dear Father for sending Your only begotten Son to purchase me back to You by shedding His own precious blood. Please fill this Your vessel with Your love for all as I choose to rejoice when persecuted for my LORD Jesus Christ's sake. In the name of Jesus, amen.

September 22

> "Bless the LORD, O my soul, and forget not all his benefits:" Psalms 103:2

The LORD **"daily loadeth us with benefits"** (Psalms 68:19) and we are not to forget from whose hands those blessings come (James 1:17). Forgetting God was a major sin of Israel about which Scripture specifically warns us.

> "Yea, they turned back and tempted God, and limited the Holy One of Israel." Psalms 78:41

> "But thou shalt remember the LORD thy God: for it is he that giveth thee power to get wealth, that he may establish his covenant which he sware unto thy fathers, as it is this day." Deuteronomy 8:18

Forgetting God simply equals not holding Christ as **"first love"** above all others, all else (Revelation 2:4-5). The LORD has warned His people not to forget Him.

Those who forget God—who do not keep the LORD first—are doomed downward, both now and in eternity.

> "The wicked shall be turned into hell, and all the nations that forget God." Psalms 9:17

Prayer: *Father, imbue my being with Your fear. Quicken me in Your holy fear. Let misery of spirit fill my heart if I ever forget, if I ever waver from following hard after You. In Jesus' name, amen.*

September 23

> "Knowing therefore the terror of the Lord, we persuade men; but we are made manifest unto God; and I trust also are made manifest in your consciences." 2 Corinthians 5:11

Christ's apostle Paul speaks up to **"persuade men"** due to **"the terror of the Lord."** In fact, just a few chapters forward, he commands God's people to **"Examine yourselves, whether ye be in the faith; prove your own selves. Know ye not your own selves, how that Jesus Christ is in you, except ye be reprobates?"** (2 Corinthians 13:5).

As a true servant of Christ, Paul knew the jeopardy of believers falling away and losing all—because that's what Jesus taught (Luke 8:13). Paul never spoke in the heretical terms as so many false teachers today who induce lukewarmness as they promulgate the myth of eternal security—guaranteeing something God never promised. All true under-shepherds of Christ will continually warn believers of **"the terror of the Lord"** coming on all who die in sin and how hell will be worse for those who once knew Christ and then fell away (Ezekiel 33:12-13; 2 Peter 2:20-21; Hebrews 10:29).

False teachers quickly pour water on the flames of the holy fear of God!

> "Serve the LORD with fear, and rejoice with trembling. 12 Kiss the Son, lest he be angry, and ye perish from the way, when his wrath is kindled but a little." Psalms 2:11-12

Prayer: *Father, instill Your holy fear in me, in Jesus' name.*

September 24

> **"For we preach not ourselves, but Christ Jesus the Lord; and ourselves your servants for Jesus' sake."**
> **2 Corinthians 4:5**

Because there is no cross, no crucified life in their own personal lives, most ministers today make it about them, not Jesus.

Many today patronize false ministries where Christ is not truly elevated but rather His holy name is used to elevate the mere organizations and the men in charge of ministries.

When is the last time you heard a message on Christ, from the Scriptures? Think about it: Most messages today are scant on Scripture and they cater to the audience's "felt needs" and comfort, to help them live their best life now (2 Timothy 4:2-4).

The grand subject of all of Scripture is the LORD Jesus Christ. Yet, ministers of Satan, posing as representatives of Christ, hide Him! Beware!

> **"Search the scriptures; for in them ye think ye have eternal life: and they are they which testify of me. 40 And ye will not come to me, that ye might have life." John 5:39-40**

Prayer: *Heavenly Father, please let me know You. May Christ truly be my all in all! In Jesus' name, amen.*

September 25

> "He that overcometh shall inherit all things; and I will be his God, and he shall be my son. 8 But the fearful, and unbelieving, and the abominable, and murderers, and whoremongers, and sorcerers, and idolaters, and all liars, shall have their part in the lake which burneth with fire and brimstone: which is the second death." Revelation 21:7-8

Without exception, Jesus warned each of the seven churches in Revelation, chapters 2 and 3, that they must overcome to be with Him eternally. Here He's warning us by citing the specific sins that clearly reveal that such transgressors are not abiding in Him. Paul lists 17 soul damning **"works of the flesh"** (Galatians 5:19-21).

Throughout Scripture the LORD names the classes of sinners going to the lake of fire. Those who will be eternally with Christ must follow Him to the end.

> "But Christ as a son over his own house; whose house are we, if we hold fast the confidence and the rejoicing of the hope firm unto the end. ... Take heed, brethren, lest there be in any of you an evil heart of unbelief, in departing from the living God. 13 But exhort one another daily, while it is called To day; lest any of you be hardened through the deceitfulness of sin. 14 For we are made partakers of Christ, if we hold the beginning of our confidence stedfast unto the end;" Hebrews 3:6, 12-14

Prayer: *Unite my heart to fear Your holy name LORD. Make me holy. In Jesus' name.*

September 26

"For we are not as many, which corrupt *(twist, misuse, manipulate)* the word of God: but as of sincerity, but as of God, in the sight of God speak we in Christ." 2 Corinthians 2:17

REFUSING TO RIGHTLY DIVIDE THE WHOLE OF GOD'S WORD: One of the ways these agents of Satan peddle their wares is when they selectively, crassly pass over and ignore certain Bible verses which contradict their evil agenda. They do this in order to keep the party line (tradition) and continue to peddle their wares! (See 2 Corinthians 2:17; 2 Timothy 2:15.)

Scripture instructs God's people to consider and never ignore **"all scripture"** (1 Corinthians 2:13; 2 Timothy 3:16). Ministers who ignore the whole of Scripture manifestly declare that they are the very wolves Christ that His holy apostles so often warned us about! Beware.

The only way to escape being deceived by the **"MANY false prophets"** Jesus warned would **"deceive many"** is to study and know God's Word for yourself (Matthew 24:11). There are no short cuts.

Memorize 2 Timothy 2:15 today from the King James Bible.

Prayer: *Father, make me an astute student, a disciple of Your kingdom. Please use me to help others, in Jesus' name!*

September 27

> "And walk in love, as Christ also hath loved us, and hath given himself for us an offering and a sacrifice to God for a sweetsmelling savour." Ephesians 5:2

To **"walk in love"** is of the highest priority to the Lord. Study this important topic, asking God to fill you with His love and all the corresponding fruit thereof (Galatians 5:22-23). How can those who claim to know He who **"is love"** not walk in His love? (See 1 John 4:8, 16.)

> "Though I speak with the tongues of men and of angels, and have not charity, I am become as sounding brass, or a tinkling cymbal. 2 And though I have the gift of prophecy, and understand all mysteries, and all knowledge; and though I have all faith, so that I could remove mountains, and have not charity, I am nothing. 3 And though I bestow all my goods to feed the poor, and though I give my body to be burned, and have not charity, it profiteth me nothing. 4 Charity suffereth long, and is kind; charity envieth not; charity vaunteth not itself, is not puffed up, 5 Doth not behave itself unseemly, seeketh not her own, is not easily provoked, thinketh no evil; 6 Rejoiceth not in iniquity, but rejoiceth in the truth; 7 Beareth all things, believeth all things, hopeth all things, endureth all things. 8 Charity never faileth." 1 Corinthians 13:1-8

Prayer: *Father, You are love. Please fill my heart and life with Your love—to pour on others. In Jesus' name, amen.*

September 28

> "But thou, when thou prayest, enter into thy closet, and when thou hast shut thy door, pray to thy Father which is in secret; and thy Father which seeth in secret shall reward thee openly." Matthew 6:6

Private prayer is essential to the disciple. Jesus reveals here that those who seek His face in prayer privately, will be used of Him publicly!

Are you at Christ's feet? Do you live a life of prayer? Have you ever studied the life of Christ and beheld the many instances of His prayer life?

> "And in the morning, rising up a great while before day, he went out, and departed into a solitary place, and there prayed." Mark 1:35

If we want to assess our true spiritual state with God, we need only look to our prayer life or lack thereof. Show me a man's prayer life, and I will show you who that man is! When God is truly first in a person's life, all else will be demoted in importance!

> "Nevertheless I have somewhat against thee, because thou hast left thy first love. [5] Remember therefore from whence thou art fallen, and repent, and do the first works; or else I will come unto thee quickly, and will remove thy candlestick out of his place, except thou repent." Revelation 2:4-5

Prayer: *Heavenly Father, I return to You now. Please forgive my sin of prayerlessness. Break me* LORD*. In Jesus' name, amen.*

September 29

> "Open rebuke is better than secret love. ⁶ Faithful are the wounds of a friend; but the kisses of an enemy are deceitful." Proverbs 27:5-6

To speak the truth that convicts and exposes evil is "better than secret love." "Secret love" is love that is deceitfully hidden to the harm of others!

Have you, like myself, ever been rebuked? And, can you relate to the fruit a godly rebuke brings to our lives?

At times, when moved upon by the LORD, we must issue forth a rebuke. Such a rebuke that comes from Heaven is meant to ultimately bring the recipient to repentance and to be soundly grounded in the truth. These two can never be separated— truth and love!

> "But speaking the truth in love, may grow up into him in all things, which is the head, even Christ." Ephesians 4:15

The divine aim of truth is always out of God's love! David cried:

> "Let the righteous smite me; it shall be a kindness: and let him reprove me; it shall be an excellent oil, which shall not break my head: for yet my prayer also shall be in their calamities." Psalms 141:5

Prayer: *Father, please rebuke me where and when needed. Like Your servant David, I ask You to let Your people rebuke my sin and error. In Jesus' name, amen.*

September 30

> **"Be careful** *(anxious)* **for nothing; but in every thing by prayer and supplication with thanksgiving let your requests be made known unto God. 7 And the peace of God, which passeth all understanding, shall keep your hearts and minds through Christ Jesus." Philippians 4:6-7**

In other words, we are to rest in the LORD's perfect providence when we've lifted something to Him in prayer. A **"supplication"** is simply a humble request we submit to the LORD. We need not be anxious, or full of care about anything after we've prayed about it! It's in God's hands now!

Those who walk with God live by faith and can gloriously **"dwell safely, and shall be quiet from fear of evil."**

> **"But whoso hearkeneth unto me shall dwell safely, and shall be quiet from fear of evil." Proverbs 1:33**

"The peace of God ... shall keep" the **"hearts"** of all who trust in the LORD instead of self.

> **"Pray without ceasing." 1 Thessalonians 5:17**

Prayer: *Father in Heaven, in Jesus' name, please forgive my sin of self-dependence and lack of faith in You! I love You LORD. You alone are my Savior, my Source, my Supply, my Sustenance and my Success! Without You I can do nothing LORD Jesus!*

October 1

> "Then said Jesus, Father, forgive them; for they know not what they do." Luke 23:34

Jesus forgave us while we had the hammer in our hand, nailing the Son of God to the cross! We are fully guilty in the eyes of a holy God. Yet, we've hypocritically judged others in our hearts. **"Father, forgive them"** is the slaying love of God that should floor us—that He would send His only begotten Son for our sins.

The LORD commands—requires—that we show His mercy and love, His forgiveness to all others. With not one exception, eternal hell awaits all who don't (Matthew 18:34).

> "And when ye stand praying, forgive, if ye have ought against any: that your Father also which is in heaven may forgive you your trespasses. 26 But if ye do not forgive, neither will your Father which is in heaven forgive your trespasses." Mark 11:25-26

God has shown us the ultimate kindness and mercy. Now He commands us to pour it out on others!

> "And be ye kind one to another, tenderhearted, forgiving one another, even as God for Christ's sake hath forgiven you." Ephesians 4:32 (memorize today).

Prayer: *Holy Father, I've been wicked. I've sinned against You grossly—in word, attitude and transgression. Now, I hang my head in shame before Your Majesty. Here this moment I ask You to forgive my sins afresh through the blood of my LORD Jesus. In Jesus' name. Amen.*

October 2

> "Now set your heart and your soul to seek the LORD your God; arise therefore, and build ye the sanctuary of the LORD God, to bring the ark of the covenant of the LORD, and the holy vessels of God, into the house that is to be built to the name of the LORD." 1 Chronicles 22:19

Setting our hearts to seek the LORD is a deliberate decision and action. God will use those who do such. Those who seek Him are known of God and will be used to build the sanctuary, to build the kingdom of God in the hearts of men.

> "If a man therefore purge himself from these, he shall be a vessel unto honour, sanctified, and meet for the master's use, and prepared unto every good work." 2 Timothy 2:21

Jesus uses crucified vessels! Being rooted in Christ, in His cross, crucified with Him, means being raised up by Him! His fruit will always result. All who seek His holy face embrace the cross. The following verse captures the truth of who is genuinely in Christ and the resulting fruit of their relationship with Him in the crucified life.

> "And the remnant that is escaped of the house of Judah shall again take root downward, and bear fruit upward:" Isaiah 37:31

Prayer: *Father, I turn afresh to You, crucified with my LORD Jesus. Please help me be perpetually dead and buried, that You might raise up this life for Your good pleasure. In Jesus' name.*

October 3

> "For if ye live after the flesh, ye shall die: but if ye through the Spirit do mortify the deeds of the body, ye shall live. ¹⁴ For as many as are led by the Spirit of God, they are the sons of God." Romans 8:13-14

LOTS of people claim to be led by the Holy Spirit. Jesus anoints His people with His Holy Ghost to put to death the deeds of the body! (See Romans 8:13-14.) If you are truly full of and led by the Holy Spirit, you are denying yourself, taking up the cross daily and authentically following Him (Luke 9:23-24, etc.). We seldom hear these things together ... yet they are biblically inseparable!

Those not learning to die to self are not being led by the Holy Spirit whatsoever. Many today sit under false leaders who do not preach the original Gospel, beginning with the essential command to repent, deny self, take up the cross and follow Jesus (Matthew 3:2; 4:17; 16:24-25, etc.).

> "Then said Jesus unto his disciples, If any man will come after me, let him deny himself, and take up his cross, and follow me. ²⁵ For whosoever will save his life shall lose it: and whosoever will lose his life for my sake shall find it." Matthew 16:24-25

Prayer: *Jesus, please let me be truly crucified with Thee this day—dead, buried, and raised up by You!*

October 4

> **"And every man that hath this hope in him purifieth himself, even as he is pure." 1 John 3:3**

Here's how you know if you are ready to meet Jesus—whether by dying or His soon return. The context of the Bible verse above is the return of Jesus and being ready for it (1 John 2:24-3:3). Those who live for Christ long to see Him and look expectantly for His soon return. This world is not their home.

Those not purifying their lives (washing daily in the blood and water of His Word), do not live daily with the hope of Christ's return. Memorize 1 John 3:3 today.

Your present spiritual state is what matters most to God. In the following passage, carefully note the state of the Church—the people for whom Jesus will soon return.

> **"Christ also loved the church, and gave himself for it; 26 That he might sanctify and cleanse it with the washing of water by the word, 27 That he might present it to himself a glorious church, not having spot, or wrinkle, or any such thing; but that it should be holy and without blemish." Ephesians 5:25-27**

Prayer: *Father, I know You are holy and will have Your holy Bride whom Jesus died to purchase. Please purify my heart, mind and life of all that defiles. Make me holy dear* LORD, *as You alone can do. In Jesus' name, amen.*

October 5

> "Therefore I will judge you, O house of Israel, every one according to his ways, saith the Lord GOD. Repent, and turn yourselves from all your transgressions; so iniquity shall not be your ruin. 31 Cast away from you all your transgressions, whereby ye have transgressed; and make you a new heart and a new spirit: for why will ye die, O house of Israel? 32 For I have no pleasure in the death of him that dieth, saith the Lord GOD: wherefore turn yourselves, and live ye." Ezekiel 18:30-32

This is yet another severe divine warning to the people of God.

As you read God's Word, pay close attention to the many warnings. As you **"study to shew thyself approved unto God,"** you will notice that there are many warnings which the honest student of Christ must synthesize in order to be **"rightly dividing the word of truth"** (2 Timothy 2:15).

Paul told us that one of the three things he did to prepare Christ's body for His soon return was to warn them (Colossians 1:28).

> **"Beware lest ye also, being led away with the error of the wicked, fall from your own stedfastness."** 2 Peter 3:17

Prayer: *Father, in Jesus' name, may Your warning resound in the hearts of Your people, to hasten them in repentance to Your feet.*

October 6

"For the Son of man is come to seek and to save that which was lost." Luke 19:10

"**That which was lost**": The relationship between God and man was severed, when Adam and Eve sinned (Genesis 3).

"But your iniquities have separated between you and your God, and your sins have hid his face from you, that he will not hear." Isaiah 59:2

The Savior solved the separation as He alone could do—by paying the full price for our sins on the cross and then coming after us, to find and restore us back to the Father and Himself!

"Godly sorrow also leads to repentance—sorrow when we realize how we have rejected His love in favor of sin (2 Corinthians 7:9-10)" A disciple

In His drawing us to Himself there is a conviction, a convincing that we are in sin which separates us from Him, His love—being **"alienated from the life of God"** and **"dead** *(separated)* **in trespasses and sin"** (Ephesians 2:1; 4:18). This is a divine granting of the gift of repentance.

Our alienation from Him and our reconciliation with the LORD are both found here— **"But now being made free from sin, and become servants to God, ye have your fruit unto holiness, and the end everlasting life. 23 For the wages of sin is death; but the gift of God is eternal life through Jesus Christ our Lord"** (Romans 6:22-23).

Prayer: *Dear LORD Jesus thank You for Your perfect sacrifice for the sins of the whole world—and for me!*

October 7

"Well; because of unbelief they were broken off, and thou standest by faith. Be not highminded, but fear: 21 For if God spared not the natural branches, take heed lest he also spare not thee. 22 Behold therefore the goodness and severity of God: on them which fell, severity; but toward thee, goodness, IF thou continue in his goodness: otherwise thou also shalt be cut off." Romans 11:20-22

The word **"if"** in Scripture always denotes condition. Salvation is conditional, not un-conditional. God is not forced to keep anyone He's saved if they rebel. And He won't. Notice this severe warning which most ministries both evade and wax over. Notice how those who are saved and choose to not **"continue"** to abide with Christ, will be **"cut off"** just as the people of God in the Old Testament rebelled and were **"cut off"** from Him.

"If a man abide *(remain, continue)* **not in me, he is cast forth as a branch, and is withered; and men gather them, and cast them into the fire, and they are burned." John 15:6**

Prayer: Holy Father, I ask You to convict and fill my innermost being with Your holy fear. Please hasten my life to be holy as You are holy. In Jesus' name, amen.

If you died today, are you 100% certain you'd be in Heaven and not hell? God wants you with Him! Check out page 381 to make sure.

October 8

> "That in the dispensation of the fulness of times he might gather together in one all things in Christ, both which are in heaven, and which are on earth; even in him: 11 In whom also we have obtained an inheritance, being predestinated according to the purpose of him who worketh all things after the counsel of his own will:" Ephesians 1:10-11

God's grand plan is stated in His Word. He is going to ultimately, in eternity, bring His children into **"the exceeding riches of his grace."**

> "That in the ages to come he might shew the exceeding riches of his grace in his kindness toward us through Christ Jesus." Ephesians 2:7

No matter what afflictions we face in this life, it's going to all be worth it when we are with Him!

> "For here have we no continuing city, but we seek one to come." Hebrews 13:14

May the Lord grant to our hearts an eternal perspective.

> "And if children, then heirs; heirs of God, and joint-heirs with Christ; if so be that we suffer with him, that we may be also glorified together. 18 For I reckon that the sufferings of this present time are not worthy to be compared with the glory which shall be revealed in us." Romans 8:17-18

Prayer: *Heavenly Father, please open the eyes of my heart's understanding to see Your grand, eternal perspective. Fill me afresh with the joy of Your beautiful salvation. In Jesus' name, amen.*

October 9

> "These are wells without water, clouds that are carried with a tempest; to whom the mist of darkness is reserved for ever." 2 Peter 2:17

A LOT of ministry, especially on the internet, is designed to touch you emotionally and yet, there's no change of life when you're all done watching and listening and reading. It doesn't contain any divine substance. If it doesn't begin with the divine command, the non-negotiable Gospel essential of repenting (Matthew 3:2; 4:17; Acts 2:38; 3:19, etc.), it's one of the prophesied ear-tickling counterfeit ministries.

> "Preach the word; be instant in season, out of season; reprove, rebuke, exhort with all longsuffering and doctrine. 3 For the time will come when they will not endure sound doctrine; but after their own lusts shall they heap to themselves teachers, having itching ears; 4 And they shall turn away their ears from the truth, and shall be turned unto fables." 2 Timothy 4:2-4

Those who refuse to get into God's Word for themselves will be turned over to **"fables"**—stories, fairy tales.

Many today would rather find someone to tell them what the Bible says instead of studying it for themselves. Deadly mistake. Hand write and memorize 2 Timothy 2:15 today!

Prayer: *Father, in Jesus' name, please forgive me for the sin of bidding God speed to Your enemies who pose as Your servants. Please teach me to discern between the true and the false.*

October 10

> "If we confess our sins, he is faithful and just to forgive us our sins, and to cleanse us from all unrighteousness." 1 John 1:9

What confessed sin of your life or anyone else's are you elevating above the blood of Christ's cross? That is idolatry! Repent now and rejoice in His forgiveness! Read Psalms 103:10-12.

> "For I will be merciful to their unrighteousness, and their sins and their iniquities will I remember no more." Hebrews 8:12

Although we cannot escape reaping according to how we have sown, the LORD's forgiveness is perfect toward those who fear and therefore obey Him by repenting and confessing all sin (Galatians 6:7-8).

> "How much more shall the blood of Christ, who through the eternal Spirit offered himself without spot to God, PURGE YOUR CONSCIENCE from dead works to serve the living God?" Hebrews 9:14

> "Brethren, I count not myself to have apprehended: but this one thing I do, forgetting those things which are behind, and reaching forth unto those things which are before, 14 I press toward the mark for the prize of the high calling of God in Christ Jesus." Philippians 3:13-14

Prayer: LORD, please let Your precious blood now, this moment, cleanse all my sins all the way to the conscience level. I lay my life in Your holy hands right this moment, without reserve. In Jesus' name, amen.

October 11

"Verily, verily, I say unto you, Except a corn of wheat fall into the ground and die, it abideth alone: but if it die, it bringeth forth much fruit. 25 He that loveth his life shall lose it; and he that hateth his life in this world shall keep it unto life eternal." John 12:24-25

Here Jesus speaks of His own death, burial and resurrection—the Gospel (1 Corinthians 15:1-4). Also, the need for believers to follow Him in their daily lives by dying to self and allowing Him to raise them up! (Death, burial, resurrection.) The Christian life will not work without the power generator of this cross principle working in the lives of God's people daily.

The Gospel key to glorifying the LORD is the cross He bled on and the one He commanded us to take up daily! There will never be victory for those who evade this truth. They will be **"Ever learning, and never able to come to the knowledge of the truth"** (2 Timothy 3:7).

The cross is at center stage in the divine economy. Is the cross at center stage in your heart and life? Are you ready to lay down and lose your life today and begin experiencing the resurrection power of Christ? (See John 11:25.) Are you ready to be engrossed in the cross and raised up by Christ's divine power and grace?

This central Gospel truth has been lost, forgotten and yet, that doesn't diminish anything from it, nor does this apostasy negate our accountability to do things God's way—the cross.

Prayer: *LORD, I count myself right now to be dead and buried—crucified with Christ. Thank You Jesus!*

October 12

> "Be not rash with thy mouth, and let not thine heart be hasty to utter any thing before God: for God is in heaven, and thou upon earth: therefore let thy words be few." Ecclesiastes 5:2

"Let thy words be few" is a good biblical phrase to commit to memory, right now.

> "A fool uttereth all his mind: but a wise man keepeth it in till afterwards." Proverbs 29:11

Ever hear someone say, "I'm an open book"? To some this means that they hold nothing back, uttering all that is in their minds. Yet God's Word instructs us that this is not wisdom and always leads to more sin.

> "In the multitude of words there wanteth *(lacketh)* not sin: but he that refraineth his lips is wise." Proverbs 10:19

Prophetically of Christ (before He came to the earth) the Word says that He would have **"the tongue of the learned"**:

> "The Lord GOD hath given me the tongue of the learned, that I should know how to speak a word in season to him that is weary: he wakeneth morning by morning, he wakeneth mine ear to hear as the learned." Isaiah 50:4

Prayer: *Heavenly Father, please circumcise my heart, cut away all that doesn't belong to You. Let this heart be purified and please set a watch before my mouth. Let my words speak Your truth and edify others. In Jesus' name, amen.*

October 13

> "And we have known and believed the love that God hath to us. God is love; and he that dwelleth in love dwelleth in God, and God in him. 17 Herein is our love made perfect, that we may have boldness in the day of judgment: because as he is, so are we in this world. 18 There is no fear in love; but perfect love casteth out fear: because fear hath torment. He that feareth is not made perfect in love." 1 John 4:16-18

The evil fear, **"the spirit of fear"** (2 Timothy 1:7) will be cast out as God's love interpenetrates the life of His saints! So, with this in mind, the focus should not be on wrestling with the fear but rather becoming more and more one with the Lord—just exactly as Jesus prayed to the Father for us in His glorious prayer recorded in John 17. Pour over this!

As we grow in the grace of Christ, knowing Him more and more, fear will have less and less a hold on us. **"Perfect love casteth out fear."**

The believer need not try to overcome fear, to wrestle with fear itself, but rather to be one with Christ whereby he who **"is love"** will drive all ungodly fear from our lives (1 John 4:16-18).

Prayer: *Father, You created me to know You. Please let me know You more and more, just like my Lord Jesus prayed for me and for all who are Yours. In Jesus' name, amen!*

October 14

"Let nothing be done through strife or vainglory; but in lowliness of mind let each esteem other better than themselves. ⁴ Look not every man on his own things, but every man also on the things of others. ⁵ Let this mind be in you, which was also in Christ Jesus." Philippians 2:3-5

The mind of Christ ... what does that mean? How do we walk in it? What is the mind or disposition, attitude of Christ? What should mine be?

HOW TO BEGIN OUR DAY ... Think heart posture. We are here on earth where the LORD has us for now, to serve Him and others and not ourselves. (Read Matthew 20:24-28.) This is how we follow Jesus!

Are you elevating other people ABOVE— "**BETTER than**"— yourself? This is the very **"mind of Christ"** (1 Corinthians 2:16).

When God is working in us, we are crucified with Christ, setting ourselves aside. This is the place He brings us, without fail (Matthew 22:37-39). Great joy and liberty are found only in the place of serving God and others above self!

Prayer: *Father, in Jesus' name, may Your people walk in the mind of Christ this day, lifting You and others above self.*

October 15

> "I am crucified with Christ: nevertheless I live; yet not I, but Christ liveth in me: and the life which I now live in the flesh I live by the faith of the Son of God, who loved me, and gave himself for me." Galatians 2:20

Memorizing this truth will change your life. Nothing works in our life with Christ, outside of the divine cross economy—where we follow Christ by consenting to our own death and burial and then He raises us upward in His grace and strength!

The cross-message Christ gave is not some nice platitude. It's a divine imperative and command to be obeyed! (Read Luke 9:23-24.) Any minister not taking up daily and preaching this cross-life Jesus preached is a fraud! (See Philippians 3:18-19.)

> "And he said to them all, If any man will come after me, let him deny himself, and take up his cross daily, and follow me. 24 For whosoever will save his life shall lose it: but whosoever will lose his life for my sake, the same shall save it." Luke 9:23-24

There can and will be no raising up by Christ without first consenting to death and burial. Are you ready to let go and let God? Satan's days are numbered in the lives of those learning to take up the cross truly and daily (Colossians 3:3).

Prayer: *Father in the name of Jesus Christ, please teach me this cross You ordain that I take up. Amen.*

October 16

"But thou, O Lord, art a God full of compassion, and gracious, longsuffering, and plenteous in mercy and truth." **Psalms 86:15**

God is **"plenteous in mercy"** and therefore has chosen to be ever so merciful to us, His people, on the sole basis of the shed blood of His only begotten Son.

Do we begin to realize that we are not forgiven by God if we refuse to forgive others? Do we realize the eternal consequences of such sinful rebellion? (Read Matthew 18:21-35.) Do you know friend that the LORD is looking at the attitudes of your heart?

MERCY. Plentifully, unsparingly release it on others—beginning in your heart attitudes—because you need it! Memorize Micah 6:8 and James 2:13 now.

"Forgiveness: It's impossible to know the complete freedom and joy it brings until you've experienced giving it to others. Forgive all, freely ... today. Glory to God." Debbie Lord

Prayer: *Father, in the name of Jesus, please forgive my own sinful hardness of heart. Please reveal to me the depravity of my own heart and my utter need for Your mercy, of which I am completely undeserving.*

There's an eternity of difference between being religious and being truly saved. Check out page 381 to make sure.

October 17

> "But he that is greatest among you shall be your servant. 12 And whosoever shall exalt himself shall be abased; and he that shall humble himself shall be exalted." Matthew 23:11-12

The greatest in Christ's kingdom is the servant of all! The greatest is not the pastor, the singer, the evangelist, etc., but rather the serving saint! Kingdom Truth: Wherever you find yourself ... ABS = Always Be Serving (humbly).

When in doubt, serve, serve, serve, serve, serve. It's the safest, most blessed place to be! Jesus came to give His life for us, and we are blessed today with the privilege to give ourselves for others—empowered by divine grace as we do. (1 Corinthians 15:10).

> "It is more blessed to give than to receive." Acts 20:35

God Himself will raise up those who choose to bow down in death and burial. His resurrection life follows, without fail! This preeminent kingdom truth is found throughout all of Scripture.

> "Humble yourselves in the sight of the Lord, and he shall lift you up." James 4:10

The deeper your death and burial, the more resurrection grace He will grant!

Prayer: *Jesus, I am crucified with You—dead and buried. Now LORD, thank You for raising me upward, propelled by Your grace to be used by You and for Your glory.*

October 18

> "But let him ask in faith, nothing wavering. For he that wavereth is like a wave of the sea driven with the wind and tossed. 7 For let not that man think that he shall receive any thing of the Lord. 8 A double minded man is unstable in all his ways." James 1:6-8

Are you authentic and consistent in your relationship with the LORD? We just read that not living and asking by faith means we shall be **"like a wave of the sea driven ... and tossed"** and receive nothing of the LORD.

> "But without faith it is impossible to please him: for he that cometh to God must believe that he is, and that he is a rewarder of them that diligently seek him." Hebrews 11:6

Nothing in the Word of God is meant to be implemented outside of a cross relationship with Christ—where His death, burial, and resurrection (the Gospel) is re-enacted in our lives daily (Romans 6; 1 Corinthians 15:1-4). It's the cross that crucifies unbelief out of our lives. Being **"double minded"** would mean to be other than cross-minded. You MUST consent to the death of your own will before the LORD will raise you upward in His grace to do His will.

Prayer: *Father, You command me to live by faith in You. Please increase my faith and crucify all unbelief out of my heart. I here and now turn back to You wholly and confess the sin of unbelief. In Jesus' name, amen.*

October 19

"But by the grace of God I am what I am: and his grace which was bestowed upon me was not in vain; but I laboured more abundantly than they all: yet not I, but the grace of God which was with me." 1 Corinthians 15:10

God's grace labors in us as we humbly submit to and obey Christ. As we serve, we can be sure that it's the ability of God—the divine enablement of the Lord laboring in and through us. Life changer!

"For it is <u>God which worketh in you</u> both to will and to do of his good pleasure." Philippians 2:13

In conjunction with the grace of God and out of a completely humble spirit we learn to serve everyone around us in every situation. That's our mission. Memorize and live the words of our Savior recorded in Matthew 23:11-12. Notice we are to serve—and yes, it must be humbly or it's in vain.

"But he that is greatest among you shall be your servant. 12 And whosoever shall exalt himself shall be abased; and he that shall humble himself shall be exalted." Matthew 23:11-12

Prayer: *Teach me Your ways dear Lord. Thank You for Your divine enablement—Your grace—working in my life. Here this moment, I lay my life in Your hands. Please use me, Father, to serve others. Minister to their hearts, bring them to You! In Jesus' name, amen.*

October 20

> "Beloved, let us love one another: for love is of God; and every one that loveth is born of God, and knoweth God. ⁸ He that loveth not knoweth not God; for God is love." 1 John 4:7-8

We are not love but **"God is love,"** and we are dependent upon Him who **"is love"** to fill us with His love. GOD's LOVE can only fill and emanate from our lives as we seek the face of Him who **"is love"** (1 John 4:7-8, 16-18). As we live in an abiding relationship with Christ, we will serve the Lord, functioning in His mission to mankind—the Great Commission He gave us to do (Matthew 28:18-20). We will not serve ourselves but rather the Savior because we are not our own. **"For ye are bought with a price: therefore glorify God in your body, and in your spirit, which are God's"** (1 Corinthians 6:19-20).

Serving God involves following Jesus—being occupied with the mind of Christ in serving others (Philippians 2:3-5).

> **"Let nothing be done through strife or vainglory; but in lowliness of mind let each esteem other better than themselves. ⁴ Look not every man on his own things, but every man also on the things of others. ⁵ Let this mind be in you, which was also in Christ Jesus:" Philippians 2:3-5**

Prayer: *Father, may the mind, the disposition of Christ be in me. This instant, I lay my life into Your holy hands. In Jesus' name, amen.*

October 21

"The fear of the LORD is the beginning of wisdom: and the knowledge of the holy is understanding." Proverbs 9:10

Do we yet have **"the knowledge of the holy"**? Does it begin to seep into our hearts that God is **"Holy, holy, holy"** and we are **"desperately wicked"**? (See Isaiah 6:3; Jeremiah 17:9.)

When we begin to understand the infinite contrast between our wretchedness and depravity, compared to God's holiness and perfection, we will then begin to understand our relationship with Him. Consequently, we will cease wrongly judging others just because the sin they committed may be a different flavor than ours!

Understanding **"the knowledge of the holy"** all begins today with the choice to fear the LORD—elevating Him for the infinite Almighty God He is.

"They rest not day and night, saying, Holy, holy, holy, Lord God Almighty, which was, and is, and is to come." Revelation 4:8

Prayer: *Father, teach me to fear Your holy name and to begin to understand the reality that You are holy, and I am wicked outside of You. Set me apart to Yourself, for Your glory. In Jesus' name, amen*

October 22

> "Holding forth the word of life; that I may rejoice in the day of Christ, that I have not run in vain, neither laboured in vain." Philippians 2:16

Are you **"holding forth,"** are you issuing forth the Word of God into the hearts of men today?

> "How then shall they call on him in whom they have not believed? and how shall they believe in him of whom they have not heard? and how shall they hear without a preacher? 15 And how shall they preach, except they be sent? as it is written, How beautiful are the feet of them that preach the gospel of peace, and bring glad tidings of good things!" Romans 10:14-15

To stand before the LORD as His ambassador, having beautiful feet which disperse His Good News, is exclusively the calling and privilege of the righteous.

> "The lips of the righteous feed many: but fools die for want of wisdom." Proverbs 10:21

> "But ye shall receive power, after that the Holy Ghost is come upon you: and ye shall be witnesses unto me both in Jerusalem, and in all Judæa, and in Samaria, and unto the uttermost part of the earth." Acts 1:8

Prayer: *Heavenly Father, thank You for saving me by the blood of Jesus Christ. In fresh surrender to You and Your will, right now, I ask You to please fill, baptize, immerse me with Your Holy Ghost. So be it in Jesus' name, amen.*

October 23

> "I have fought a good fight, I have finished my course, I have kept the faith:" 2 Timothy 4:7

How could the LORD's apostle Paul be so confident, so secure in his spiritual state and readiness to meet Christ? Nearing the end of his time on earth, Paul says:

I have … **"<u>fought</u> a good fight, I have <u>finished</u> my course, I have <u>kept</u> the faith."**

Finishing strong is what matters most in the continuum of our relationship with Christ! If you are reading these words, you are blessed because you possess the bless-ed opportunity, the privilege to serve God and finish strong! *How* we finish is most important. The Bible says:

> "Better is the end of a thing than the beginning thereof: and the patient in spirit is better than the proud in spirit." Ecclesiastes 7:8

Samson was a man who was all too eager to sin against God during his earthly life and yet finished strong and ended up in the list of the heroes of faith in Hebrews 11! THAT should give us all great encouragement to finish strong! (See Hebrews 11:32.)

Prayer: *Father, please quicken a deep hunger in me and the desire to know and serve You authentically. Bless me to sprint to the finish on Your terms so that I can hear from You* **"Well done"** *in the end. In Jesus' name, amen.*

October 24

> **"But the fruit of the Spirit is love, joy, peace, longsuffering, gentleness, goodness, faith, Meekness, temperance: against such there is no law. And they that are Christ's have crucified the flesh with the affections and lusts." Galatians 5:22-24**

God's fruit, good fruit, is borne out of the cross relationship we have with Christ. Nine dimensions of this divinely produced fruit are listed above. Does your life look like this?

These are the **"fruit"** produced in the lives of all who are truly abiding in Christ (John 15:1-16). If these fruit are not growing in your life, there's a disconnect—a life void of truly being rooted in Christ.

The fruit of being born again and remaining, abiding in Christ, is always according to Galatians 5:22-23. Abiding in Him will without fail yield this beautiful produce.

Our works are the good fruit born out of Christ's salvation and present work in our lives (Philippians 1:6; 2:12-13). The good fruit, the good works do not save us but are the outworking of His great salvation in us.

> **"Work out** *(not for)* **your own salvation with fear and trembling. 13 For it is God which worketh in you both to will and to do of his good pleasure." Philippians 2:12-13**

Prayer: *Father, in the name of Jesus, I desire to truly abide in Christ today—on Your terms. I love You Jesus.*

October 25

"Then look up, and lift up your heads; for your redemption draweth nigh." Luke 21:28

Jesus told us to **"look up, and lift up your heads"** when we see the signs of the end which would indicate His soon return. Rather than being overly preoccupied with the signs and Satan's agents that Christ told us would be most evident just before his return, we should be all the more seeking the face of the Lord. Jesus is coming which should hasten us to do the ministry commission He left us to do—edify, nourish, teach and send forth His people into ministry to make Him known to the lost (Matthew 28:18-20; John 21:15-17; Ephesians 4:11-15, etc.).

> **"But exhort one another daily, while it is called To day; lest any of you be hardened through the deceitfulness of sin." Hebrews 3:13**

> **"And let us consider one another to provoke unto love and to good works: 25 Not forsaking the assembling of ourselves together, as the manner of some is; but exhorting one another: and so much the more, as ye see the day approaching." Hebrews 10:24-25**

Are you nourishing your heart daily in God's Word? Who will you build up in Christ today?

Prayer: LORD, please root me soundly in You this day. Produce the fruit and good works in this vessel that glorify You. Help me to nourish, edify, and equip others of Your beloved people. In Jesus' name, amen.

October 26

> "Not by works of righteousness which we have done, but according to his mercy he saved us, by the washing of regeneration, and renewing of the Holy Ghost; 6 Which he shed on us abundantly through Jesus Christ our Saviour;" Titus 3:5-6

Returning His Mercy to others:

> "And be ye kind one to another, tenderhearted, forgiving one another, even as God for Christ's sake hath forgiven you." Ephesians 4:32

GOD requires that we forgive others, not because they deserve it but rather because He requires it of us. Did WE deserve, do we deserve His mercy, His forgiveness? NO! Memorize Ephesians 4:32 and Titus 3:5-6 today (KJB).

The cross of Christ is the greatest love ever shown! While fallen man was committing the greatest crime ever—the murder of the sinless Son of God—Jesus cried out from that cross for God to be merciful: **"Father, forgive them; for they know not what they do"** (Luke 23:34).

Prayer: *Father, forgive me for my hardness of heart. Break me Jesus, please. Take away the stony places of my heart and replace them with a heart of flesh. I lay my life in Your hands this moment. In Jesus' name. Amen.*

Have you been saved by God's mercy? Check out page 381 to make sure.

October 27

> "Sow to yourselves in righteousness, reap in mercy; break up your fallow ground: for it is time to seek the LORD, till he come and rain righteousness upon you." Hosea 10:12

Drawing close to God begins at repentance and receiving Jesus—the moment He saves us. And yet, continually drawing close to the LORD is taught throughout Scripture and essential in the abiding relationship Jesus ordained for each of His children (John 15). To His own, through James, the LORD beckons:

> "Draw nigh to God, and he will draw nigh to you. Cleanse your hands, ye sinners; and purify your hearts, ye double minded. ^{9} Be afflicted, and <u>mourn</u>, and weep: let your laughter be turned to mourning, and your joy to heaviness *(the cross)*. ^{10} Humble yourselves in the sight of the Lord, and he shall lift you up *(resurrection)*." James 4:8-10

Prayer: *Father, please let the hard, dry parched places of my heart be broken up. Let them be plowed, turned over, and ready to humbly receive Your Word of truth. Pour the oil of Your Holy Spirit on my heart dear LORD and make me Yours. In Jesus' name, amen.*

October 28

> "If thou faint in the day of adversity, thy strength is small. [11] If thou forbear to deliver them that are drawn unto death, and those that are ready to be slain; [12] If thou sayest, Behold, we knew it not; doth not he that pondereth the heart consider it? and he that keepeth thy soul, doth not he know it? and shall not he render to every man according to his works?" Proverbs 24:10-12

Never evade or cower from a need another has when it's placed before you. This is an opportunity and a test.

> "Pure religion and undefiled before God and the Father is this, To visit the fatherless and widows in their affliction, and to keep himself unspotted from the world." James 1:27

> "We love him, because he first loved us. [20] If a man say, I love God, and hateth his brother, he is a liar: for he that loveth not his brother whom he hath seen, how can he love God whom he hath not seen? [21] And this commandment have we from him, That he who loveth God love his brother also." 1 John 4:19-21

Prayer: *Father, I am here to be Your servant. Please posture my heart to be Your ambassador and open doors to use me to help others. In Jesus' name, amen.*

October 29

"Blessed are they that mourn: for they shall be comforted." Matthew 5:4

Mourning then comfort: We must be willing to **"mourn"** in order to experience divine comfort and joy. We must be willing and obedient to do things God's way—to die in order to experience resurrection.

The daily cross life brings the **"comfort"** of Christ's resurrection grace in our lives, which is utterly priceless. No matter what we may be walking through **"the God of all comfort"** will fill us as we remain rooted and grounded in the cross He prescribed (Luke 9:23-24).

"Blessed be God, even the Father of our Lord Jesus Christ, the Father of mercies, and the God of all comfort." 2 Corinthians 1:3

The words **"mourn,"** and **"mourning"** appear 96 times in God's Word. Ever heard a message on it?

Regrettably, the biblical doctrine of mourning is seldom heard in the modern "church" along with the doctrine of suffering. Why? Well, these truths don't entertain the goats that modern pastors have deceitfully corralled for their own self-serving purposes (Isaiah 30:9-10; Philippians 3:18-19; 2 Timothy 4:2-4). Please read Ecclesiastes 7:1-5.

Prayer: *Father, You are the God of all comfort. You comforted Jesus in the unfathomable afflictions He suffered, and we thank You for comforting Your people in the earth. In Jesus' name, amen.*

October 30

> "Which things also we speak, not in the words which man's wisdom teacheth, but which the Holy Ghost teacheth; comparing spiritual things with spiritual." 1 Corinthians 2:13

The word **"comparing"** here speaks of *stacking, collating*—**"comparing spiritual things with spiritual."** Gathering every Scripture on a topic is vital to correctly understand the truth of God.

> **"For precept must be upon precept, precept upon precept; line upon line, line upon line; here a little, and there a little." Isaiah 28:10**

Topically studying God's Word is extremely beneficial—as Scriptures are gathered on a certain topic to be considered. There is great safety in following our Lord's prescription here for apprehending His truth: **"rightly dividing the word of truth"** (2 Timothy 2:15).

This Biblical method is imperative in the study of God's Word which each individual believer is to diligently, daily engage in.

> **"Study to shew thyself approved unto God, a workman that needeth not to be ashamed, rightly dividing the word of truth." 2 Timothy 2:15**

Prayer: *Father, please lead me into the correct understanding of Your Word and every doctrine therein. In Jesus' name, amen.*

October 31

> "And take heed to yourselves, lest at any time your hearts be overcharged with surfeiting, and drunkenness, and cares of this life, and *so* that day come upon you unawares. ³⁵ For as a snare shall it come on all them that dwell on the face of the whole earth. ³⁶ Watch ye therefore, and pray always, that ye may be accounted worthy to escape all these things that shall come to pass, and to stand before the Son of man." Luke 21:34-36

Make no mistake, Jesus gave us a severe warning in this riveting passage. Keep it close. Read it often. Pour over it prayerfully, crying out to God to make you ready!

"Watch ye therefore, and pray always." Prayer is perpetual fellowship with our Lord Jesus who came and died that we might know Him and the Father (John 17:3). Prayer is not merely a privilege granted to believers to call on God in the time of crisis or to obtain their heart's desires for temporal things—though it certainly is one aspect of prayer. Prayer is saving faith in action—the obedience of engaging in an abiding, personal, perpetual relationship with the Savior. Praying is an absolute imperative of fellowship with Jesus and overcoming, which is essential to receiving final salvation. If prayer were not so important in present abiding, victory, and of eternal consequence, there would have been no reason that the Son of God would have uttered the words of warning He issued forth in Luke 21:34-36.

Prayer: *Lord, draw me nigh to You. Grant my heart to be engrossed with communing with You. In Jesus' name, amen.*

November 1

> "The time of my departure is at hand. 7 I have fought a good fight, I have finished my course, I have kept the faith: 8 Henceforth there is laid up for me a crown of righteousness, which the Lord, the righteous judge, shall give me at that day: and not to me only, but unto all them also that love his appearing." 2 Timothy 4:6-8

As an ambassador of Christ, Paul was nearing the end of his mission on earth and said he had **"fought," "finished"** and **"kept."** IF YOU DON'T FIGHT YOU WILL FALL, YOU WILL FAIL! With God, failure is never final unless you don't get back up.

> "For a just man falleth seven times, and riseth up again: but the wicked shall fall into mischief." Proverbs 24:16

You must choose daily to **"FIGHT the good fight of faith, lay hold on eternal life, whereunto thou art also called, and hast professed a good profession before many witnesses."** (1 Timothy 6:12)

> "Brethren, I count not myself to have apprehended: but this one thing I do, forgetting those things which are behind, and reaching forth unto those things which are before, 14 I press toward the mark for the prize of the high calling of God in Christ Jesus." Philippians 3:13-14

Prayer: LORD, imbue in my innermost being the resolve to know You, to walk with You, to love You supremely as the first love of my life. In Jesus' name, amen.

November 2

> "Which say, Stand by thyself, come not near to me; for I am <u>holier than thou</u>. These are a smoke in my nose, a fire that burneth all the day." Isaiah 65:5

The phrase **"holier than thou"** here expresses a divine hatred for self-righteousness which was confirmed in the ministry of Jesus when He lambasted the Pharisees (Matthew 21:31; 23:1-25; Luke 18:9-14).

There is never an excuse for sin (James 1:13-15). We must not self-righteously feign holiness. Being absolutely honest concerning our own frailty and need for the LORD is not about making excuses or false humility, but rather, realizing and admitting our ever present need for the grace of God to live a life that is pleasing to Him (Psalms 38:18; Romans 7:18).

> "For I will declare mine iniquity; I will be sorry for my sin." Psalms 38:18

The walk of the true follower of Christ is not denying sin and failure but rather readily admitting and denouncing it as one draws nigh afresh to Christ! Getting Honest: Memorize Luke 8:15; Proverbs 28:13.

Prayer: *Father, please purge all self-righteousness out of my life. Make me Your authentic disciple, stripping all falsity and iniquity. In Jesus' name, amen.*

November 3

"Now the God of peace, that brought again from the dead our Lord Jesus, that great shepherd of the sheep, through the blood of the everlasting covenant," Hebrews 13:20

JESUS alone bought with His blood His beloved Church and He alone is the **"Great Shepherd of the sheep"** and knows exactly what each of His people need and when! He NEVER misses His que! Jesus Christ is LORD! In His discourse on the Good Shepherd, Jesus says:

"I am the good shepherd: the good shepherd giveth his life for the sheep. ... I am the good shepherd, and know my sheep, and am known of mine. 15 As the Father knoweth me, even so know I the Father: and I lay down my life for the sheep. 16 And other sheep I have, which are not of this fold: them also I must bring, and they shall hear my voice; and there shall be one fold, and one shepherd. 17 Therefore doth my Father love me, because I lay down my life, that I might take it again. 18 No man taketh it from me, but I lay it down of myself. I have power to lay it down, and I have power to take it again. This commandment have I received of my Father." John 10:11-18

Read Psalms 23.

Prayer: *LORD, thank You for giving Your very life for Your sheep and for leading, guiding, equipping and feeding Your beloved people. In Jesus' name, amen.*

November 4

"And be ye kind one to another, tenderhearted, forgiving one another, even as God for Christ's sake hath forgiven you." Ephesians 4:32

Those who seek God to be **"tenderhearted"** —to have His heart—will readily forgive all others. This they do in light of the unfathomable love God showed them by sending His only begotten Son for their sins, in the face of their rebellion against Him!

God *chose* to send His only begotten Son for our sins. Our LORD Jesus *chose* to come and to die for us rather than live without us! What love! Unfathomable mercy! WE nailed the Savior to that cross! The cross of Christ is the greatest love ever shown! While fallen man was committing the greatest crime ever—the murder of the sinless Son of God—Jesus cried out for their mercy from that cross **"Father, forgive them; for they know not what they do"** (Luke 23:34).

With this preeminent Gospel truth in mind, HOW could we not show mercy on others? How could we possibly turn from the cross of divine mercy and not bestow it lavishly upon others as He poured it out on our undeserving wretched souls?

Prayer: Heavenly Father, in the name of Jesus, I implore You to grant me a heart of flesh. Please change me Lord, beginning right now. I love You Jesus.

November 5

> "Therefore if thou bring thy gift to the altar, and there rememberest that thy brother hath ought against thee; 24 Leave there thy gift before the altar, and go thy way; first be reconciled to thy brother, and then come and offer thy gift." **Matthew 5:23-24**

Get up! Do not bother with fake praying when you have sin in your life. Never cover your sins, only turn back to God and confess them (Proverbs 28:13). Make amends where needed.

Crucified servants of Christ do not hold any grudge or unforgiveness. They are forgiven out of the sheer mercy of God and abide ever-ready to meet their LORD, knowing that if they do not forgive, God will not forgive them (Matthew 18:21-35; Mark 11:25-26, etc.).

> "Be patient therefore, brethren, unto the coming of the Lord. Behold, the husbandman waiteth for the precious fruit of the earth, and hath long patience for it, until he receive the early and latter rain. 8 Be ye also patient; stablish your hearts: for the coming of the Lord draweth nigh. 9 Grudge not one against another, brethren, lest ye be condemned: behold, the judge standeth before the door." **James 5:7-9**

Prayer: *Father, I know You are holy, and I now come to you in Jesus' name and ask You to forgive the exceeding wickedness of my heart. Please forgive me for the hypocritical, merciless hatred of despising others in my attitudes while ignoring my own sin. No one is more in need of Your saving mercy than I am. Please wash me now and establish Your love in this heart. Thank You Lord for finding and saving me. In Jesus' name. Amen.*

November 6

> **"And they shall teach my people the difference between the holy and profane, and cause them to discern between the unclean and the clean." Ezekiel 44:23**

The reason a minister doesn't teach you to discern by Holy Scripture is because he doesn't want you to find out who he really is—a wolf!

Discernment is needed and all truly God-fearing ministers *will* teach it. Does this not remind us of what Solomon and Peter warned us about?

So many today in ministry boast of their gifts, build their own empires and exploit people. They do this all while using the name of the LORD in vain, as they feign to be representing Christ while merely using His holy name for their own self-serving enterprises.

> **"Whoso boasteth himself of a false gift is like clouds and wind without rain." Proverbs 25:14**

The phrase **"clouds and wind without rain"** concerns the lack of substance. Merely sprinkling in a Bible verse or two is not preaching the Word. The true servant of the LORD will remain specifically in the text of Holy Scripture, unwaveringly. **"Preach the word"** (2 Timothy 4:2).

Prayer: *Father, in Jesus' name, please help me discern Your few true servant-disciples and those wolves You so often warned us of.*

November 7

"And that repentance and remission of sins should be preached in his name among all nations, beginning at Jerusalem." Luke 24:47

Here Jesus commissions and mandates that His people preach repentance and the ensuing **"remission of sins."** This is how He requires that men be saved. **"I tell you, Nay: but, except ye repent, ye shall all likewise perish"** (Luke 13:3).

Do we know the original Gospel message? What is the first divine command for sinners to appropriate the justification of God? Repentance is essential (Matthew 3:2; 4:17; Acts 2:38, etc.)

John the Baptist: **"And saying, Repent ye: for the kingdom of heaven is at hand"** (Matthew 3:2).

Jesus: **"From that time Jesus began to preach, and to say, Repent: for the kingdom of heaven is at hand"** (Matthew 4:17).

Peter: **"Repent ... for the remission of sins"** (Acts 2:38).

> **"Repent ye therefore, and be converted, that your sins may be blotted out, when the times of refreshing shall come from the presence of the Lord;"** Acts 3:19

Paul: **"And the times of this ignorance God winked at; but now commandeth all men every where to repent:" Acts 17:30**

Prayer: *Father, please teach me sound doctrine, purity of doctrine, exactness of Your doctrine, the exact astuteness of Your words. In Jesus' name, amen.*

November 8

> "When Jesus therefore had received the vinegar, he said, It is finished: and he bowed his head, and gave up the ghost." John 19:30

This revelation in the above words of the Messiah— "**It is finished**"—is consistent with the whole divine unveiling of Holy Scripture—the redemption of mankind after the fall. Jesus came to do something and that's why while dying on the cross for the sins of the world, He declared "**It is finished**" (John 19:30). These are the three most powerful words ever spoken! *What* exactly was "**finished**"?

> "For then must he often have suffered since the foundation of the world: but now once in the end of the world hath he appeared to put away sin by the sacrifice of himself." Hebrews 9:26

Jesus declared mercy and forgiveness over mankind while He was dying to provide redemption on that cross: "**It is finished**" (John 19:30). This simply means "paid in full." The price for sin has been fully paid. The claims of the Father's justice were perfectly satisfied, paid in full by the precious, sinless blood of the Son of God. All men are now invited to come to Him, repent and believe upon the LORD Jesus Christ for redemption—mercy and forgiveness (Colossians 1:14). On that cross, the LORD Jesus declared: "**It is finished**" and "**Father, forgive them; for they know not what they do**" (John 19:30; Luke 23:34).

Prayer: *Father I rejoice in the precious blood of Jesus shed for my sin—to bring me to You for an eternal relationship.*

November 9

> "Search the scriptures; for in them ye think ye have eternal life: and they are they which testify of me. 40 And ye will not come to me, that ye might have life." John 5:39-40

Satan's plan is to divert your attention, the affections of your heart. He uses false leaders (the majority of leaders today) to do this. Satan came **"to steal, to kill, and to destroy"** by getting you to look to mere man to tell you what the Bible says, instead of reading God's Word for yourself and letting the LORD speak for Himself to your heart (John 10:10). Jesus told you to **"Search the scriptures"** for yourself (John 5:39). Paul said the same (2 Timothy 2:15). Read God's Word for yourself—the King James Bible. Jesus calls all men to search His Word and to come to Him—to know and walk with Him.

> "Thy word is a lamp unto my feet, and a light unto my path." Psalms 119:105

The LORD has unveiled His will to us through the counsel of His Word.

> "**The counsel** *(Word)* **of the LORD standeth for ever, the thoughts of his heart to all generations.**" Psalms 33:11

Prayer: *Father, may Your Word be the highest and final authority of my life from this moment forward. In Jesus' name. I declare with Paul,* **"Let God be true and every man a liar."**

November 10

> "For it became him, for whom are all things, and by whom are all things, in bringing many sons unto glory, to make the captain of their salvation perfect through sufferings." Hebrews 2:10

Christ alone won the day, triumphed in victory over sin and Satan at the cross (Colossians 2:14-17). He is the unique, only begotten Son of the living God, and is alone **"the captain of their salvation perfect through sufferings."**

Jesus alone is Savior and Sanctifier! Jesus saves. Jesus sanctifies those whom He saves!

> **"The LORD will perfect** *(bring to full maturity)* **that which concerneth me: thy mercy, O LORD, endureth for ever: forsake not the works of thine own hands." Psalms 138:8**

He continues that good work of salvation He granted—that He exclusively provided—in the lives of all who abide, **"continue"** with Him (John 8:31-32; 15:1-6).

> **"Then said Jesus to those Jews which believed on him, <u>IF ye continue in my word</u>, then are ye my disciples indeed; ³² And ye shall know the truth, and the truth shall make you free." John 8:31-32**

Prayer: *Father, You gave Jesus for my sins. You found me in my sin and saved me to Yourself. Thank You LORD for continuing that good work You began. In Jesus' name, amen.*

November 11

> "For I know that in me (that is, in my flesh,) dwelleth no good thing: for to will is present with me; but how to perform that which is good I find not." Romans 7:18

Do we not attempt to do/accomplish God's will in and through our bankrupted flesh? Are we, in and of ourselves, sufficient for such? If so, we then must ask why Jesus even bothered to come to the earth. Jesus not only came to do something we couldn't possibly do—dying in our place on that cross. He's the Head of His body (our life) and He alone can accomplish His will in us as we participate with Him in the daily Gospel of the cross where we lay down our own lives (will) and allow Him to reign.

We cry with John the Baptist— **"He must increase but I must decrease"** (John 3:30), and with Paul— **"I am crucified with Christ: nevertheless I live; yet not I, but Christ liveth in me: and the life which I now live in the flesh I live by the faith of the Son of God, who loved me, and gave himself for me"** (Galatians 2:20), and with Jesus— **"Not my will but thine be done"** (Luke 22:42).

Prayer: LORD, I need You. Please help me (as only You can) to grasp this reality in a much deeper fashion. I love You Jesus. You must increase this day in my life, and I must decrease. I am crucified with Christ, in Jesus' name. amen.

November 12

> "I exhort therefore, that, first of all, supplications, prayers, intercessions, and giving of thanks, be made for all men; 2 For kings, and for all that are in authority; that we may lead a quiet and peaceable life in all godliness and honesty. 3 For this is good and acceptable in the sight of God our Saviour; 4 Who will have all men to be saved, and to come unto the knowledge of the truth. 5 For there is one God, and one mediator between God and men, the man Christ Jesus; 6 Who gave himself a ransom for all, to be testified in due time." 1 Timothy 2:1-6

God here instructs His people to pray for **"all men"** and **"all that are in authority."** We are instructed to pray daily for those in authority while we obey God by making known the **"one mediator between God and men"**—Jesus Christ. God mandates that His people continually do His Great Commission and also be involved in prayer for our civil leaders (Romans 13; 1 Peter 2:13-15).

> "And seek the peace of the city whither I have caused you to be carried away captives, and pray unto the LORD for it: for in the peace thereof shall ye have peace." Jeremiah 29:7

Three things God instituted: 1. The family; 2. The Body of Christ; 3. Civil governmental authority.

Prayer: *Father, In Jesus' name, please bless the leaders of this nation to be wise, to fear You and do Your bidding. Establish justice and quicken Your Word in Your people, preparing their hearts to repent and receive Your truth, amen.*

November 13

> "And it came to pass, when Moses held up his hand, that Israel prevailed: and when he let down his hand, Amalek prevailed. ¹² But Moses' hands were heavy; and they took a stone, and put it under him, and he sat thereon; and Aaron and Hur stayed up his hands, the one on the one side, and the other on the other side; and his hands were steady until the going down of the sun. ¹³ And Joshua discomfited Amalek and his people with the edge of the sword." Exodus 17:11-13

God's servant Moses needed the ministry of Christ through His other saints—just as we do. Amalek represents the flesh which can only be defeated via the crucified Savior and cross life He instructed us to participate in with Him **"daily"** (Luke 9:23-24). True fellowship includes exhorting one another **"daily"** to deny self, take up the cross and follow Jesus—the way He prescribed.

> "But exhort one another daily, while it is called To day; lest any of you be hardened through the deceitfulness of sin. ... And let us consider one another to provoke unto love and to good works: ²⁵ Not forsaking the assembling of ourselves together, as the manner of some is; but exhorting one another: and so much the more, as ye see the day approaching." Hebrews 3:13; 10:24-25

Prayer: *Father, I am crucified with Jesus this day. Let my life be dead and buried and raised up by You dear LORD. Help me humbly receive the exhortation of other disciples. Amen.*

November 14

> **"Nevertheless I have somewhat against thee, because thou hast left thy first love. 5 Remember therefore from whence thou art fallen, and repent, and do the first works; or else I will come unto thee quickly, and will remove thy candlestick out of his place, except thou repent." Revelation 2:4-5**

As I truly repent, that means my life is laid down and Christ is my **"first love"** and not self! Jesus ordains that my life be His, not mine.

> **"What? know ye not that your body is the temple of the Holy Ghost which is in you, which ye have of God, and ye are not your own? 20 For ye are bought with a price: therefore glorify God in your body, and in your spirit, which are God's." 1 Corinthians 6:19-20**

At the moment He saves us, our lives are no longer our own, all things are now **"of God."**

> **"Therefore if any man be in Christ, he is a new creature: old things are passed away; behold, all things are become new. 18 And all things are of God, who hath reconciled us to himself by Jesus Christ, and hath given to us the ministry of reconciliation" 2 Corinthians 5:17-18**

Prayer: *Father, in Jesus' name, please breathe into me Your revelation, your distinct divine reason for sending Your only begotten Son to save me to Yourself, for Your purposes. I am all Yours LORD Jesus!*

November 15

> "Let no corrupt communication proceed out of your mouth, but that which is good to the use of edifying, that it may minister grace unto the hearers." Ephesians 4:29

God wants His people to use the tongue He gave them to edify others, to **"minister grace unto the hearers."** This makes it obvious that the tongue is a tool which can be used either for evil or for good. Read James 3.

The LORD alone can tame the tongue and He does, in the hearts of those who are known of Him. As they seek Him daily, He purifies their hearts.

> "Blessed are the pure in heart: for they shall see God. ... for out of the abundance of the heart the mouth speaketh." Matthew 5:8; 12:34

No man can singlehandedly tame the unruly tongue. He must submit himself to the LORD daily for this to be accomplished.

> "But the tongue can no man tame; it is an unruly evil, full of deadly poison." James 3:8

Prayer: *Dear LORD, I openly acknowledge my sin before You this moment. Please forgive me and clean this heart, purify it for Your glory. Please let my tongue be used by You to bless others. In Jesus' name, amen.*

November 16

"For I determined not to know any thing among you, save Jesus Christ, and him crucified." 1 Corinthians 2:2

Paul preached Christ—Paul's only identity!

"But God forbid that I should glory, save in the cross of our Lord Jesus Christ, by whom the world is crucified unto me, and I unto the world." Galatians 6:14

When the topic of God, Christianity, religion or spirituality surfaces, the disciple must think JESUS! There are far too many mere *professors* of Christianity who are not possessed by the living revelation of Jesus Christ. They are yet religious and void of a real relationship with the living LORD.

Those who talk about their "church" or "pastor" and not Christ are being called to the LORD, to genuinely repent—to turn *from* their sin of self-idolatry and *to* Him as the highest priority of their life, their supreme love (Revelation 2:4-5). When Jesus is authentically our **"first love,"** we delight in Him, we rejoice in our nail scarred risen Savior alone (1 Corinthians 2:2; Galatians 6:14). The kingdom of God is ALL about Jesus, Heaven's KING!

Prayer: *Dear Father, in the name of Jesus, please forgive my sins of unbelief, pride, self-righteousness, self-idolatry and self-love. I repent, turning my heart to You now LORD Jesus, confessing You alone as the Master of my life, my Savior and LORD. Amen.*

November 17

"I have BLOTTED OUT, as a thick cloud, thy transgressions, and, as a cloud, thy sins: return unto me; for I have redeemed thee." Isaiah 44:22

God's promise is to blot out—completely expunge all of the sins of His people—in the flood of the precious blood of Jesus. No sin could possibly stand in the power of that divine flood. His people who are repentant, confess their sins, fear, obey, worship and love Him supremely, are granted divine mercy.

When you've repented, your sins are blotted out! GONE forever!

> "Repent ye therefore, and be converted, that your sins may be BLOTTED OUT, when the times of refreshing shall come from the presence of the Lord;" Acts 3:19

> "For I will be merciful to their unrighteousness, and their sins and their iniquities will I remember no more." Hebrews 8:12

> "He hath not dealt with us after our sins; nor rewarded us according to our iniquities. 11 For as the heaven is high above the earth, so great is his mercy toward them that fear him. 12 As far as the east is from the west, so far hath he removed our transgressions from us." Psalms 103:10-12

Prayer: *Heavenly Father, in the name of Jesus Christ, I thank You for His perfect, cleansing blood washing me clean of all sin and for finding and saving me!*

November 18

"O wretched man that I am! who shall deliver me from the body of this death?" Romans 7:24

Romans 7 details how the great apostle Paul continually grappled with the flesh, having to learn to **"mortify the deeds of the body"** so Christ could reign supreme (Romans 6-8).

"But I keep under my body, and bring it into subjection: lest that by any means, when I have preached to others, I myself should be a castaway." 1 Corinthians 9:27

Walking with our Lord requires a **"daily"** dying, the denial of self in preference for our **"first love"**—Jesus (Luke 9:23-24; 1 Corinthians 15:36; Revelation 2:4-5).

The Lord would have us realize just how wicked and depraved our hearts are and fall afresh at the foot of the cross on the mercy of God poured out through the shed blood of our Lord Jesus Christ (Genesis 6:5, 12; Jeremiah 17:9; Titus 3:5-7, etc.).

Prayer: *Jesus, You alone were crucified, buried and raised again from the dead to bring me back from the dead into life in You! Thank You Lord for the redemption You alone were qualified to provide. Here this moment, I admit that I am not enough, not sufficient to merit justification or sanctification. I lay my life in Your holy hands, resting in You alone.*

November 19

> "And the Spirit and the bride say, Come. And let him that heareth say, Come. And let him that is athirst come. And whosoever will, let him take the water of life freely." Revelation 22:17

The Holy Spirit, working in the people of God, is saying to all those outside of Christ's kingdom, to **"Come."** Jesus beckons:

> "Come unto me, all ye that labour and are heavy laden, and I will give you rest. 29 Take my yoke upon you, and learn of me; for I am meek and lowly in heart: and ye shall find rest unto your souls. 30 For my yoke is easy, and my burden is light." Matthew 11:28-30

Jesus is preparing a place for His Bride to be with Him forever and is presently using us to call others to Himself.

> "And he said unto them, Go ye into all the world, and preach the gospel to every creature." Mark 16:15

Prayer: *Father, please fill me with Your Holy Ghost afresh and use me. Open the hearts of men to receive Your Word and to respond in repentance and faith. In Jesus' name, amen.*

Have you been saved by responding to the call of God in repentance and faith? Read more about it on page 381 of this book.

November 20

> "The LORD will perfect that which concerneth me: thy mercy, O LORD, endureth for ever: forsake not the works of thine own hands." Psalms 138:8

God is going to continue to do His beautiful work in the lives of His abiding children (John 15; Philippians 1:6; 2:12-13). This is the work of God. He requires man's participation and yet, it's in a responder posture.

The LORD confronts and rebukes us straight up this hour with, **"Are ye so foolish? having begun in the Spirit, are ye now made perfect by the flesh?"** (Galatians 3:3).

It is Jesus alone who both saves and sanctifies. We **"abide,"** remain and grow in intimacy with Him, and the fruit of His will and Spirit is produced in our daily lives (John 15:1-6, 16).

> "For we ... have no confidence in the flesh. ... 8 and I count all things but loss for the excellency of the knowledge of Christ Jesus my Lord: for whom I have suffered the loss of all things, and do count them but dung, that I may win Christ, 9 And be found in him, not having mine own righteousness, which is of the law, but that which is through the faith of Christ, the righteousness which is of God by faith: 10 That I may know him, and the power of his resurrection, and the fellowship of his sufferings, being made conformable unto his death." Philippians 3:3, 8-10

Prayer: *Father, in Jesus' name, please sanctify this life. Set me apart for Your eternal glory.*

November 21

> "O generation of vipers, how can ye, being evil, speak good things? for out of the abundance of the heart the mouth speaketh." Matthew 12:34

How can any person speak words that authentically glorify God while they are evil hearted? Impossible. The words of our mouths come forth out of the reservoir of our hearts. The pure in heart, those whose hearts are being purified by the LORD, will glorify God with their words.

> "A good man out of the good treasure of the heart bringeth forth good things: and an evil man out of the evil treasure bringeth forth evil things. 36 But I say unto you, That every idle word that men shall speak, they shall give account thereof in the day of judgment. 37 For by thy words thou shalt be justified, and by thy words thou shalt be condemned." Matthew 12:35-37

The authentic disciple of Jesus will teach his mouth.

> "The heart of the wise teacheth his mouth, and addeth learning to his lips. 24 Pleasant words are as an honeycomb, sweet to the soul, and health to the bones." Proverbs 16:23-24

Memorizing Scriptures from Proverbs, etc. has immensely helped this disciple.

Prayer: *Father, in Jesus' name, please purify my heart and help me to speak words that bring You glory and edify others. Amen.*

November 22

"Always bearing about in the body the dying of the Lord Jesus, that the life also of Jesus might be made manifest in our body. ¹¹ For we which live are alway delivered unto death for Jesus' sake, that the life also of Jesus might be made manifest in our mortal flesh. ¹² So then death worketh in us, but life in you."
2 Corinthians 4:10-12

Many feel hopeless, like they can never overcome the flesh. Yet, we know that God is able to bring the victory He ordained in our lives through the crucified life He commanded that we walk in. **"For ye are dead, and your life is hid with Christ in God"** (Colossians 3:3).

Powerful ministry that bears fruit for the glory of God only comes out of the cross life with Christ whereby you are dead and buried and Christ is raising you up by His grace, and His power is filling, propelling and flowing through your life to minister His truth and love to others (2 Corinthians 4:10-12).

As we consent to our own death and burial, Jesus raises us upward in HIS divine strength. Divine empowerment in the life of the disciple of Jesus comes from His resurrection grace working in our lives as we consent to our own dying—death and burial. Death and burial precede God raising us up. God cannot raise us up if we aren't dead and buried. This cross concept is at the center of our walk with Jesus, whose death, burial and resurrection are enacted in our own lives daily (Romans 6).

Prayer: *Father, in Jesus' name, I am here and now crucified with Christ. I am dead and my life is hidden with Christ in God.*

November 23

> "Judge not according to the appearance, but judge righteous judgment." John 7:24

Many who misuse Jesus' words in Matthew 7:1-5 (below), have no idea this verse above exists. Are God's people to judge? Yes! That's what Jesus says and He's the final divine authority. This is a command of Jesus. Keep in mind that the meanings of **"judge"** and **"judgment"** vary according to their context. For example, we are to judge, to discern according to the LORD's **"righteous judgment"** and not the outward **"appearance"**—because **"the LORD seeth not as man seeth; for man looketh on the outward appearance, but the LORD looketh on the heart"** (1 Samuel 16:7; John 7:24).

Jesus is rebuking *hypocritical* judgment, not *all* judgment.

> **"Judge not, that ye be not judged. 2 For with what judgment ye judge, ye shall be judged: and with what measure ye mete, it shall be measured to you again. 3 And why beholdest thou the mote that is in thy brother's eye, but considerest not the beam that is in thine own eye? 4 Or how wilt thou say to thy brother, Let me pull out the mote out of thine eye; and, behold, a beam is in thine own eye? 5 Thou hypocrite, first cast out the beam out of thine own eye; and then shalt thou see clearly to cast out the mote out of thy brother's eye." Matthew 7:1-5**

> Prayer: *Father, please purify my heart. Teach me to get the log out of my own eye, in Jesus' name.*

November 24

"Behold, I come as a thief. Blessed is he that watcheth, and keepeth his garments, lest he walk naked, and they see his shame." Revelation 16:15

The sojourning disciple must live in the state of readiness for the return of Christ. This truth is imparted throughout the teaching of Jesus and His holy apostles. ANY leader who has you relaxed— **"lukewarm"**—about the return of Christ is an agent of Satan (Revelation 3:15-16).

> "Let your loins be girded about, and your lights burning; 36 And ye yourselves like unto men that wait for their lord, when he will return from the wedding; that when he cometh and knocketh, they may open unto him immediately. 37 Blessed are those servants, whom the lord when he cometh shall find watching: verily I say unto you, that he shall gird himself, and make them to sit down to meat, and will come forth and serve them. 38 And if he shall come in the second watch, or come in the third watch, and find them so, blessed are those servants. 39 And this know, that if the goodman of the house had known what hour the thief would come, he would have watched, and not have suffered his house to be broken through. 40 Be ye therefore ready also: for the Son of man cometh at an hour when ye think not." Luke 12:35-40

Prayer: *Jesus, You are my Savior and Sanctifier. Please let me be alwaysr ready to meet You!*

November 25

"And that REPENTANCE and REMISSION OF SINS should be preached in his name among all nations, beginning at Jerusalem." Luke 24:47

What two things did Jesus tell us to preach?

1. Repentance
2. Remission of sins

Not just repentance but also, to those who repent we can declare with full assurance that if they have truly repented, all their sins are remitted!

The following words of our Lord to His apostles, when also giving them the Great Commission, seem to come into focus:

"Whose soever sins ye remit, they are remitted unto them; and whose soever sins ye retain, they are retained." John 20:23

Prayer: Precious Father, dear Lord Jesus, thank You so very much for providing perfect salvation to all who will come to You on Your stated terms. Thank You for dying for my sins Jesus. Purify my life by Your precious blood this moment. Bless my life to truly, sincerely worship and serve You to the end. I love You Jesus.

Have you been truly saved? Check out page 381 to make sure.

November 26

"For we are not as many, which corrupt the word of God: but as of sincerity, but as of God, in the sight of God speak we in Christ." 2 Corinthians 2:17

Here we are once again warned about men in our midst who twist God's Word and pretend to represent Christ. In other words, they use it to accomplish their own agenda and mislead others in doing so.

We can cherry-pick Scripture to justify nearly anything. Men can deceitfully extrapolate and prove nearly anything they wish using the right mixture of Scripture verses taken out of the context of the whole counsel of God's Word. This is why it is essential for each of us, as individual disciples of Jesus, to be established in our very own daily study of God's Word. Otherwise we *will* be deceived.

"Study to shew thyself approved unto God, a workman that needeth not to be ashamed, rightly dividing the word of truth." 2 Timothy 2:15

Are you in God's Word daily?

Prayer: *Father in Heaven, please convict my heart, quicken me to know You through my own study of Your Word. Protect me from the wolves You so often warned Your people about. In Jesus' name, amen.*

November 27

"Jesus said unto her, I am the resurrection, and the life: he that believeth in me, though he were dead, yet shall he live: 26 And whosoever liveth and believeth in me shall never die. Believest thou this?" **John 11:25**

The crux (centrality) of the New Testament message is the cross of Christ and all else in the divine economy being produced out of that daily cross experience—**"the resurrection and the life"**—Himself raising our lives upward (now and for eternity) as we agree to be dead and buried. This is the down and up of the Gospel of Jesus in our daily life. That's you saint! You are a child of the King who came to die for you so that you could experience His resurrection life today. He raises up your life from that prostrate disposition of humility, even the mind of Christ which manifests in you serving God and others first and foremost (Philippians 2:3-5). Jesus is **"the resurrection and the life"** (John 11:25), which means He is raising you up as you lay down your will and according to His example, cry **"Not my will but thine be done"** (Luke 22:42).

Jesus saved you to serve HIM and others, not yourself (Ephesians 5:25-27). Your life in Christ will not work outside of the principle of the cross that Christ gave us as the prescription for following Him—the **"daily"** death, burial and raising up (Luke 9:23-24; 2 Corinthians 4:10-12).

Prayer: *Jesus, let me be dead and buried with You today. Into Your hands I submit my spirit. In Jesus' name, amen* LORD.

November 28

> "Thou art my servant; I have chosen thee, and not cast thee away. ¹⁰ Fear thou not; for I am with thee: be not dismayed; for I am thy God: I will strengthen thee; yea, I will help thee; yea, I will uphold thee with the right hand of my righteousness."
> Isaiah 41:10

There are 10 elements to behold in this passage from Isaiah:

- "Thou art my servant"
- "I have chosen thee"
- "and not cast thee away"
- "Fear thou not"
- "I am with thee"
- "be not dismayed"
- "for I am thy God"
- "I will strengthen thee"
- "I will help thee"
- "I will uphold thee with the right hand of my righteousness"

The soul that prospers is that one who clings to, trusts in and relies upon Christ alone, day by day, walking ever nearer to the soon coming Savior. He is with us and promises to **"never leave thee, nor forsake thee"**—that is, for those who abide with Christ (Hebrews 13:5).

Prayer: *Dear LORD, thank You for helping me today, and continuing the good work of salvation You began in me the moment You saved me. In Jesus' name, amen.*

November 29

"And the angel said unto them, Fear not: for, behold, I bring you good tidings of great joy, which shall be to all people. ¹¹ For unto you is born this day in the city of David a Saviour, which is Christ the Lord. ¹² And this shall be a sign unto you; Ye shall find the babe wrapped in swaddling clothes, lying in a manger. ¹³ And suddenly there was with the angel a multitude of the heavenly host praising God, and saying, ¹⁴ Glory to God in the highest, and on earth peace, good will toward men." Luke 2:10-14

From the time of His birth, **"Great joy ... to all people"** is what Christ brings to us all! Jesus is the Prince who came to bring peace. God sent His only begotten Son to bring peace between God and His fallen creation. When Jesus was born into this earth the announcement from Heaven was one of great joy and peace which is God's intention and will for **"all men"** (John 12:32).

Do you believe that God is good? What did He communicate to us is His will for all of mankind? What is God's will for you? **"GOOD will."**

> "Having predestinated us unto the adoption of children by Jesus Christ to himself, according to <u>the good pleasure of his will</u>." Ephesians 1:5

Prayer: *Father, in Jesus' name I thank You that You chose, out of Your good pleasure, to send Your only begotten Son to save the world from sin! I love You Lord!*

November 30

"For the wrath of man worketh not the righteousness of God." James 1:20

The LORD Jesus Christ rebuke our wicked hearts this day! How we've hypocritically judged others while we ourselves have a desperate, deep need for God's mercy and workings in our own lives! (Read Matthew 7:1-5.)

"The wrath of man" is completely wicked. Just what stone do we have to throw, being that we ourselves are fully guilty of gross sin in the eyes of a holy God? Realizing our own wicked iniquity and the myriad of our own sins against a holy God is more than enough motivation to forgive others! Today is your day to turn back to the LORD in true repentance and to make every relationship in your life right—to forgive all. God requires us to take responsibility for our own sins, not that of others.

> **"Let all bitterness, and wrath, and anger, and clamour, and evil speaking, be put away from you, with all malice: 32 And be ye kind one to another, tenderhearted, forgiving one another, even as God for Christ's sake hath forgiven you." Ephesians 4:31-32**

> **"For he shall have judgment without mercy, that hath shewed no mercy; and mercy rejoiceth against judgment." James 2:13** (memorize)

Prayer: *Father, please grant this heart to be broken and contrite before You in utter humility. Cleanse me of everything that does not glorify You. In Jesus' name, amen.*

December 1

"Every branch in me that beareth not fruit he taketh away: and every branch that beareth <u>fruit</u>, he purgeth it, that it may bring forth <u>more fruit</u>." John 15:2

Like the farmer who expands his operation, so the LORD purges His people, in order to further prepare them to bear a progressively expanding harvest. The LORD desires a growing yield of fruit to be produced in the lives of His people. Notice the order in John 15:

- **"Fruit"** v. 2
- **"More fruit"** v. 2
- **"Much fruit"** vv. 5, 8

"I am the vine, ye are the branches: He that abideth in me, and I in him, the same bringeth forth <u>much fruit</u>: for without me ye can do nothing. ... ⁸ Herein is my Father glorified, that ye bear <u>much fruit</u>; so shall ye be my disciples." John 15:5, 8

Ministry comes forth out of relationship. Ministry that glorifies God, that bears divine fruit, is the work of God in and through the abiding, crucified believer. Ministry is not a work of the flesh. Yes, it non-negotiably involves the agreement and participation of faith-filled, worshipful obedience of the saint. Many today labor in the flesh. Though the motive may be right (the desire to serve God) many times we go forth in our own feeble strength, instead of God's.

Prayer: *Father, thank You for saving me into Your kingdom and for purging, correcting and chastening me, thereby increasing fruit in this vessel. In Jesus' name, amen.*

December 2

"Now the end of the commandment is charity out of a pure heart, and of a good conscience, and of faith unfeigned:" 1 Timothy 1:5

"Charity out of a pure heart." The term **"end of the commandment"** refers to the highest goal for God giving us His commandments in His Word. It speaks of the chief aim of the purpose of God's Word. His highest objective is that divine charity flows out of hearts purified by the LORD, being full of **"faith unfeigned"** (pure, sincere faith, having no hypocrisy).

The seat of charity is a pure heart. As God purifies the hearts of His saints, they are increasingly prepared to house, to facilitate His love! Is God's love finding an increasing place in your heart?

Note: **"Charity out of a pure heart." "Charity"** flows out of **"a pure heart."** A pure heart is the bottle into which the new wine of His love is poured and from which it flows (Mark 2:22).

Prayer: *Father, please purify my heart. Create in me a clean heart and fill this life with Your love. In Jesus' name, amen.*

December 3

> "Lay not up for yourselves treasures upon earth, where moth and rust doth corrupt, and where thieves break through and steal: 20 But lay up for yourselves treasures in heaven, where neither moth nor rust doth corrupt, and where thieves do not break through nor steal: 21 For where your treasure is, there will your heart be also." Matthew 6:19-21

Here Jesus instructs His people to lay up treasure in Heaven and not to waste His resources. As we lay up treasure in Heaven instead of on the earth, our hearts will be deeply, richly invested in Christ and His kingdom.

Make no mistake, this is a divine incentive to lay up treasure in Heaven while we can, using the supply He's put into our hands temporarily in this brief life (Matthew 6:19-21).

> "But this I say, He which soweth sparingly shall reap also sparingly; and he which soweth bountifully shall reap also bountifully. 7 Every man according as he purposeth in his heart, so let him give; not grudgingly, or of necessity: for God loveth a cheerful giver. 8 And God is able to make all grace abound toward you; that ye, always having all sufficiency in all things, may abound to every good work." 2 Corinthians 9:6-8

Prayer: *Father, please teach me Your wisdom. Everything I have came from You. Please grant that my heart be a giving one, like Yours. In Jesus' name, amen.*

December 4

"I am not worthy of the least of all the mercies, and of all the truth, which thou hast shewed unto thy servant;" Genesis 32:10

It was when Jacob was broken before God, having wrestled with the LORD all night, that he was made to be dependent upon the LORD as we shall be as He allows hardships, trials and afflictions. It's then that we begin to understand divine mercy and how the LORD (who made, found and saved us) is everlasting in His mercy toward us and that we are completely undeserving (John 15:5).

"Not by works of righteousness which we have done, but according to his mercy he saved us, by the washing of regeneration, and renewing of the Holy Ghost; 6 Which he shed on us abundantly through Jesus Christ our Saviour." Titus 3:5-6

It's only those who are shown by God just how evil they are without Christ that can begin to understand and appreciate divine mercy—the cross of Jesus Christ! (Read Romans 3:23-25; 7:18, 24.)

Prayer: *Holy Father, in the name of Jesus, please grant this heart to be a heart of flesh, contrition and authentic sincerity. I lay my life in Your hands dear LORD and thank You for giving Your very life to save mine. Amen.*

Are you truly saved? Any doubts? Go to page 381 of this book.

December 5

"Behold, I come quickly: hold that fast which thou hast, that no man take thy crown." Revelation 3:11

Jesus warns: **"hold that fast which thou hast, that no man take thy crown"** which clearly reveals that losing the crown of glory is possible. Scripture is full of divine warnings like this and yet most ignore them which shall be their own undoing. *Initial salvation* does not guarantee *final salvation* into Heaven.

"Behold, I come as a thief. Blessed is he that watcheth, and keepeth his garments, lest he walk naked, and they see his shame." Revelation 16:15

God's Word is full of warnings to protect you! This is the divine design by Him who is **"NOT willing that any should perish, but that all should come to repentance"** (2 Peter 3:9).

He saved you which involved an act of faith on your part—and God never removed your free will. **"Abide,"** remain, continue with Christ to the end of your life or all will be lost (John 15:6; Hebrews 10:26-39; 2 Peter 2:20-21).

Prayer: *Father, please unite my heart to fear Thy holy name. Open my eyes to the false teachings that lead to lukewarmness and unholy living. Use me for Your glory. In Jesus' name, amen.*

December 6

"And that from a child thou hast known the holy scriptures, which are able to make thee wise unto salvation through faith which is in Christ Jesus. 16 All scripture is given by inspiration of God, and is profitable for doctrine, for reproof, for correction, for instruction in righteousness: 17 That the man of God may be perfect, throughly FURNISHED unto all good works." 2 Timothy 3:15-17

"Furnished" means *fully equipped*. And according to this passage, the only way to be **"throughly furnished"** (furnished through and through) is by being full of God's Word and obedient to it, to Him.

To "furnish" also means *to fill*, just like we fill our living room with specific furniture, so most importantly, we are to fill, to furnish our hearts with the furniture of God's Word. Are you putting the furniture of God's Word in your heart daily? Are you furnishing the vessel that He made you to be?

True, seasoned disciples are **"furnished"** not only with the head knowledge of God's Word but also the outward enactment of the workings of God in their daily lives. They are **"doers of the word, and not hearers only"** and therefore **"by reason of use have their senses exercised to discern both good and evil"** (Hebrews 5:14; James 1:22).

Prayer: *Father, may there be an insatiable hunger for Your truth in my heart. In Jesus' name, amen.*

December 7

"Nevertheless I have somewhat against thee, because thou hast left thy first love. ⁵ Remember therefore from whence thou art fallen, and repent, and do the first works; or else I will come unto thee quickly, and will remove thy candlestick out of his place, except thou repent." Revelation 2:4-5

Is Jesus the very **"first love"**—the foremost burning love that consumes your life, everything you think, dwell on, and do?

"If any man come to me, and hate not his father, and mother, and wife, and children, and brethren, and sisters, yea, and his own life also *(compared to how much he loves Jesus—his first love)*, **he cannot be my disciple. ²⁷ And whosoever doth not bear his cross, and come after me, cannot be my disciple."** Luke 14:26-27

This is yet another hard truth that false teachers purposely dodge, ignore. Do no such thing beloved. It will cost your eternal soul. Are you ready to surrender afresh? Here you go. Seek Him with everything within you, right this moment beloved.

Prayer: *Dear LORD, this very moment, I return to You as my first love, the most important Person in my life. I lay my life in Your holy hands, right now, if never before. Please wash me of all sin. Cleanse me dear LORD. In Jesus' name.*

December 8

> "This is a faithful saying, and worthy of all acceptation, that Christ Jesus came into the world to save sinners; of whom I am chief." 1 Timothy 1:15

It was the greatest rescue mission ever when the Father **"reconciled us to himself by Jesus Christ"** (2 Corinthians 5:18). And now He uses us to reach others. We call it the Great Commission … **"Go ye"** (Mark 16:15).

> "And all things are of God, who hath reconciled us to himself by Jesus Christ, and hath given to us the ministry of reconciliation; … [20] Now then we are ambassadors for Christ, as though God did beseech you by us: we pray you in Christ's stead, be ye reconciled to God." 2 Corinthians 5:18, 20

As His ambassadors, and as Jesus leads us, we are blessed to humbly help apply the healing oil of salvation to those who are sick, separated from God in sin.

"How we walk with the broken speaks louder than how we sit with the great." Unknown

Isn't that exactly what Jesus did when He came to rescue us?

Prayer: LORD Jesus, it was the greatest rescue mission ever when You came and died for me. Thank You my LORD. Please use me to help others know You.

December 9

> "A new commandment I give unto you, That ye love one another; as I have loved you, that ye also love one another. 35 By this shall all men know that ye are my disciples, if ye have love one to another." John 13:24-35

The divine mandate to **"love one another"** appears 13 times in the New Testament Scriptures.

The people of God are known by their **"love one to another."**

Walking in God's love is the distinct, cardinal fruit of all who are known of God. **"God is love"** and those who have **"known God, or rather are known of God,"** are possessed with His love for others (1 Corinthians 8:3; Galatians 4:9).

> "Beloved, let us love one another: for love is of God; and every one that loveth is born of God, and knoweth God. 8 He that loveth not knoweth not God; for God is love." 1 John 4:7-8

Reading 1 Corinthians 13 (the love chapter) regularly, is of immense benefit to the saints of Christ.

Prayer: *Heavenly Father, You alone are love. I am not love, yet I ask You now to permeate this life with Your love, as You alone can do. In Jesus' name, amen.*

December 10

"For the Son of man is not come to destroy men's lives, but to save them." Luke 9:56

As His disciples, we must prayerfully seek to understand the mind of Christ—the perspective of our God toward mankind—revealed to us in His Word (Psalms 33:11). Is He a harsh angry God or is our LORD tenderhearted toward those He made in His own image?

"For God sent not his Son into the world to condemn the world; but that the world through him might be saved." John 3:17

When Peter, one of the twelve, was restored, forgiven, and set forth into Christ's ministry after the gross sin of openly denying the holy One of Israel (the very Messiah), his ministry was empowered by the Holy Ghost as he preached and led 8,000 souls to Jesus in one day! And that was only the beginning of Peter's ministry. Did this same God not forgive Moses and use him mightily AFTER he murdered a man? Isn't this the same Savior who forgave David's gross sinning, used him, and in the end said David was **"a man after mine own heart, which shall fulfil all my will"**? (See Acts 13:22.) The consequences of our sin linger and yet, God forgives when we come to Him on the basis of Christ's perfect sacrifice, returning to Him (repenting), and confessing sin (1 John 1:9).

Prayer: *Father, thank You for loving Your creation, for loving me. Jesus, thank You for dying to bring me back to Yourself and the Father. Teach me dear LORD, in Jesus' name.*

December 11

> "Work out your own salvation with fear and trembling. 13 For it is God which worketh in you both to will and to do of his good pleasure." Philippians 2:12-13

God alone is the Initiator and we are the responders— **"We love him, because he first loved us"** (1 John 4:19). He is the One who began a good work in us and is also **"the author and finisher of our faith"** (Philippians 1:6; Hebrews 12:1-2).

> "Being confident of this very thing, that he which hath begun a good work in you will perform it until the day of Jesus Christ." Philippians 1:6

He who alone began the good work of His salvation in us can continue the work He alone began in us!

> "Wherefore seeing we also are compassed about with so great a cloud of witnesses, let us lay aside every weight, and the sin which doth so easily beset us, and let us run with patience the race that is set before us, 2 Looking unto Jesus <u>the author and finisher of our faith</u>; who for the joy that was set before him endured the cross, despising the shame, and is set down at the right hand of the throne of God." Hebrews 12:1-2

Prayer: *Thank You Jesus for dying for me. Thank You for finding, saving and sanctifying me. I am set apart unto You dear* LORD. *I love You Jesus!*

December 12

> "And in the morning, rising up a great while before day, he went out, and departed into a solitary place, and there prayed." Mark 1:35

Seeking the Father early is what our LORD did while He was where we are—on the earth. The psalmist did the same. Jesus got up early to commune with His Father in intimate prayer.

> "My voice shalt thou hear in the morning, O LORD; in the morning will I direct my prayer unto thee, and will look up." Psalms 5:3

Show me one's prayer life, their life of prayer, and I will show you exactly who they truly are. One cannot rightly claim to love God if they spend no time with Him.

Jesus gives us His very own instructions on how He sought the Father while in the days of His flesh.

> "But thou, when thou prayest, enter into thy closet, and when thou hast shut thy door, pray to thy Father which is in secret; and thy Father which seeth in secret shall reward thee openly." Matthew 6:6

Prayer: *LORD, please impress deeply upon my heart the necessity of seeking Your holy face, knowing You more and more. In Jesus' name, amen.*

December 13

"But now thus saith the LORD that created thee, O Jacob, and he that formed thee, O Israel, Fear not: for I have redeemed thee, I have called thee by thy name; thou art mine." Isaiah 43:1

You are His and because we are Christ's, your identity and future are not determined by the lies told about you or the afflictions you've suffered. Rather your identity and future are determined by the One who made and died to save you!

"He that spared not his own Son, but delivered him up for us all, how shall he not with him also freely give us all things? 33 Who shall lay any thing to the charge of God's elect? It is God that justifieth. 34 Who is he that condemneth? It is Christ that died, yea rather, that is risen again, who is even at the right hand of God, who also maketh intercession for us." Romans 8:32-23

No matter what His true children go through in this life, the LORD is with them. **"Lo, I am with you alway, even unto the end of the world. Amen"** (Matthew 28:20).

"When thou passest through the waters, I will be with thee; and through the rivers, they shall not overflow thee: when thou walkest through the fire, thou shalt not be burned; neither shall the flame kindle upon thee." Isaiah 43:2

Prayer: *Thank You Father that You will never leave or forsake Your own. I love You Jesus.*

December 14

> "They shall be abundantly satisfied with the fatness of thy house; and thou shalt make them drink of the river of thy pleasures." Psalms 36:8

Is **"the river of thy pleasures"** flowing into your life? First, do we realize that God made all, and He did so for His own good pleasure?

> "Thou art worthy, O Lord, to receive glory and honour and power: for thou hast created all things, and for thy pleasure they are and were created." Revelation 4:11

The LORD delights in bestowing His blessings upon His people.

> "He that spared not his own Son, but delivered him up for us all, how shall he not with him also freely give us all things?" Romans 8:32

> "Fear not, little flock; for it is your Father's good pleasure to give you the kingdom." Luke 12:32

The term **"good pleasure"** appears five times in the New Testament concerning the goodness of our God (Luke 12:32; Ephesians 1:5, 9; Philippians 2:13; 2 Thessalonians 1:11).

Prayer: *Father, You are so very good! So much so that You gave Your only begotten Son to die for the sins of the whole world, for my sins—to bring us back to You. Please use me today to pour out Your love on others, in Jesus' name, amen.*

December 15

"But by the grace of God I am what I am: and his grace which was bestowed upon me was not in vain; but I laboured more abundantly than they all: yet not I, but the grace of God which was with me." 1 Corinthians 15:10

As God's people—found and saved by Christ—we are what we are, by His saving grace. And, as His kingdom servants, we are empowered by divine grace. Capturing this truth is life changing as you do Christ's work in this life. Notice: **"but I laboured more abundantly than they all: yet <u>not I, but the grace of God which was with me</u>."** Paul, out-serving all others, was empowered by God's grace. Our labor in the LORD has upon it the influence and the divine enablement of God's grace! Astounding!

The power of God's grace is what Paul attributed as the divine ability working in and through his life as he served the LORD in ministry. In fact, as he suffered, being downed—dead and buried—the grace of God was **"sufficient"** and increased in and through his life (2 Corinthians 12:7-10).

Prayer: *Father, thank You for forgiving all my sins by the precious blood of Jesus, my LORD and Savior. Please multiply Your grace, Your divine enablement and empowerment in my life to minister Your saving truth and grace to others, in Jesus' name, amen.*

December 16

> "And by knowledge shall the chambers be filled with all precious and pleasant riches. 5 A wise man is strong; yea, a man of knowledge increaseth strength." Proverbs 24:4-5

When someone comes to your home, do you have a cupboard stocked with good food to share with your guests? When you meet someone new or gather with others, do you have lots of biblical food to nourish them with? See Acts 2:42; Colossians 3:16.

God's Word is an inexhaustible treasure chest of divine nuggets. The rich treasures of God's Word fill and supply His saints with plentiful blessings to nourish their hearts and to share with others concerning **"ALL things that pertain unto life and godliness"** (2 Peter 1:3-4).

> "Therefore every scribe which is instructed unto the kingdom of heaven is like unto a man that is an householder, which bringeth forth out of his treasure things new and old." Matthew 13:52

> "Let the word of Christ dwell in you richly in all wisdom; teaching and admonishing one another in psalms and hymns and spiritual songs, singing with grace in your hearts to the Lord." Colossians 3:16

Prayer: *Father, help me to lay up the treasure of Your Word in my heart and mind to share with others. Let my vessel be full of Your blessed precepts, overflowing onto others. In Jesus' name, amen.*

December 17

"For the wages of sin is death" Romans 6:23

Sin knocks at every door, every day. The consequences of the sin you are being tempted to commit are hidden, except by Scripture, history, and experience. And it's not good.

"Seek the Lord and his strength, seek his face continually." 1 Chronicles 16:11

Sin will ...

- Take you further than you want to go ...
- Keep you longer than you want to stay, and ...
- Charge you more than you want to pay.

Seeking the Lord is always the right thing, at all times. His divine **"strength,"** His power for holy living, will permeate our lives. It's the only way we can dwell in and abide with Him and overcome the flesh, the world, and the devil (James 4:7). As we abide in Christ the fruit of His holiness manifests in our lives (John 15).

Jesus will soon return for a Bride, **"a glorious church, not having spot, or wrinkle, or any such thing; but that it should be holy and without blemish."** (Ephesians 5:25-27). Are you remaining **"ready"**? (See Luke 12:40.)

Prayer: *Father, in Jesus' name, please purify my heart and life. Probe the depths of my being. May this life be set in perfect order, beginning now. I look for Your soon return Lord Jesus.*

December 18

"A wise man is strong; yea, a man of knowledge increaseth strength." Proverbs 24:5

Increasing in divine strength integrally involves increasing in the Word of God. The correlation is direct. Strength in God doesn't come outside of the knowledge of God—knowing Him via walking in His holy Word. Those not increasing in the knowledge of God's Word, are not only not increasing in divine strength, but they are also sliding backward, slipping and in danger of falling away.

Do you have the inner resolve to diligently study, know and live out the Word of God? Do your days begin early, in the Word and prayer?

Increasing strength requires remaining hungry, teachable, correctable, and obedient to the LORD.

"A wise man will hear, and will increase learning; and a man of understanding shall attain unto wise counsels:" Proverbs 1:5

Are you constantly increasing in your learning? The human tendency seems to be to learn a bit and then pridefully, vainly imagine ourselves to be "experts." Such is completely incompatible with kingdom humility.

Prayer: *Heavenly Father, I repent of pride. Please bless this heart to be a heart of flesh. Help me to grow in the grace and knowledge of Jesus Christ and to humbly serve You by serving others. In Jesus' name, amen.*

December 19

> "If ye abide in me, and my words abide in you, ye shall ask what ye will, and it shall be done unto you." John 15:7

Walking with Jesus, seeking and abiding in relationship with Him—according to His Word, His terms—has many benefits. One is answered prayer. As we **"delight"** ourselves in the LORD, being made more and more one with the LORD, our hearts will become imbued, consumed with His desires and no longer our own.

> "Delight thyself also in the LORD; and he shall give thee the desires of thine heart. 5 Commit thy way unto the LORD; trust also in him; and he shall bring it to pass." Psalms 37:4-5

The **"benefits"** of God for His people are for here and are but a mere foretaste of glory divine!

> "Blessed be the Lord, who daily loadeth us with benefits, even the God of our salvation. Selah." Psalms 68:19

Prayer: *Father, thank You so much for loading Your people with Your benefits which were all purchased with the precious blood of my LORD Jesus Christ. Help me to always abide in You dear LORD, according to Your definition of this vital relationship. In Jesus' name, amen.*

December 20

> "Ye have not chosen me, but I have chosen you, and ordained you, that ye should go and bring forth fruit, and that your fruit should remain: that whatsoever ye shall ask of the Father in my name, he may give it you." John 15:16

God alone ordains His people to His work and brings them through many purging seasons to cause His fruitfulness in them, preparing them to bear more of His fruit.

God chose us and blessed us with the ability to repent and receive Christ. As His people, He's also ordained us to **"go and bring forth fruit, and that your fruit should remain."**

As we read this discourse from our LORD (John 15 and 17), we discover that He is speaking of that abiding fellowship we have with Him, and how out of it is borne the good fruit of His ministry in and through our life.

Being rooted in that oneness, the abiding relationship with Christ, is all-important to our relationship with Him and the Father. As his student, His disciple, may the reader be encouraged to pour prayerfully over these truths captured, and given to us in John, chapters 15 and 17.

Prayer: *Heavenly Father, in the name of Jesus, please make me one with You. Please deeply root and establish my life in an abiding fellowship with You dear LORD.*

December 21

"Now the Spirit speaketh expressly, that in the latter times some shall depart from the faith, giving heed to seducing spirits, and doctrines of devils; 2 Speaking lies in hypocrisy; having their conscience seared with a hot iron;" 1 Timothy 4:1-2

"Having their conscience seared with a hot iron" makes it clear that there does exist a point of no return for a person's conscience.

The importance of a **"good conscience"** cannot be over emphasized. The word **"conscience"** appears 31 times in the New Testament! Here's a sampling:

"But have renounced the hidden things of dishonesty, not walking in craftiness, nor handling the word of God deceitfully; but by manifestation of the truth commending ourselves to every man's conscience in the sight of God." 2 Corinthians 4:2

"Now the end of the commandment is charity out of a pure heart, and of a good conscience, and of faith unfeigned:" 1 Timothy 1:5

"Holding faith, and a good conscience; which some having put away concerning faith have made shipwreck:" 1 Timothy 1:19

"Holding the mystery of the faith in a pure conscience." 1 Timothy 3:9

Prayer: L ORD *please purify my heart and conscience. Make it super sensitive to Your voice, leading and conviction, in Jesus' name, amen.*

December 22

"If we confess our sins, he is faithful and just to forgive us our sins, and to cleanse us from all unrighteousness." 1 John 1:9

Excuse me: **"ALL"** means **ALLLLL** saints!

Never cover sin—confess it! God sees all anyway. Nothing is hidden from Him. Get honest now. The results are amazing!

"He that covereth his sins shall not prosper: but whoso confesseth and forsaketh them shall have mercy." Proverbs 28:13 (Good to memorize this one right now!)

"Let not any iniquity have dominion over me." Psalms 119:133b

Washed afresh in the blood of Jesus! Today! Now dip your robe! Return to Him, confess, and He will clean!

Prayer: *Father, I come to You, confessing my sin of self-idolatry, returning my heart affections to You now. I lay my life in Your hands dear* LORD*. Please wash me clean, afresh, right this moment. Cleanse away all evil from my life, in Jesus' name, amen.*

Have you been genuinely saved? See page 381 at the end of this book.

December 23

"Give us a King." 1 Samuel 8:6

The Israelites were led by God. They were supposed to be led directly by the Lord Himself. Yet in their rebellion they cried out **"Give us a king"**—a human king or leader (1 Samuel 8:6).

The critical lesson for us to learn is that wolves step right in on the wings of this evil desire to put away the Lord and exchange Him for a mere human leader (2 Timothy 4:3). Ear-tickling charlatans now occupy the vacuum created as Jesus is rejected as the supreme **"Head"** of His body (Colossians 2:18-19).

In the days of the kings, when God's people rejected His leadership and sought a mere human leader, they were led into great trouble. We see the same transpiring today as we see church goers who emphatically declare they know the Lord and yet are in reality submitted to men and not God. The lack of kingdom fruit in their daily lives makes this clear. Their energies and supplies are wasted on helping build the kingdoms of mere men, and not Christ's eternal kingdom!

Prayer: *Father, I here and now repent before Your Majesty for elevating men to the place of leadership reserved only for You. Father, please forgive my sin of idolatry. I now ask You alone to reign in my heart and life. In Jesus' name, amen.*

December 24

"Now once in the end of the world hath he appeared to put away sin by the sacrifice of himself." Hebrews 9:26

The LORD is **"Holy, holy, holy"** and therefore takes sin seriously (Isaiah 6:3; Revelation 4:8). The coming of Jesus to die on that cross reveals how holy and loving God is and how personally He takes sin. The LORD therefore **"appeared to put away sin by the sacrifice of himself."** The Son of God came in person to pay the full debt for the sin of mankind— **"It is finished"** which means *paid in full* (John 19:30).

Jesus **"obtained eternal redemption for us"**—**"by his own blood."**

> "Neither by the blood of goats and calves, but BY HIS OWN BLOOD he entered in once into the holy place, having obtained eternal redemption for us." Hebrews 9:12

> "And from Jesus Christ, who is the faithful witness, and the first begotten of the dead, and the prince of the kings of the earth. Unto him that loved us, and washed us from our sins IN HIS OWN BLOOD," Revelation 1:5

> "WHEN HE HAD BY HIMSELF purged our sins, sat down on the right hand of the Majesty on high." Hebrews 1:3

Prayer: *Jesus, I thank You for washing me in Your precious blood afresh right now.*

December 25

> "This is a faithful saying, and worthy of all acceptation, that Christ Jesus came into the world to save sinners; of whom I am chief." 1 Timothy 1:15

Jesus came and died to save the souls of fallen mankind, the whole human race. And, when He left to go back to His Father in Heaven, having accomplished redemption, He sent us forth as His ambassadors, His witnesses—to tell the world!

He said that it is actually better that He was going back to Heaven because then He was going to (and did) send the divine Person of the Holy Ghost to fill every one of His people!

> "Nevertheless I tell you the truth; It is expedient for you that I go away: for if I go not away, the Comforter will not come unto you; but if I depart, I will send him unto you." John 16:7

Jesus is on his rescue mission today and **"we** (that's us) **are labourers TOGETHER with God"** (1 Corinthians 3:9).

Prayer: *Father, this moment, I thank You for sending your Son for me and for all men. I now lay down my life before You. I lay my life in Your holy hands. I repent of my sinful rebellion of doing things my own way instead of Yours. Please forgive my sin and take over my life completely dear LORD. Please fill and use me LORD. In Jesus' name, amen.*

December 26

"If a man therefore purge himself from these, he shall be a vessel unto honour, sanctified, and meet for the master's use, and prepared unto every good work." 2 Timothy 2:21

Do you possess the desire to be used mightily by our LORD? Are you a **"vessel unto honour, sanctified, and meet for the master's use, and prepared unto every good work"**? Are you willing to meet His conditions?

"Every branch in me that beareth not fruit he taketh away: and every branch that beareth fruit, he purgeth it, that it may bring forth more fruit. 3 Now ye are clean through the word which I have spoken unto you." John 15:2-3

Did you catch what our LORD just said? Wow! GOOD NEWS: If God is purging you it proves that you are truly in Christ and have borne good fruit and now, He is purging you so that even more good fruit will be produced in your life! Victory!

Are you truly humbled, teachable, correctable, repentant and obedient to the LORD today?

"I would rather be purged now, than burned later!" Brother Charles Pray

Prayer: *Heavenly Father, right now, I submit to You afresh, to Your divine authority over my life. Please forgive all my sinful rebellion against You. Into Your hands I now submit my spirit, my life. Please prepare and use me dear LORD. In Jesus' name.*

December 27

"Not every one that saith unto me, Lord, Lord, shall enter into the kingdom of heaven; but he that doeth the will of my Father which is in heaven." Matthew 7:21

Does our obedience save us? No, Jesus saves us. Obeying God isn't earning our own salvation, it's an expression of true love for Him and saving faith (Matthew 7:21; 22:37-40; Luke 6:46; John 15:14; James 2, etc.). "Faith" that doesn't result in a changed life and the good fruit of good works, is not saving faith! — **"Faith without works is dead"** (James 2:26).

"He that saith, I know him, and keepeth not his commandments, is a liar, and the truth is not in him. 5 But whoso keepeth his word, in him verily is the love of God perfected: hereby know we that we are in him." 1 John 2:4-5

"And why call ye me, Lord, Lord, and do not the things which I say?" Luke 6:46

Prayer: *Father, I ask You to try my heart, then purge, cleanse and purify it. Please remove every trace of falsity and establish my heart to be sincere before You. Please conform my life to the image of Christ and make me Your authentic disciple, in Jesus' name, amen.*

December 28

"And by knowledge shall the chambers be filled with all precious and pleasant riches." Proverbs 24:4

O the **"precious and pleasant riches"** of our God! Are the chambers of your heart, your vessel being filled today via communion with Him? Remember the ten virgins of Jesus' parable? (Read Matthew 25:1-13.) Getting into God's Word today means God's Word is getting into you!

How can I possibly bless others today with the **"precious and pleasant riches"** of the treasure chest of God's Word if those riches of His Word aren't being replenished into the chambers of my heart today?

Are you hungering and thirsting for the righteousness of the LORD? Are you a man or a woman after God's own heart like David was? Are you filling your vessel continually with the treasure of God's Word?

> "And he said unto me, Son of man, cause thy belly to eat, and fill thy bowels with this roll *(God's Word)* that I give thee. Then did I eat it; and it was in my mouth as honey for sweetness. 4 And he said unto me, Son of man, go, get thee unto the house of Israel, and speak with my words unto them." Ezekiel 3:3-4

Prayer: *Father, I repent of self-idolatry and unbelief, and not seeking You. Today I seek You. I lay my life in Your hands and choose to hunger and thirst after more of You, more of Your Word. Please use me for Your glory, in Jesus' name.*

December 29

> "Then said Jesus, Father, forgive them; for they know not what they do. And they parted his raiment, and cast lots." Luke 23:34

WHAT did Jesus do while suffering a horrible death on that cross for our sins—for the sins of His very enemies? He said, "Father, forgive them; for they know not what they do."

WHAT did Jesus command us to do toward our very enemies?

> "But I say unto you, Love your enemies, bless them that curse you, do good to them that hate you, and pray for them which despitefully use you, and persecute you;" Matthew 5:44

Doing things HIS way means humbling ourselves, forgiving and praying right now for our enemies. Is that not following Jesus—His example?

Remember that your enemies are in darkness and know not what they do—just as we once were, before someone lifted us in prayer and Jesus found and rescued us from sin, separation, and eternal damnation! THANK YOU, JESUS!

Prayer: *Dear LORD please reduce me to love. Make me one with You dear LORD. Let my life be an offering to You. I love You LORD, in Jesus name.*

December 30

"Whosoever shall seek to save his life shall lose it; and whosoever shall lose his life shall preserve it." Luke 17:33

Releasing our lives to Him, losing them to Him instead of retaining our lives, is the key to Christ's victory prevailing in our lives. You must let go of your life to release it into the care of the Almighty. Faith.

If Jesus isn't reigning strongly enough to conquer any and all sin in our lives, it's because there's the need for the cross—to truly let go and let God.

All who follow Christ abandon their own lives in this world and genuinely repent of all that offends Him (Ezekiel 18:30; Luke 14:33; 17:33). Holiness is the work of God in the yielded, abiding born-again saint (John 15; Romans 8:12-14; 1 Peter 1:15-16, etc.). Think about it: When the HOLY Spirit is ruling a person's yielded life, that vessel will be HOLY (1 Peter 1:15-16).

"So likewise, whosoever he be of you that forsaketh not all that he hath, he cannot be my disciple." Luke 14:33

Prayer: *Father, I repent now of trying to keep my own life and not losing it to You. I love You* LORD. *Right this instant, I lay my life in Your hands. In Jesus' name, amen.*

December 31

"For a just man falleth seven times, and riseth up again: but the wicked shall fall into mischief." Proverbs 24:16

True disciples, like beloved David, know what it means to fall, to sin, to repent, to re-turn to the Lord and be restored by the Lord. They therefore can help you. They encourage, admonish, and warn you to hasten to the throne of grace to obtain mercy and grace—and the cross, the crucified life.

IF you choose to sin, it's going to cost you (Romans 6:23). We must all reap what we sow (Galatians 6:7-8). Yet, the transgressor should run TO God, not AWAY from Him.

> **"My little children, these things write I unto you, that ye sin not. And if any man sin, we have an advocate with the Father, Jesus Christ the righteous:" 1 John 2:1**

> **"Let us therefore come boldly unto the throne of grace, that we may obtain MERCY, and find GRACE to help in time of need." Hebrews 4:16**

Though there is mercy to forgive our sins and grace to divinely enable us to overcome them, the consequences of sin are lasting. This is clear in the life of Moses and David and others throughout biblical history. David reaped horrid consequences on himself and his household after he committed adultery and had Uriah murdered. Satan will never warn you of the cost of your sin.

Prayer: *Father, let Your holy fear consume me, hastening me to You to escape the lure of sin. In Jesus' name. Amen.*

Making Peace with God

Are you ready to pass from death to life? The most astounding event of human history occurred when this man, Jesus Christ, died on a Roman cross. When He died, an untimely darkness covered the land at 3:00 p.m. and an earthquake occurred as He took His final breath. This man called Jesus was crucified. Three days later He was raised from the dead! Here's why He died:

"But your iniquities (sins) **have separated between you and your God, and your sins have hid his face from you, that he will not hear." ~ Isaiah 59:2**

God is holy, and our sins separate us from Him. We have all broken God's laws by lying, dishonoring our parents, cheating, hating, committing a sex act (even in our mind) with someone we are not married to, stealing, coveting, taking His holy name in vain, etc. These are all sins against God, and we are all guilty. Committing any single one of these sins makes us guilty of breaking the whole law and worthy of death.

Divine justice demands that our violations be punished. Because we are guilty of breaking God's holy law, we deserve to be fairly repaid for our offenses. God doesn't want us to be punished in hell forever though, so He sent His Son to pay the debt for us, so we would not have to pay for our own sins in eternal hell as we clearly deserve, but rather live now and forever with Him. What love!

At the end of a perfect (sinless) life, Christ carried the very cross He was to be nailed to. His infinite love for you, along with the nails driven through His hands and feet, held Him to that cross as He agonized for 6 hours in pain—to pay for your sins. He was crucified to make peace between God and man. The Son of God bridged the gap that sin had caused. This wonderful man named Jesus chose to shed His life blood (die— in excruciating pain) for you rather than live without you. He loves you.

"For the wages of sin is death; but the gift of God is eternal life through Jesus Christ our Lord." ~ Romans 6:23

Christ died to fully pay for the sins of the human race (John 19:30). God loves us and wants us to experience relationship with Him, now and forever (John 17:3). Friend, who else has ever died for you but Jesus, the Good Shepherd?

"**For when we were yet without strength, in due time Christ died for the ungodly** *(that's you).*"
~ **Romans 5:6**

Jesus Christ bears those scars in His holy hands and feet which prove how much He loves you (Romans 5:6-9; 2 Corinthians 5:19-21; 1 John 3:16). No one else ever died for your sins on a cruel cross—to buy you back to Himself. He **"gave himself a ransom for all, to be testified in due time"** ~ (1 Timothy 2:6).

"Christ Jesus came into the world to save *(rescue)* **sinners."** ~ **1 Timothy 1:15**

No religion or religious figure can save your soul from hell (no matter what they claim). Jesus didn't come to start a religion but rather to establish His eternal kingdom in the hearts of men, granting them a relationship with God. Jesus Christ is the only One who bears nail-scarred hands and feet for your sins. He is the only way to God and your only hope.

"For there is ONE God, and ONE mediator between God and men, the man Christ Jesus." ~ **1 Timothy 2:5**

The Son of God died and rose again to take away all your sins. He was the only One qualified for the job and He is the only One worthy of your worship.

Peace with God Happens When We Meet the Prince of Peace.

It is by no accident you are reading this message. This is your moment in history to be saved. Praying and doing good deeds and going to church will save no person from eternal punishment. **"For by grace** *(undeserved favor)* **are ye saved through faith; and that not of yourselves: it is the gift of God: Not of works, lest any man should boast"** (Ephesians 2:8-9). Only the good work of Christ shedding His sinless blood on the cross for you will save your soul as you repent before a holy and righteous God and Judge.

If you are going to get right with the LORD and go to Heaven, there must be a moment of reckoning. Now is your time to be saved. No one will ever through a life of good works earn God's favor. There must, of necessity, be that divinely defining moment when you lay your whole life/being/existence into His perfect, holy hands.

Apply His holy blood to your life so that you may be saved, forgiven, and live eternally with Him. You must completely turn your life over to Him in repentance and faith.

In a moment of sincere solitude, get alone with God or pray with another true born-again Christian. Take yourself away from all else to honor the One who made you, bowing your heart to speak in prayer with Him who is Your God and Judge. He is listening. In fact, He's the very One who orchestrated all of this and brought you to this place.

Below is a model prayer. If you will pray to God sincerely and from the depths of your heart, in sincere repentance in turning to the LORD with all that is in you, the LORD will hear and answer your prayer and save you.

Your Prayer of Repentance to God to be Saved

Dear heavenly Father, right now, if never before, I come to you as a broken and sinful person. Thank You for sending Your only begotten Son to die in my place for my sins. Thank You Jesus for coming to this earth to die and rise again to rescue me from sin and eternal hell and to save me for Your eternal glory. Right this moment, if never before, I receive You Lord Jesus. Come in and take over my whole life. I am all Yours and You are all mine. I love You Jesus and I will follow You from this moment forward till I am with You in Heaven forever! Please use me to help others know You dear Lord. In Jesus' name, Amen.

——— • ———

Tell another Christian that you've been born again! Find a group of Christ-loving, Bible-living believers. Be water baptized. Read your King James Bible, daily, and talk with God in prayer. Follow Christ to the end of your life.

- Give Him thanks—preferably with uplifted heart and hands, give forthright, verbal thanksgiving to the LORD daily for finding and saving you from sin and hell and for His glory and eternal purpose.
- Ask the LORD to fill you with His Holy Spirit (Acts 1:48; 2:14; 2:38-39; 19:1-6).

- Tell another Christian that the LORD has saved you (Luke 12:8 -9).
- Find a group of Christ-centered believers who love God's Word and study it unceasingly. Stay clear of those who are proud of their church, their pastor, or their denomination. Fellowship with those who unceasingly magnify Jesus Christ, the nail-scarred risen Savior above all else (Colossians 2).
- Be water baptized (Acts 2:38).
- Obtain a copy of the booklet titled: *What Next? Now that You are Saved* (at SafeGuardYourSoul.com.)
- Read your King James Bible daily and talk with God in prayer. Read at least four chapters every morning as soon as you awake. Have a Bible reading and feeding plan.
- Follow Christ to the end of your life (Matthew 24:13).
- Read and obey God's Word (James 1:22).
- Read articles, listen to audios & radio programs, etc., and sign up for the free email devotional. All of which are available at SafeGuardYourSoul.com, to help you to grow in grace as a born-again disciple of Jesus (Colossians 2:6-10).

Sharpen your personal discernment for the building up of His saints. *Let's grow in His grace together!*

Get your supply of soul-winning Gospel tracts and copies of this book to share with others.

Sign up to receive *Moments with Our Master* email devotional for the edification of the body of Christ in this late hour. It is sure to help you grow in His grace and in the knowledge of our LORD and Savior Jesus Christ (2 Peter 1:2; 3:18).

Sign up at: **info@SafeGuardYourSoul.com**

SafeGuardYourSoul.com

Mailing Address:

>SafeGuardYourSoul
>9201 Warren Pkwy. Ste. 200
>Frisco, Texas 75035

Made in the USA
Columbia, SC
23 September 2024